Accession no.
36122412

WITHDRAWN

D1344494

Interpreting

How is Britain governed? *Interpreting British Governance* develops a novel approach and answer to this question. It argues that political practices can be understood only by grasping the beliefs on which people act. It offers a governance narrative as a challenge to the Westminster model of British government and searches for a more accurate and open way of speaking about British government.

Part I defines the authors' interpretive approach, their epistemology and governance. Part II provides an extended illustration of their approach by using the concepts of tradition and dilemma to re-analyse critically public sector reform as enacted by politicians. Part III uses history and ethnography to decentre public sector reform as constructed by civil servants.

This controversial and innovative volume argues that there is no necessary or given pattern of governance but only the constructions of various traditions. The authors thus reject the concept of a positivist 'political science' for an interpretive approach which finds the study of politics rooted in history, philosophy and ethnography. This book will appeal to students and researchers of British government, public administration and political science methods.

Mark Bevir is an Associate Professor in the Department of Political Science, University of California, Berkeley. He is the author of *The Logic of the History of Ideas*. **R.A.W. Rhodes** is Professor of Political Science at the Research School of Social Science, Australian National University, Canberra. He is the author or editor of twenty books and has been editor of the journal *Public Administration* since 1986. He is President of the Political Studies Association of the UK.

Interpreting British Governance

Mark Bevir and R.A.W. Rhodes

LIS - LIBRARY

Date	Fund
7/6	H

Order No.

2123472

University of Chester

Routledge
Taylor & Francis Group

LONDON AND NEW YORK

First published 2003
by Routledge
11 New Fetter Lane, London EC4P 4EE

Simultaneously published in the USA and Canada
by Routledge
29 West 35th Street, New York, NY 10001

Routledge is an imprint of the Taylor & Francis Group

© 2003 Mark Bevir and R.A.W. Rhodes

Typeset in Sabon by Exe Valley Dataset Ltd, Exeter
Printed and bound in Great Britain by MPG Books Ltd, Bodmin

All rights reserved. No part of this book may be reprinted or reproduced or
utilised in any form or by an electronic, mechanical, or other means, now
known or hereafter invented, including photocopying and recording, or in
any information storage or retrieval system, without permission in writing
from the publishers.

British Library Cataloguing in Publication Data
A catalogue record for this book is available from the British Library

Library of Congress Cataloging in Publication Data
A catalog record has been requested

ISBN 0–415–30451–2 (hbk)
ISBN 0–415–30452–0 (pbk)

Contents

Tables

Preface and acknowledgements

This book combines the skills of a political theorist and intellectual historian with those of a student of British government and administration. We share responsibility for all that follows, believing that it would be invidious to try to specify who had what ideas. Even when one of us has taken the lead in writing a section of the book, the other has read and commented on it at various stages in ways that have altered its tone and content. We hope the combination provides a distinctive take on how to understand British government.

Many people have helped us over the past four years. Mark Bevir thanks the University of California, Berkeley for the award of a faculty research grant. Rod Rhodes thanks the Economic and Social Research Council: the research for this book was done while he was director of its Whitehall Programme. For help and comments, we also thank Chris Ansell, Peter Barberis, Laura Bevir, Andrew Dunsire, Andrew Gamble, Carsten Greve, Colin Hay, Torben Beck Jørgensen, Lotte Jensen, Tim Knudsen, Patrick Le Galès, Janice McMillan, David Marsh, David O'Brien, Cynthia Rhodes, Shannon Stimson, Gerry Stoker, Simon Walker, Bertram Welker and Pat Weller. The last thank you goes to Sir Robin Mountfield and Sir Richard Mottram for giving so generously of their time.

While we have drawn on several essays published jointly and singly since 1998, the book is not a collection of our earlier work. Rather, every chapter has been revised extensively – no chapter is just a reprint of previously published material – to create a new and continuous whole. The essays on which we have drawn are:

Bevir, M. (2002) 'Una Teroria Decentrata della "Governance"' [A Decentred Theory of Governance], *Stato e Mercato*, 64: 467–93.

Bevir, M. and O'Brien, D. (2001) 'New Labour and the Public Sector in Britain', *Public Administration Review*, 61: 535–47.

Bevir, M. and Rhodes, R.A.W. (1998) 'Narratives of "Thatcherism"', *West European Politics*, 21, 1: 97–119. Reproduced with the permission of Frank Cass Publishers.

Bevir, M. and Rhodes, R.A.W. (1999) 'Studying British Government: Reconstructing the Research Agenda', *British Journal of Politics and*

International Relations, 1, 2: 215–39. Reproduced with the permission of Blackwell Publishers.

Bevir, M. and Rhodes, R.A.W. (2001) 'Decentring Tradition: Interpreting British Government', *Administration and Society*, 33, 2: 107–32. Reproduced with the permission of Sage Publications, Inc.

Bevir, M. and Rhodes, R.A.W. (2002) 'Interpretative Approaches', in D. Marsh and G. Stoker (eds), *Theory and Methods in Political Science*. London: Macmillan. Reproduced with the permission of Palgrave Macmillan.

Rhodes, R.A.W. (1999) 'Understanding Governance: Comparing Public Sector Reform in Britain and Denmark', *Scandinavian Political Studies*, 22, 4: 341–70. Reproduced with the permission of Blackwell Publishers. Copyright: Nordic Political Science Association.

Rhodes, R.A.W. (1999) 'Public Administration and Governance', in J. Pierre (ed.) *Debating Governance*. Oxford: Oxford University Press. Reproduced with the permission of Oxford University Press.

Rhodes, R. A. W. (2000) 'New Labour's Civil Service: Summing-up Joining-up', *Political Quarterly*, 71, 2: 151–66. Reproduced with the permission of Blackwell Publishers. Copyright: The Political Quarterly Publishing Company.

Rhodes, R.A.W. (2001) 'Everybody But Us: Departmental Secretaries in the UK, 1970–99', in R.A.W. Rhodes and P. Weller (eds) *Mandarins or Valets? The Changing World of Top Officials*. Buckingham: Open University Press. Reproduced with the permission of Open University Press.

Mark Bevir and R.A.W. Rhodes
Berkeley, California, and Spital Tongues, Newcastle
September 2002

1   Introduction

On governance

Interpretation

Interpretive approaches begin from the insight that to understand actions, practices and institutions, we need to grasp the relevant meanings, the beliefs and preferences of the people involved. As John Stuart Mill (1969 [1840]: 119–20) remarked:

> By Bentham . . . men have been led to ask themselves, in regard to any ancient or received opinion, Is it true? And by Coleridge, What is the meaning of it? The one took his stand outside the received opinion, and surveyed it as an entire stranger to it: the other looked at it from within, and endeavoured to see it with the eyes of a believer in it . . . Bentham judged a proposition true or false as it accorded or not with the result of his own inquiries . . . With Coleridge . . . the very fact that any doctrine had been believed by thoughtful men, and received by whole nations or generations of mankind, was part of the problem to be solved, was one of the phenomena to be accounted for.

In this book we ask, after Coleridge, 'what is the meaning of it', where 'it' is British governance.

We use an anti-foundational epistemology and an interpretive approach to understand changes in British government, critically assessing the claim that there has been a shift from government of a unitary state to governance in and by networks. We develop the argument that people can engage in a practice only because they hold certain beliefs or concepts. So, political scientists can explore that practice by unpacking the relevant beliefs and explaining why they arose. For example, our electoral practices assume participants have a shared understanding of such notions as voting, candidate and polling. We can explore electoral practices by examining the content of these concepts and their historical roots. When political scientists so interpret practices, they lump beliefs together in discourses, ideologies, or traditions. They abstract from the beliefs of particular individuals to depict aggregates – the patterns of thought that inform a political practice. Alternatively, when individuals vote for the Labour Party, they may do so believing Labour will promote redistributive policies that are socially desirable and from which they will benefit. We can explore their voting behaviour by examining their webs of beliefs and how they came to hold them. When political scientists so interpret beliefs, they provide insights into the behaviour of particular individuals. They describe the particular sets of reasons that led the relevant individual to act.

The distinction between aggregate and individual analysis is artificial. An interpretive approach moves back and forth between aggregate concepts and the beliefs of particular individuals. Whether we focus on aggregates such as traditions or on the beliefs of individuals will depend on the questions we seek to answer. The choice will depend on the topic to be studied. On the one hand, we will argue individuals are not autonomous, so they necessarily come to hold the beliefs they do within a social context that influences them. To explain the beliefs of a particular individual, we have to appeal to an aggregate concept, such as tradition, that evokes this social context. On the other hand, we will argue discourses, ideologies or traditions have no existence apart from in the contingent beliefs of particular individuals. To appeal to a tradition is always explicitly or implicitly to make claims about the beliefs of particular individuals.

In this book, we concentrate on an aggregate analysis of British political traditions. One of the dangers of so working is that we can neglect the differences in the beliefs of the individuals lumped together in a tradition. Recognition of this danger prompts us to decentre aggregate concepts such as tradition. To decentre is to highlight the diversity of an aggregate concept by unpacking the actual and contingent beliefs and actions of those individuals who fall under it (see Chapter 4 pp. 63–7). So, within the British political tradition, we distinguish Tory, Whig, Liberal and Socialist traditions. Within the Tory tradition, we distinguish the One Nation and statecraft strands. We could have gone on to analyse the beliefs of particular individuals. Yet we do not do so. Our aim is to trace the patterns of thought informing British governance, and to do so we provide an aggregate analysis. In Chapter 9, we unpack the beliefs of two senior civil servants about governance. Elsewhere we do not unpack the beliefs that inform the actions of particular individuals but concentrate on the broader traditions informing general changes in the practices of British government.

Our interpretive approach differs sharply from present-day practice in British political science. It may be true that British political science continues to reveal its 'insular', Whiggish roots despite 'homoeopathic doses of American political science' (Hayward 1991: 104). Even if we can detect a Whiggish historiography behind the Westminster model, the links between the epistemology of present-day political science and its analysis of British government and the nineteenth century have weakened. The attention now given to pressure groups, elections and public policy analysis shows the vast influence of the modernist empiricism and even positivism more usually associated with American political science. The interpretive approach discussed in Chapter 2 relies on an alternative epistemology to both modernist empiricism and positivism. It represents a challenge to this dominant or mainstream tradition.

Our criticisms focus mainly on the modernist empiricism, and even positivism, that informs much political science.[1] Positivism and modernist empiricism – from now on referred to as 'positivism' – share a broadly similar epistemology. They postulate given facts divorced from theoretical contexts as the basis of legitimate claims to knowledge. In contrast, as anti-foundationalists, we reject explicitly the idea of given truths whether based on pure reason or pure experience: all perceptions, and so 'facts', arise within the context of a prior set of beliefs or theoretical commitments. As a result, we typically look suspiciously on any claim to describe neutrally an external reality. We stress the constructed nature of our claims to knowledge (Rorty 1980). Adherents of a positivist epistemology study political actions and institutions as atomised units, which they examine individually before assembling them into larger sets. They assemble such units into larger sets by comparing and classifying their similarities and differences. In contrast, anti-foundationalists stress interpreting political actions and institutions to reveal how they are constructed by prior webs of belief informed by traditions.

Although we defend an interpretive approach by appealing to an anti-foundational epistemology, there are other reasons for doing so. We are sympathetic to the historical and philosophical approach to British politics found in the work of Beer (1965) and Birch (1964). More generally, constructivist theories of the human sciences also suggest these disciplines contain an 'irreducible and inexpungeable element of interpretation' (White 1978: 51 and 82). For example, Collingwood (1939, 1993) argues that historians ask questions and then answer them with stories that make sense out of 'facts', which in their raw form make no sense at all. He summarises his position by saying,

> history should be (a) . . . an answering of questions; (b) concerned with human action in the past; (c) pursued by interpretation of evidence; and (d) for the sake of human self-knowledge.
>
> (Collingwood 1993: 10–11)

Again, Collingwood insists knowledge is '*created*, not *discovered*, because evidence is not evidence until it makes something evident' (Collingwood 1965: 99, emphasis in original). This does not mean there are no 'facts', only that historians in part construct those facts. The human sciences are constructed and shaped by their concepts and theories. The resulting interpretations are always incomplete and always open to challenge. Such a view of the human sciences contrasts markedly with those commonly found in political science where the influence of models drawn from natural science is great.[2]

Although our interpretive approach resembles those of Beer (1965) and Birch (1964), we deploy it to study governance and thus highlight the growing limitations of the Westminster model, which their studies take for granted. The term 'governance' signals that important changes have and are taking place. There are, however, many different accounts of these changes, each of which gives different content to the concept of governance. Governance can refer to a new process of governing, a changed condition of ordered rule, or the new method by which society is governed (cf. Finer 1970: 3–4). One colleague described it as a 'weasel' word – slippery and elusive, used to obscure, not to shed light. He has a point, so in Chapter 3 we identify its various meanings to clear the way for our account. This ground-clearing exercise carries the danger that, as authors, we dictate what words mean. We have no wish to wear such a mantle of linguistic omniscience. We do not believe that our account should be privileged because, as political scientists, we have a means of deciding which accounts are true, which are false. Other political scientists are free to use the same words to mean something else. We are simply describing the content we will attach to our terms. That content will both guide and receive support from the rest of our work. Its reasonableness should depend, not on our having access to given facts, but on a comparison with alternative studies of governance.

The content we attach to governance reflects our interpretive approach. So in Chapter 4 we will decentre it. We will open a positivist, institutional account to questions of meaning. We will indicate how governance is created and recreated as a meaningful practice through beliefs informed by traditions and modified in response to dilemmas. There is, however, the danger we will only tear down the positivist account and put nothing in its place. We must show what an interpretive approach can add to existing accounts of governance. We will indicate the distinctive light our decentred account casts on key issues in the literature as well as on the concerns of practitioners. We will offer, first, an account of British governance focused on networks; second, an interpretive critique of the positivist analysis of governance as networks; and, third, a decentred analysis of governance, which focuses on beliefs, traditions and dilemmas. In effect, we take apart the positivist account of governance as networks by contrasting it with an interpretive approach to networks understood through agents and their beliefs.

Our interpretive approach prompts us to explore governance through beliefs, traditions and dilemmas. We explain the rise and development of governance by the beliefs that informed the policies and practices through which networks arose alongside, and even supplanted, hierarchies and markets. We begin in Chapter 5 by contrasting Britain and Denmark to provide a broad picture of the tradition against which British governance arose. Next, in Chapter 6, we decentre the British tradition into various constituent traditions – Tory, Whig, Liberal and Socialist – showing how each of these understands Thatcherism differently. The first wave of reforms in British governance was the programme of neo-liberal reforms associated with Thatcherism. We explore these reforms and their effects by unpacking the diverse beliefs, concepts and traditions through which Tories, Whigs, Liberals and Socialists construct them. The second wave of reforms to British governance was New Labour's turn to joined-up governance. So we also explore New Labour's policies, in Chapter 7, by unpacking the beliefs it adopted in response to dilemmas thrown up by Thatcherism.

Our interpretive approach explains the rise of governance in part by reference to the beliefs embedded in the Tory, Whig, Liberal and Socialist traditions. When we describe these beliefs, we retell their theories of governance. Our account thus resembles at times a metanarrative: it describes the different narratives of Thatcherism and governance. Yet this resemblance is only superficial. An interpretive approach provides a distinctive, alternative analysis, rather than an account of the field as a whole. It analyses governance by unpacking its constituent ideas and locating them in traditions and dilemmas. Inevitably, the interpretive nature of our alternative analysis means we must unpack and explain other concepts, theories and beliefs in a way that sometimes makes our approach seem like a metanarrative. This elision of alternative narrative and meta-narrative cannot be avoided because it follows from telling stories about other people's stories.

To tell stories about other people's stories, we have to recover their stories and explain them. Although we cannot separate the practices of understanding and explanation in this way, the analytic distinction high-lights that we use two modes of inquiry. Understanding needs an ethno-graphic form of inquiry: we have to read practices, actions, texts, interviews, and speeches to recover other people's stories. Explanation needs a historical form of inquiry: we have to locate their stories within their wider webs of belief, and these webs of belief against the background of traditions they modify in response to specific dilemmas. In our analysis of governance, we merge these two modes of inquiry, reading a wide range of texts in relation to traditions and dilemmas. When we turn from governance in general to the higher civil service, we make more effort to distinguish between them. So we begin in Chapter 8 by reading texts to construct the historical background to present-day debates on civil service reform. Next, in Chapter 9, we use interviews as a basis for an ethno-graphic study of the beliefs permanent secretaries hold about the reforms and their impact on the higher civil service.

The ethnographic study of permanent secretaries also allows us to illustrate how our interpretive approach works at a micro-level. In our analysis of governance, we provide mainly an aggregate analysis. We focus on traditions, invoking individuals as exemplars, rather than on the individual agents who compose traditions. The theory informing our interpretive approach includes a powerful emphasis on individual agency, and we want to show this emphasis is compatible with aggregate studies. Interpretation, as we suggested earlier, covers shared understandings that inform a practice as well as the particular beliefs that inform an individual's actions. While our comparison of Britain and Denmark, and our studies of Thatcherism, New Labour and the roots of civil service reform are examples of the former, our work on permanent secretaries goes some way towards illustrating the latter.

British governance

We use our interpretive approach to explore changes in the British state since 1979. Our story has three parts.

First, we take as our starting point the claim there has been a shift from government by a unitary state to governance by and through networks. In this period the boundary between state and civil society changed. It can be understood as a shift from hierarchies, or the bureaucracies of the welfare state, through the marketisation reforms of the Conservative governments of Thatcher and Major to networks. This emphasis on networks contrasts markedly with accounts of British government rooted in the Westminster model.

Second, we use our anti-foundational approach, with its notions of tradition and dilemma, to decentre this governance story; that is, we identify the several ways in which individuals construct governance. History and ethnography are the best tools for constructing our story of other people's constructions of what they are doing; that is, thick descriptions of individual beliefs and preferences.

Finally, we will thus argue that governance has arisen out of contingent and contested narratives. We present four narratives of governance: intermediate institutions, networks of communities, reinventing the constitution and joined-up government. The actions of individuals are informed by their beliefs in one or other of these narratives. Contemporary British governance is an unintended effect of these actions and the competing narratives.

The notion of governance signals, therefore, change in British government but, in our account, the stress falls on how these changes arose out of competing webs of belief informed by different traditions. Governance refers to the informal authority of networks as constitutive of, supplementing or supplanting the formal authority of government. The concept of governance thus overlaps with those of the core executive, the hollow state and the differentiated polity, all of which point to a more diverse view of state authority as being located at the boundary of state and civil society.

We recognise that others have also sought to explore this broader notion of governance.[3] Harris (1990: 66–7) argues that one of the 'tacit understandings' about political community was 'a belief among politicians of all complexions that the relationship between government and society was essentially a limited one'. Civil society was 'the highest sphere of human existence', while the state was 'an institution of secondary importance'. The corporate life of society 'was expressed through voluntary associations and the local community'. She argues that these beliefs had 'enormous tenacity' (ibid.: 69). Between the wars, they were sustained not just by professional civil servants, who favoured a return to more limited government, but also by the British public who 'resumed their Victorian habits of voluntary action and self-help' (ibid.: 77). However, the Second World War led Britain to develop 'a far more powerful centralised wartime state than any of her more metaphysical-minded, state-exalting continental enemies' (ibid.: 91). It also fuelled a reformist mood, which led to a 'profound break with some of the major conventions of the previous hundred years' (ibid.: 96). 'Promises, programmes and planning' became the new norm (ibid.: 97). Harris concludes that by the 1950s, 'the common constitutional culture based on tacit acceptance of common history and unspoken assumptions about the nature of political behaviour which had been so pervasive earlier in the century had virtually ceased to exist' (ibid.: 111). We should not write the history of the twentieth century as a battle between collectivism and the free market because they 'advanced in tandem at the expense of other more traditional social arrangements such as philanthropy, the family and the local community' (ibid.: 113). 'The ethos of voluntarism was … subtly transformed over the course of the twentieth century':

> They [voluntary associations] were the very sinews of autonomous 'civil society', supported by the state only through a general framework of law. This unpretentious and invisible private collectivism continued in some spheres throughout the period, largely falling through the meshes of the history of government. In many voluntary organisations, however, such autonomy progressively dwindled: they became increasingly the agents and clients of the state, holders of state licenses, beneficiaries of state tax concessions, recipients and competitors for state financial aid – or simply pressure groups urging government to change its policies on some deserving cause. The boundary between public and private spheres became more confused than in the late nineteenth century.
>
> (Ibid.: 114)

Harris is describing the spread of organisational networks tied to the state. These networks are common to both the days of centralised planning and giant corporations and the days of governmental minimalism and neo-liberal economics.

Lowe and Rollings (2000: 101) similarly argue the balance between state and civil society, 'between government and governance', was disrupted by two contradictions. First, British government had a limited or minimalist role in practice but unlimited power in theory. Although there were no constitutional checks on the powers of government, 'public compliance depended on their non-use'. Second, the state was supposed to be neutral between classes but it was partial whenever it intervened on controversial economic and social issues. Britain enjoyed 'an exceptional degree of continuity and order', but this was 'an achievement of governance broadly defined, rather than government' (ibid.: 105). The crisis of the 1950s saw the breakdown of this broader governance as the government responded to perceptions of relative decline by pursuing a policy of modernisation through centralisation. Thus, the history of British government during the twentieth century appears as a shifting balance between government and governance:

> There was a rolling back of the state in the inter-war period; and between 1957 and 1964 far from being a hollowing out of the state there was a heroic attempt at centralisation . . . Governance was a core concept at the start of the century. In the 1920s it was classed as incipiently obsolete. In the 1960s it was then declared wholly obsolete. Its current reinvention needs to be placed in a proper historical context.
>
> (Ibid.: 117)

Our analysis does not remain so abstract. We try to ground the changing boundaries of state and civil society in an account of patterns of government or the mechanisms for authoritatively allocating resources and for exercising control and co-ordination. In other words, we focus on markets, hierarchies and networks. Bureaucracy remains the prime example of hierarchy or co-ordination by administrative order. Despite all the recent changes, it is still a major way of delivering services in British government; for example, the Benefits Agency remains a large bureaucracy. Privatisation, market testing and the purchaser-provider split are examples of government using market or quasi-market ways of delivering services. Price competition is deemed the key to efficient and better quality services. Competition and markets are now a fixed part of the landscape of British government. It is less widely recognised that British government now works through networks characterised by trust and mutual adjustment to provide welfare services. The shifts from hierarchy to markets and then to networks involved changing the boundaries between state and civil society. Indeed, the Conservative government explicitly defended its use of market mechanisms as a way of redefining the boundaries of the state, while New Labour is almost equally explicit about its use of networks.

We also ground our analysis of patterns of government in specific public sector reforms. Policies such as contracting-out are the specific means that brought about the change from hierarchy to markets. Thus, while we focus on governance, the study of the several rounds of public sector reform during the 1980s and 1990s is central to an understanding of governance. Nonetheless, we do not use the examples of the civil service or public management reform for their own sake. Rather, we treat them as instances of reforms to patterns of government and, therefore, to changes in the boundaries between state and civil society.

So, governance refers, to employ shorthand, to governing with and through networks at the boundary of the state and civil society. We use this shorthand in three contexts. First, it describes the changes in British government during the 1980s and 1990s. Second, it interprets British government, directly implying we need to revise radically the Westminster model to include the notion of the differentiated polity. Third, it prescribes the next round of reforms currently proposed by various voices in Britain. For example, the terms holistic governance and joined-up governance refer to measures designed to improve co-ordination between government departments and other agencies. However, whether we use the term 'governance' to describe, to interpret or to prescribe, we take it to refer to the changing boundary between the British state and civil society, in particular to the ways in which the informal authority of networks constitutes, supplements and supplants the formal authority of the state.

A new language

An interpretive approach shifts from familiar concepts such as 'institution' to those of 'decentring', 'tradition' and 'dilemma'. Similarly, 'governance' is not only an alternative to the more familiar 'government' but also one that relies on other new concepts such as 'core executive', 'hollow state' and 'differentiated polity'. Not everyone welcomes these new concepts. Commenting on research into British central government, for example, Peter Riddell, political editor of *The Times*, said:

> The language in which political scientists operate is divorced from that of practitioners and commentators. Every time I see the word 'governance' I have to think again what it means and how it is not the same as government. Terms such as 'core executive', 'differentiated polity' and 'hollowed out executive' have become almost a private patois of political science, excluding outsiders, rather like the jargon of management reform in the civil service. The current generation of political scientists should look back a century to the elegance and clarity – though not the views – of Dicey and Bryce, and even perhaps the wit of a Bagehot.
>
> (Riddell 2000)

Clearly we use the 'private patois of political science' while adding to it the patois of an interpretive approach. We do so because we are convinced the old vocabulary for describing Westminster and Whitehall is at best a partial description of how British government works, and the old positivism is philosophically unsound. We need a new language – our 'private patois' – to capture changes both in our theories and in the state itself. In defending this patois, our objective is not to repair the wounded pride of political science. It matters how we understand British government. Such understandings are not the privilege of the chattering classes. If our existing map of our institutions and how they work is faulty, we mislead citizens and undermine representative democracy. Such maps are about how we are governed and politicians with faulty maps will make promises they cannot keep, not because they are venal, but because, unwittingly, they travel in the wrong direction. We are trying to make corrections to the existing map of British government so citizens and politicians alike know what journeys they can and cannot take.

We defend the concepts in our interpretation of governance because they provide a more accurate and fruitful map of British government than the more familiar concepts of the Westminster model. Yet Riddell rejects a new language less because he thinks it inaccurate than because it lacks the familiarity and the clarity of that of earlier political scientists such as Bagehot. To respond to his concerns, we have to examine the nature of concepts.

What makes concepts familiar? Familiarity obviously comes from use. Here lies a puzzle; the new vocabulary is not acceptable until approved by everyday use but it cannot be so approved until we start using it. Clearly, then, a lack of familiarity cannot be a serious objection to new concepts. We must be able to translate our ideas into ones other political scientists and practitioners recognise. Indeed, such translation is central to the debate, reconfirmation and comparison so integral to an anti-foundationalist epistemology. However, translating our concepts must not entail a slavish adherence to the existing, mainstream language of the Westminster model because it would restrict debate and innovation in political science.

What gives concepts clarity? From an anti-foundationalist perspective, any concept derives meaning in large part from its place within a body of concepts. In isolation, all concepts are vague. Just as the differentiated polity gains clarity when filled out with ideas such as the hollowing-out of the state and the core executive, so the Westminster model gains clarity when filled out with ideas such as the unitary state and cabinet government. No doubt people unfamiliar with a concept such as the hollowing-out of the state might need us to relate it explicitly to processes such as the erosion of the authority of the state by international interdependencies. Equally, however, people who are unfamiliar with the concept of a unitary state might need us to contrast it with federal systems. Although concepts such as the hollow state can sound like metaphors, that too need not be a matter of concern. After all, they are metaphorical only in that they apply novel names to processes and practices that we can unpack in more literal terms, such as international pressures and organisations eroding the authority of the state. What is more, all concepts begin as metaphors in this sense. They start out as novel names, such as loyal opposition, to describe a set of parliamentary practices, only later to acquire familiarity. Gradually, our new concepts might become as much a part of the everyday language of practitioners and commentators as the terms embedded in the Westminster model.

Interpreting British governance

Part I is a ground-clearing exercise. We review the several concepts of governance and describe our approach to its analysis. Chapter 2 explains why interpretation is necessary. We identify and introduce briefly the main varieties of interpretation – hermeneutics, ethnology, post-structuralism and postmodernism. We then offer a sketch and critique of the Westminster model, covering the traditional version and its modifications at the hands of sceptics, social science approaches, the radical alternative and the new public management. We argue there are many weaknesses in this model, most notably its failure to accommodate recent changes. After that we fill out our interpretive approach by analysing traditions and dilemmas and invoking an anthropological concept of objectivity. Finally, we consider the most common criticisms of interpretive approaches.

Chapter 3 provides a survey of the notion of governance. We describe seven uses of the term – corporate governance, the new public management, 'good governance', international interdependence, socio-cybernetic systems, the new political economy and networks. We then provide an outline of the governance narrative of British government. To highlight the differences between this narrative and current versions of the Westminster model, we focus on the four key notions of governance, the core executive, hollowing-out and the differentiated polity. We argue there have been significant shifts in the mix of governing structures in Britain, shifts we summarise as a movement from hierarchy to markets and then to networks.

Throughout the book we compare and contrast positivist and interpretive approaches. In Chapter 4 we use this contrast to decentre the account of governance provided in Chapter 3. Governance appears here as a meaningful practice informed by competing sets of beliefs adopted against the background of various traditions and dilemmas. We then ask five questions about the analysis of policy networks and governance: Is governance new? What is the content of governance? How do we explain changes in governance? How does the centre manage networks? And, is governance failure inevitable? Throughout we stress that the key question posed by an interpretive approach is 'whose story within which tradition'.

In Part II we provide three examples of how to use the concepts of tradition and dilemma to understand present-day governance. Our concept of tradition is a pragmatic one. In Chapters 5–7 we illustrate our approach by analysing public sector reform and its implications for how we understand governance. We show it is possible to decentre the idea of tradition and analyse traditions at several levels. In each chapter we also discuss the problems that arise when we analyse traditions at each level of generality. These problems include reifying traditions, essentialism and explaining change within traditions.

In Chapter 5 we analyse the governmental traditions, or webs of belief about the institutions and history of government, of Britain and Denmark. We argue the Anglo-Saxon governmental tradition constructs public sector reform differently to the *rechtsstaat*, participatory tradition of Denmark. These different constructions lead to reforms characterised by different aims, measures and outcomes. We identify six dimensions to public sector reform: privatisation, marketisation, corporate management, regulation, decentralisation and political control. We describe public sector reform in Britain and Denmark using these dimensions, before comparing the two governmental traditions. We argue the key differences lie in beliefs about the constitution, bureaucracy and relations between the state and civil society. Finally, we suggest that the different governmental traditions not only shape the aims, measures and outcomes of public sector reform, but also lead to different constructions of the dilemmas the reforms have thrown up. In Britain, the key dilemma concerns the steering capacity of the centre. In Denmark, the main dilemma is democratic accountability. Finally, we argue that, while a broad notion of tradition enables us to compare national governmental traditions and so to describe the differences between countries, it runs into the problems of reifying traditions and a relative lack of explanatory power.

In Chapter 6 we reinterpret the legacy of Thatcherism by exploring how the dominant traditions of British government construct the notion. We introduce the Tory, Liberal, Whig and Socialist traditions, arguing each incorporates a distinctive narrative – a map, questions, language and historical story – about British government. We discuss several narratives of Thatcherism to show it has no essential core. There is no one Thatcherism because each tradition constructs its own version. Rather, the legacy of Thatcherism lies in the dilemmas to which it was a response. Thatcherism highlighted the political salience of these dilemmas for each tradition. The main dilemmas concern community, the overloaded state, inflation and globalisation. These dilemmas forced a reconsideration of the existing beliefs characteristic of each tradition, producing individual narratives of Thatcherism, which lives on, therefore, not as a tradition in its own right but in the changes it has wrought in the evolving traditions of British government. Equally important for the argument of this book, we suggest the Liberal tradition developed a distinctive construction of the dilemma of state overload and of the reforms needed to cope with it. These reforms changed British government: they helped to introduce contemporary governance, and they posed dilemmas for the other traditions, which also had to respond to state overload. Finally, we point out that the use of tradition at this level of generality still has problems. We raise, in particular, the issues of essentialism and of explaining the ways in which traditions change through time.

In Chapter 7 we compare the ways in which the New Right and New Labour construct public sector reform. We briefly review their different reform proposals before examining the problems these reforms are meant to solve. We suggest the corporate management and marketisation reforms of the 1980s and 1990s had unintended consequences of, fragmentation, steering, accountability, politicisation and managerial roles. We then ask if New Labour's reforms, as outlined in the White Paper, *Modernising Government*, will resolve these problems. We argue that New Labour has a pragmatic approach to New Right reforms, accepting only some of them. More distinctively, New Labour stresses joined-up policy-making precisely to deal with dilemmas such as fragmentation and a loss of control by the centre. It favours the delivery of public services by steering networks of organisations. It seeks a shift to an enabling state.

In Part II we progressively unpack the idea of tradition to show that no one level of analysis is suitable for answering all questions. Adopting a pragmatic account of tradition means that to explore the rise of any set of beliefs we have to explore how agents respond to dilemmas and so modify the relevant traditions. New Labour's vision, for example, is the outcome of a political struggle, not an ineluctable outcome of globalisation and competition between states.

Part I defines our interpretive approach, governance and our preferred epistemology. Part II provides an extended application of our approach by using the concepts of tradition and dilemma to re-analyse critically governance, especially public sector reform. However, properly to decentre governance, we have to portray it as a product not only of the beliefs and actions of politicians but also of the beliefs and actions of civil servants, service providers and service users. Part III begins to provide such a decentred view of governance. It uses ethnography to explore the ways civil servants received and enacted the reforms. And it uses history – the concepts of tradition and dilemma – to explain why they did so in the ways they did.

In Chapter 8 we explore the historical roots of governance by examining the inherited ideas that underpin present-day debates about civil service reform. We seek to show that present-day debates are not new; they are not an invention of the New Right. So, briefly, we argue the Tory, Liberal, Whig and Socialist traditions tell distinctive stories about present-day civil service reform. We then concentrate on their shared intellectual heritage in themes surrounding the nineteenth-century administrative revolution.

These themes are: British exceptionalism, the generalist civil servant, collectivism, gradualism, elitism, local self-government and efficiency. We show that these themes remain central to understanding present-day constructions of governance.

In Chapter 9 we illustrate the use of ethnographic methods in constructing our constructions of how other people see the world. Permanent secretaries remain white, male, middle-aged lifers, and yet their beliefs about their job have changed markedly. We suggest the best way to understand how an individual's beliefs and preferences change is often to examine their actions, writings, lectures and interviews. If an analysis of the socio-economic characteristics of the administrative elite can be called an outside-in analysis – with the academic outsider looking in – then we offer an inside-out analysis – the permanent secretary insider looking out at his world. We do so by providing lengthy extracts from interviews with two permanent secretaries that show how they understand the changes in their world.

Finally, in Chapter 10, we return to the broader themes of the book to summarise our view of the relative merits of positivist and interpretive approaches. We point out what each approach can tell us about changes in British governance and how we understand such changes. In doing so, we argue there is no necessary or given pattern of governance, but only the constructions of various traditions. An analysis of these constructions is, however, 'edifying'; it is a way of finding 'new, better, more interesting, more fruitful ways of speaking about' British government (Rorty 1980: 360).

Notes

1 For a fuller account of modernist empiricism and its place in British political science see Bevir 2001. Smith 2000 explores the study of international relations, contrasting the rationalist mainstream and its reflectivist alternatives in a way that resembles our contrast between the positivist mainstream and interpretive approaches. In doing so, he emphasised that, although the mainstream often seeks to disavow positivism, it remains committed to a naturalism that effectively excludes interpretive approaches. The mainstream might deny its debt to positivism, but its work continues to exhibit the quantitative, classificatory and empirical biases of what we call modernist empiricism.

2 For a political science view of the uses of history see Kavanagh 1991; and for an equivalent view from a historian see Lowe 1999: 5 and 37.

3 See Bevir 2000b; Clarke 1996, especially the bibliographical essay (pp. 411–31); Harrison 1996; Hennessy 1992; Middlemas 1979; Perkin 1969; Porter 1994; Pugh 1994; Thompson 1990; and Thomson 1950.

Part I

The approach

On interpretation

2   An interpretive agenda

Introduction

Interpretive approaches to political science focus on the meanings that shape actions and institutions, and the ways in which they do so. Different varieties of interpretive theory understand meanings to be expressions of, for example, reason, intentions, beliefs, the unconscious or systems of signs. They seek to explain meanings using notions such as logical progression, the dispositions of individuals, the structural links between concepts and power. Behind the different types of interpretive theory, however, there lies the shared assumption that we cannot understand human affairs properly unless we grasp the relevant meanings. Thus, interpretive approaches do not merely study beliefs, ideas or discourses. They study beliefs as they appear within, and even frame, actions, practices and institutions. Interpretive theory applies to all of political science.

Most political scientists would acknowledge the inevitability of one type of interpretation. In October 1943, the Danes rescued 7,200 Jews by taking them in small boats across the Øresund, which separated Nazi-occupied Denmark from neutral Sweden. These widely shared 'facts' lie at the heart of a heated debate. According to the 'Heroic Danes' theory, the brave Danes, at risk of life and liberty, rescued the Danish Jews from the murderous Nazis. Other theories, however, try to demythologise Danish actions. According to the 'Good Germans' theory, the deportation policy was set up by the top brass of the Nazi regime but sabotaged by brave local Germans, perhaps influenced in part by Denmark's democratic way of life. Finally, according to the 'Berlin' theory, Hitler's orders to remove the Danes from Denmark were interpreted creatively with Himmler's knowledge and approval. Because Himmler was the most loyal of Hitler's top Nazis, he cannot be suspected of frustrating Hitler's policy, so we should assume the Danes merely did what Hitler wanted as opposed to what he said he wanted. The debate rages from how much the fishermen charged the Jews to take them to Sweden to whether the documentation supports the view that Berlin approved the rescue. It often revolves around the motives of key actors and is hampered only in part by inadequate source material. It is widely agreed the Danes took many Jews to Sweden but it is less clear what these agreed 'facts' mean (Kirchhoff 1995; Paulsson 1995).

While most political scientists would acknowledge the inevitability of such debates about how to interpret 'facts', we want to insist on the inevitability of another type of interpretation. We can understand and explain practices and actions adequately only by reference to the beliefs and desires of the relevant actors. Hence to study political life adequately we have to engage in the interpretation of the beliefs and desires of those we study.

Political science has its origins in disciplines such as history, law and philosophy where this second type of interpretation often plays a dominant role. Historians focused on particular events as they unfolded chronologically. Often they sought to unpack the beliefs and motives of those involved in their story. Lawyers looked at the formal nature of institutions. Often they sought to unearth the intentions of lawmakers to decide how to apply the law. Philosophers explored the normative side of social life. Often they sought to discover the ideals by which others had lived as a guide to how we should do so. Alongside these interpretive forms of political science, however, there also arose approaches more defiantly indebted to the natural sciences. These latter approaches tried to find laws or regularities that governed social life irrespective of the beliefs of individuals or the meanings found in a society (Bevir 2001). After the Second World War, political science witnessed the emergence, and gradual dominance, of behaviourism, structuralism and, most recently, rational choice theory, all of which embody positivist ambitions.

Present-day interpretive theory has two main strands. First, there are the interpretive approaches rooted in the humanities, notably history. They draw on hermeneutic and phenomenological philosophies. Second, new approaches to interpretive theory flourished as disillusionment with the positivist aims of behaviourism and structuralism grew. These approaches draw on post-structuralist and postmodern philosophies.

This chapter has five sections. The first section outlines why political scientists should adopt an interpretive approach. The second identifies some of the main varieties of interpretation, as well as exploring some of the issues that divide them. The third section outlines and criticises the dominant approach to the study of British government. The fourth section outlines the main concepts that define our preferred approach to interpretation. The final section counters the main criticisms levelled at interpretive approaches to political science.

Why interpretation is necessary

An interpretive approach follows from two premises. The first straightforward premise is that people act on their beliefs and preferences. People vote for the Labour Party, for example, because they share its values, or they believe its policies will improve their well-being. Similarly, when politicians raise interest rates they do so because they think they will bring down inflation, or they believe doing so will get them a reputation for financial prudence, or they want to save money for a pre-election binge. Because people act on beliefs and preferences, it is possible to explain their actions by referring to the relevant beliefs and preferences. Few political scientists would deny that such explanations have some force. Yet many would complain that such explanations lack the power of general applicability, and anyway that beliefs and preferences are impossible to corroborate. Thus, they seek to bypass beliefs by correlating actions with objective facts about people: they might point, for example, to a correlation between voting for the Labour Party and being working class. Alternatively they seek to build models on basic assumptions about the rationality of human actors: they might suggest, for example, that rational people will raise interest rates when inflation increases.

The second premise common to interpretive approaches undercuts attempts to bypass beliefs. This premise is that we cannot read-off people's beliefs and preferences from objective facts about them such as their social class, race or institutional position. The impossibility of pure experiences implies that we cannot reduce beliefs and preferences to mere intervening variables. When we say that a person – Sir Humphrey Appleby – in a position – Permanent Secretary managing the Department of Administrative Affairs – has an interest in preserving the staffing and spending levels of his department, we necessarily bring our particular theories to bear to identify his position and deduce what interests go with it. People with different theories might believe that this top civil servant is in a different position. He is not a manager but a political and policy adviser and so has different interests – for example, protecting the minister from political flack and fire-fighting policy disasters. Or people with different theories might believe that this top civil servant has different interests; for example, launching and promoting the department's long-standing policy preferences. Indeed, our theories may lead us to views contrary to a person's own view of his or her position and its associated interests. For example, some working-class voters might consider themselves to be middle class with an interest in preventing further redistributive measures. Others might consider themselves to be working class while believing redistributive measures are contrary to the true interests of the workers because they delay the revolution.

These two premises are all we need to show that interpretation is necessary. However, there are reasons for insisting on a special role for interpretation in spelling out some features of social life. One obvious area is the ideology that political actors use to legitimate their actions irrespective of their real motivations. When politicians use human rights to justify a policy, we cannot understand that justification and its effectiveness, irrespective of its truth, unless we grasp the content and role of ideas about human rights in the relevant society. Another such area is that of speech-acts because they usually presume shared linguistic conventions (Skinner 1970, 1988). A final area where interpretation plays a special role is in analysing the concepts that underpin social practices (Koselleck 1998; Richter 1995). When a priest pronounces a couple married, for example, they become married only because of settled conventions about the legal authority of the church, the religious nature of marriage and the binding power of contracts. To understand and explain what happens at such times, we have to grasp the relevant conventions and beliefs. A marriage can be contracted only within a set of meanings or concepts drawn from theology, law and morality. We can study statistical rises and falls in the number of marriages only after we take for granted a whole series of interpretations.

Arguments for the ineluctable role of interpretation are tied closely to arguments against the possibility of a political science modelled on the natural sciences. People choose to act on some of their preferences in accord with beliefs they adopt for their own reasons. Thus, when we try to explain the link between preferences, beliefs and actions, there is no causal necessity equivalent to that characteristic of explanations in the natural sciences. However, we can still explain social action: we can do so by pointing to the conditional and volitional links between the relevant beliefs, preferences, intentions and actions. Political science thus relies largely on a narrative form of explanation (Bevir 1999a: 252–62 and 301–8). We account for actions, practices and institutions by telling a story about how they came to be as they are and perhaps also about how they are preserved. Narratives are thus to political science what theories are to the natural sciences. Although narratives may have a chronological order and contain setting, character, actions and events, their defining characteristic is that they explain actions by the beliefs and preferences of the actors. Political science relies on narrative structures akin to those found in works of fiction. However, the stories told by political scientists are not works of fiction. The difference between the two lies not in the use of narrative but in the link between the narratives invoked to our objective knowledge of the world.

Varieties of interpretation

As political science developed and separated itself from other disciplines, the concern with meaning became associated with hermeneutics and ethnology. More recently, post-structuralist and postmodern philosophies have inspired other varieties of interpretation. The latter two forms of interpretation shift our focus from individuals and mind to systems of signs and how they work in society.

Hermeneutics and ethnology

In the early part of the twentieth century, an analytical and atomistic form of positivism increasingly dominated Anglo-American philosophy. Typically this positivism helped to inspire a behavioural social science with little interest in beliefs or meanings. Those philosophers who inherited the idealist mantle of the late nineteenth century, and those who turned to continental traditions such as phenomenology, provided the main alternatives to positivism. Idealists such as Oakeshott (1975) and Collingwood (1993) favoured hermeneutic approaches to history and by extension to the human sciences as a whole. Phenomenology inspired sociologists and anthropologists who wanted to understand the meanings people in their own or other societies attached to social practices. It resulted in the ethnology of Berger and Luckman (1971) and Geertz (1973).

Hermeneutics emerged within Biblical scholarship. It has come, however, to refer to the theory of understanding, especially interpreting texts and actions (Bauman 1978; Gadamer 1979). So, hermeneutics often overlaps with an interest in the history of ideas (Collingwood 1993; Oakeshott 1962, 1975). Typically, hermeneutic theorists explore the existential nature of understanding while recognising it is embedded in tradition. Collingwood argued all history was 'thought', where thought was a series of answers to specific questions arising in a historically specific set of taken-for-granted ideas. Oakeshott insisted, against rationalists and positivists, that political knowledge could come only from history. Political activity should be explained by the wisdom and moral claims embedded in the relevant tradition of behaviour. Greenleaf's (1983a and b, 1987) grand vision of British politics in the twentieth century represents a self-conscious application of Oakeshott's hermeneutic theory. Greenleaf traces the rise of collectivism, the ideological tensions that then surrounded the growth of government, and the impact of such growth on the political system. He moves outwards from the intimations of a tradition to the practices and institutions it inspires.

Husserl, the originator of phenomenological philosophy, argued the life world of everyday common sense provides the ontological basis of any possible experience (Husserl 1931). Later theorists suggested our common-sense knowledge was always incomplete and variable. We only ever hold such knowledge provisionally. Contingent social processes produce it. Thus, ethnology focuses on the different forms of common-sense knowledge and practical reasoning that occur in diverse social contexts. It has appealed mainly to sociologists such as Berger and Luckman (1971) and cultural anthropologists such as Geertz (1973).

For Clifford Geertz, humans live suspended in the webs of significance they have spun. Anthropologists practise ethnology to discover the relevant weaves of meaning. Doing ethnography involves using techniques such as transcribing texts and keeping a diary. More important, it is about 'thick descriptions', about explicating 'our own constructions of other people's constructions of what they and their compatriots are up to'. The everyday phrase is 'seeing things from the other's point of view'. The key point is that the ethnographer provides his or her own interpretation of what the informants believe they are up to, so his or her accounts are second- or even third-order interpretations.

Ethnographic description has four characteristics: it is interpretive; it interprets the flow of social discourse; it records that discourse commonly by writing it down; and it is microscopic. It is a soft science that guesses at meanings, assesses the guesses and draws explanatory conclusions from the better guesses. Yet it is still possible for ethnographers to generalise. Theory provides a vocabulary with which to express what symbolic action has to say about itself. Although ethnography rarely aims at prediction, theory still has to 'generate cogent interpretations of realities past' and 'survive . . . realities to come'. The task of the ethnographer is to set down the meanings that particular actions have for social actors and then say what these thick descriptions tells us about the society in which they are found. And this analysis is always incomplete.

> An Englishman (in India) who, having been told that the world rested on a platform which rested on the back of an elephant which rested in turn on the back of a turtle, asked . . . what did the turtle rest on? Another turtle. And that turtle? 'Ah Sahib, after that it is turtles all the way down.'

The ethnographer will never get to the bottom of anything. Ethnographic anthropology is a science 'marked less by a perfection of consensus than by a refinement of debate' – 'what gets better is the precision with which we vex each other'. (This summary paraphrases and quotes Geertz 1973: Chapter 1.)

Post-structuralism and postmodernism

Interpretive approaches indebted to hermeneutics and ethnology persisted even during the heyday of positivism. More recently, post-structuralist and postmodern philosophies have resulted in new varieties of interpretive theory. While these new approaches provide powerful challenges to the scientific hopes of behaviourists and rational choice theorists, proponents of the hermeneutic and ethnographic alternatives have not always welcomed them. The labels post-structuralist and postmodernist refer to a broad range of theorists who challenge foundationalism in philosophy and the human sciences.[1] Unfortunately the clear differences among them makes these labels singularly unhelpful. Many of the theorists involved have renounced the labels for their own work. We can try only to give the reader a feel for the interpretive theories inspired by post-structuralism and postmodernism and we will do so by looking more closely at the work of Foucault.

Like most post-structuralists and postmodernists, Foucault is implacably hostile to the grandiose claims that characterise the so-called modern project. This project claims to ground our knowledge and ethics on objective and essential foundations. Typically it does so by appealing to either pure experience of the world or the pure nature of human subjectivity. In doing so, it relies on other positions about, say, the transparent nature of language and the progressive nature of human history. How accurate it is to equate modernity with such claims and positions need not concern us. What does concern us is the way in which post-structuralists and post-modernists analyse the necessary limits of this modern project. Foucault's work displays a continuing hostility to two modern concepts – the subject and reason (Bevir 1999b and c).

Foucault's hostility to the modern project leads him to adopt an inter-pretive approach to social life. In opposing pure experiences, he suggests we have experiences only within a prior discourse. Objects and actions acquire meaning, become real, only when they have a place in a language, a wider web of meanings. Thus, to understand an object or action, political scientists have to interpret it in the wider discourse of which it is a part. They cannot dismiss discourse as a passive reflection of social or economic forces. However, Foucault does not seem to credit a significant role to human agency in constructing such discourses. Rather, he appears to suggest that discourses develop randomly as products of time and chance. There is no cosmic logic from which we might read-off a discourse from our know-ledge of human history. Political scientists have to interpret objects and actions in their historically specific circumstances. Human life is under-standable only in a framework of meaning, and this framework of meaning cannot be reduced to an objective process or structure.

In his early writings, Foucault sometimes argued an episteme structured the particular meanings or objects of a given era (Foucault 1973, 1986). Even here, however, the episteme only limited rather than fixing the particular meanings found in it. In his later work, moreover, Foucault turned from the notion of an episteme to that of a discursive practice (1972). A discourse consists of endlessly multiplying meanings, many statements and events, none of which are stable, none of which constitutes the essence of that discourse. From a post-structuralist perspective, the key to understanding a social practice is neither its formal legal character nor the objective characteristics of those involved. Rather, these characteristics, like the practice itself, can only be understood as part of the cluster of meanings that make them possible. For example, Foucault argues the modern state gets its character from the way in which it brings together the concepts of sovereignty, discipline and pastorship (Foucault 1991).

The distinctive nature of Foucault's interpretive approach owes much to his hostility to the subject and reason. For a start, his hostility to the subject means he stresses the ways in which regimes of power and epistemes construct individuals and their beliefs. Foucault rejected the idea of an autonomous subject; the subject does not have its own foundation or meaningful experiences, reasoning, beliefs and actions outside a social context. Equally, he rejected the Hegelian and Marxist vision of history as realising an autonomous subject. For Foucault, the subject is inherently a contingent product of a particular discourse, a particular set of techniques of government and technologies of the self (Foucault 1982). So, he stresses social discourses rather than the beliefs of individuals. In addition, Foucault's hostility to reason means he decentres discourses to show how they arise out of the more or less random interactions of all sorts of micro-practices (Foucault 1978–85). In his later works, he rejected the notion that structural relationships, essential characteristics or a logical develop-ment ever governed social practices. The modern state, for example, arose by adapting various techniques – such as the pastoral power of the church – which clearly are not integral to the state (Foucault 1991).

There are, therefore, many varieties of interpretive theory; we are not alone. But postmodern, post-structuralist and constructivist approaches have made few inroads in the political science of British government. As Hay (2003, forthcoming) notes, the contribution of interpretive approaches

> is very unevenly distributed between political science and international relations. For whilst it has yet to make much of an impact in political science, it has proved far more influential within international relations theory.

Because international relations is organised in separate disciplinary departments, has its own professional organisation, the British International Studies Association (BISA), and 'is not wedded to political science either in disciplinary roots or professional organisation' (Smith 2000: 396), we treat it as a separate discipline from political science. Given our focus on the political science of British government, we are confident that interpretive approaches have had little influence.[2] Still, we need to spell out our version of an interpretive approach. Before so doing, however, we also need to cast a critical eye over existing accounts of British government.

The Westminster model

The key difference between positivists and anti-foundationalists lies in their answer to the question, 'how do we know what we know about pure facts?' Positivism covers both strict positivists who believe in pure facts and modernist empiricists who believe in atomised facts (Bevir 2001). Positivism tries to discover pure facts, and strives after successive approxi-mations to a given truth. In Hayward's (1986: 8) acerbic tones, political science has been pervaded by 'portentous claims, methodological obsession and paltry performance' as it has tried to live up to its name. We reject all absolute truth claims, accepting there are no grounds for conclusively asserting the superiority of one interpretation over another. Our objective is to broaden the research agenda by showing how an anti-foundationalist epistemology raises distinctive and interesting questions about British government.

The phrase 'Westminster model' refers to the concepts, questions and historical story used to capture the allegedly essential features of British government that, mainly through sheer longevity, form the present-day, conventional or mainstream view.[3] The term 'mainstream' will always cause problems. Critics will reply that, because they reject some of the shared ideas, they are not part of the mainstream. Any general characterisation of any position courts this danger. Also, it is no part of our remit to set out other people's epistemological position, especially as most proponents of the political science of British government do not do so, content to leave their views implicit.[4] We draw on Wittgenstein's (1972) view that our concepts often cover diverse contents connected by family resemblance rather than a single, essential idea. We think the Westminster model refers to a set of ideas with strong family resemblances. It should be rewritten to make it explicitly a narrative. Instead of objectifying institutions, it should explain how British government works with the beliefs and preferences of the relevant actors as the basic building blocks. This contrast between a model and a narrative is instructive. The notion of a model evokes a monolithic and unchanging object of study that fits well with positivist attempts to ignore meaning, difference and contingency. Our concept of a narrative points to the need to decentre institutions and practices. By so doing, narratives reveal the diversity of beliefs and traditions on which institutions rest. They also show the contingent and changing nature of institutions as they are constantly recreated through particular actions. We refer to the Westminster model, not narrative, in part because that is what people are used to and in part to dramatise the difference between a positivist approach that works with models and an anti-foundational one that uses narratives.

It is only recently that the language of narratives has appeared in studies of British government (see, for example, Marsh *et al.* 1999; Hay 2002). There are related notions. For example, Gamble (1990: 405) appeals to 'an organising perspective' that precedes theory and provides 'a map of how things relate, a set of research questions'. It provides the frame within which we draw the map and pose the questions. Similarly, Tivey (1988: 3) deploys the concept of 'the image' to denote 'a set of assumptions about "the system" . . . and how it works'. Each image contains 'operative concepts' or 'operative ideals': 'the views of the authors are taken', moreover, 'to be of some influence; what they have said has to some extent become operative'. Indeed, his images 'have gained currency among those who study politics, and diluted and distorted they have reached the practitioners' (Tivey 1988: 1; see also Beer 1965: xiii and 404). It could be argued that the Westminster model is the pervasive image shared by British politicians and civil servants.

The ideas of an 'organising perspective' and 'an image' bear a family resemblance not only to our concept of a narrative but also to White's (1973: 4) notion of 'visions of the historical field'. To the question 'what is the correct approach to history?', White answers:

> It does not depend upon the nature of the 'data' they used to support their generalisations or the theories they invoked to explain them; it depends rather upon the consistency, coherence and illuminative power of their respective visions of the historical field. This is why they cannot be 'refuted', or their generalisations 'disconfirmed', either by appeal to new data that might be turned up in subsequent research or by elaboration of a new theory interpreting the set of events that comprise their objects of representation and analysis.

It follows, therefore, that an organising perspective is not falsifiable. It never provides a definitive account; it is an approximation, a map where maps 'can guide . . . even when they are and are known to be grossly inaccurate' since they can be corrected on the way (MacIntyre 1983: 32; Loughlin 1992: 37–8).

We prefer the term 'narrative' because it signals the distinctive nature of explanation in the human sciences. Narratives explain actions by reference to the beliefs and preferences of the relevant individuals. In addition, narratives encompass the maps, questions, languages and historical stories used to explain British government.

In discussing present-day versions of the Westminster model, we court the danger of erecting a straw man. Still we need a benchmark before we can discuss variations on it, so we begin with the obvious – a dictionary definition:

> The characteristics of the Westminster model . . . include: strong cabinet government based on majority rule; the importance attached to constitutional conventions; a two-party system based on single member constituencies; the assumption that minorities can find expression in one of the major parties; the concept of Her Majesty's loyal opposition; and the doctrine of parliamentary supremacy, which takes precedence over popular sovereignty except during elections.
>
> (Verney 1991: 637)

There are many similar definitions. For example, Gamble (1990: 407) lists a unitary state characterised by parliamentary sovereignty, strong cabinet government, accountability through elections, majority party control of the executive – that is, prime minister, cabinet and the civil service – elaborate conventions for the conduct of parliamentary business, institutionalised opposition and the rules of debate. Obviously every author varies both the list of characteristics and their relative importance.[5] The model has been criticised and adapted. For example, Marsh (1999: 1–2) argues British political science needs to be theoretically informed but empirically grounded, to be less prone to heroic generalisations and to have an explicit epistemological position. By implication, the Westminster model has none of these attributes.[6] But although there are many critics, nonetheless there remains not only a clear baseline to any discussion of the Westminster model but also marked family resemblances between its several variants. Among the most prominent family characteristics are the focus on rules and institutions, the use of legal-historical methods, a Whiggish historiography and a personalised view of power.

The Westminster model focuses on institutions – that is, the rules, procedures and formal organisations of government. Indeed, institutions with political thought are the long-standing objects of study in political science (Leftwich 1984: 16). Greenleaf (1983a: 7–9) argues that constitutional law, constitutional history and the study of institutions form the 'traditional' approach. Indisputably these topics are central to the Westminster model with its language of machine metaphors and phrases such as 'the machinery of government'.

The Westminster model also contains a widely shared set of methodological assumptions. These assumptions involve using the inductive tools of the lawyer and the historian to explain the constraints on both political behaviour and democratic effectiveness. It firmly rejects the deductive approach of the economist. Indeed, as Gamble (1990: 409) highlights, it sometimes embodies an idealist moment, seeing 'institutions as the expression of human purpose' and focusing, therefore, on the interaction between ideas and institutions. For example, Johnson (1975: 276–7) defends the study of political institutions, arguing that:

> political institutions express particular choices about how political relationships ought to be shaped; they are in the nature of continuing injunctions to members of a society that they should try to conduct themselves in specific ways when engaged in the pursuit of political ends.

At times, the Westminster model goes with a Whig historiography that comes perilously close to telling the story of a single, unilinear, progressive idea, reason or spirit underlying the evolution of British government. It emphasises gradualism and the capacity of British institutions to evolve and cope with crises. It provides 'capacity for independent action, leadership and decision' while ensuring that 'British political institutions would remain flexible and responsive'. This implicit Whig historiography probably added to the appeal of the model for political scientists. They 'were largely sympathetic', 'convinced that change needed to be evolutionary', and willing to celebrate 'the practical wisdom embodied in England's constitutional arrangements' (Gamble 1990: 411 and 409).

The Westminster model also makes some important, if implicit, assumptions about power. As Smith (1999a) argues, it focuses on behaviour, motivations and institutional position. Power is an object that belongs to the prime minister, cabinet or civil service. 'Power relationships are a zero-sum game where there is a winner and a loser' and power is 'ascribed to an institution or person and fixed to that person regardless of the issue or the context'. Personality is a key part of any explanation of an actor's power.

The family: variations on a theme

Norton and Hayward (1986) identify three periods in the development of British political science. First, there was the formative period before 1961 with its dominant philosophical and historical approach. A self-conscious community emerged between 1961 and the early 1970s with its 'reformist optimism' and 'scientific expectations'. Finally, there was a maturing phase during which the discipline has 'muddled its way forward' to become more analytical (but see Bevir 2001). Much of the literature prefers positivism to the philosophical and historical version of the Westminster model to be found, for instance, in Beer (1965) and Birch (1964).[7] We now describe the allegedly maturing phase with its several variations on, and arguably alternatives to, the Westminster model. There are some important challengers, including American behaviouralism, Marxism and the New Right, and the new public management (NPM), and the model has also been vigorously criticised from within.

The traditional sceptics

The optimism of the classical Westminster model with its belief in the resilience of British institutions foundered on recurrent crises. The sceptics flourished in the 1970s. They bemoaned government overload (King 1975), adversary politics (Finer 1975a), the cultural basis of Britain's decline (Barnett 1986) and elective dictatorship (Hailsham 1978). They called for constitutional reconstruction. Beer (1982) and Birch (1989) reassessed their analyses of the state of British government with jaundiced eyes. Beer pointed to pluralistic stagnation, class decomposition and the revolt against authority to explain the paralysis of British government, invoking no less an example than the Beatles on the way. In more phlegmatic tones, Birch commented on the implications for representative and responsible government of loosening party discipline, intra-party democracy, electoral reform, civil disobedience, referenda and the erosion of local democracy. During the 1980s, the literature on constitutional reform began to take on the proportions of an avalanche. All was not as it should be. The classical

Westminster model came under attack from within as political scientists catalogued the growing divergence between constitutional theory and political practice. Some sceptics sought to bury the model and its Whig story. But most political scientists continued to subscribe to some variant of it, if only to explain Britain's relative decline. Thus, for Marquand (1988: 154), Britain failed to become an adaptive, developmental state because of its 'political culture suffused with the values and assumptions of whiggery'.

American behaviouralism

The influence of American political science and its methods also prompted questions about the Westminster model. The preferred method of working was to frame hypotheses that, at least in principle, could be refuted or falsified. Gamble (1990: 412) notes behaviouralism 'introduced new rigour into British political science and widened the range of research questions but had no alternative organising perspective to propose'. Behavioural methods were used, but the tacit historiography was still often Whiggish, a point amply illustrated by the regular use of such phrases as Britain's 'traditionally modern political culture' (Kavanagh 1990b: Chapter 4; Norton 1984: Chapter 2; Rose 1985: Chapter 1).

Behaviouralism inspired a greater diversity of subjects. Gamble (1990: 414–18) and Tivey (1988) identify five important developments: public policy, political economy, political behaviour, especially the several theories of voting behaviour, Thatcherism and managerialism. Amid this diversity, however, there are important continuities. Common major themes include institutional continuity, the growth of government, and relative economic decline. For example, Bulmer and Burch (1996: 8) describe the British system as 'evolutionary, flexible, unitary (as opposed to federal), centralised, and adversarial with substantial power concentrated in a "collective" central executive'. Clearly, the Westminster model has not disappeared. Overall American political science received a 'cool reception' and its impact was 'muted'.

The radical alternative

For most of the post-war period, the main radical challenge came from Marxism, which broadened to encompass many varieties of state theory. The main challenge now comes from the New Right. Both state theory and the New Right offer distinct narratives of the British polity.

For Leys (1983: 15) the Marxist perspective focuses on the social totality, tries to rethink the present historically and seeks the social origins and effects of ideas. These are the basic tenets of the materialist interpretation of history. This focus on economic forces and class, allied to a critique of capitalism, characterises the Marxist challenge to the Westminster model and its Whig story.[8] However, the label Marxist is now too confining because it does not adequately capture burgeoning state theory.[9] All of these radical accounts of British politics dispute the factual accuracy of the Westminster model and challenge specific interpretations, although they typically prefer to talk of counterfactuals rather than falsification and refutation. Ironically, although their historical story is anti-Whig, their account continues to be shaped, arguably even distorted, by themes of Whig historiography. They accept that Britain has a unique political tradition characterised by stability and continuity. The British political tradition thus domesticates them even though they focus on crises. For example, Miliband's (1972, 1982) analysis of the Labour Party and parliamentarism stresses its key role in managing conflicts and discontents by expressing grievances. However, it also contained demands from below because it accepted the validity and legitimacy of the state and rejected radicalism for moderation. The similarities of Marxist alternatives with the mainstream Westminster model also extend to subject areas. The factual and interpretive challenges to the Westminster model focus on, for example, the unitary state, parliamentary sovereignty, bureaucratic neutrality, ministerial responsibility and the impact of Thatcherism. So, the Westminster model shapes other narratives through the questions it poses and the concepts used to answer them.

Central tenets of the New Right are a suspicion of the state, the primacy of markets and the importance of protecting the individual from state intervention and the state from domination by producer interests. The narrative often draws heavily on rational choice theory, including the assumptions of methodological individualism and the deductive approach of the economist. Although it has exercised much influence on the practice of British government, there are few texts that provide an interpretation of British government.[10] The New Right literature rarely goes beyond critiques of government policy, such as in health and education, or of British political institutions, such as the civil service and local government. We agree with Gamble's (1990: 420) assessment that 'the New Right model is far from gaining the ascendancy which the Westminster model once enjoyed'.

The new public management

NPM is a global phenomenon and a policy ambition for international organisations (see, for example, OECD 1995). The label also received the seal of approval from many academics (see, for example, Hood 1991). Although it covers many varieties of public sector reform (see Hood 1995), the existing literature identifies six main changes relevant to describing and analysing trends in British government: privatisation, marketisation, corporate management, decentralisation, regulation and political control.[11]

The literature on the changes is enormous, but the consistent even pervasive storyline is the problems posed for the Westminster model by NPM. Thus, the search for greater economy, efficiency and effectiveness led to agencification, which separated policy from operational management. Ministers delegated responsibility to agency chief executives but remained accountable to parliament for policy. Obviously many commentators welcomed this search for greater efficiency, but typically they bemoaned weakened ministerial responsibility to parliament. Again, NPM is a member of the family of perspectives associated with the Westminster model because it draws on the key beliefs about the constitution to interpret change.

So, traditional sceptics, behaviouralists, radicals and managerialists alike have highlighted factual and theoretical problems in the Westminster model. Yet despite the force of these criticisms, it survives. For example, most textbooks offer a critical variation, not a coherent alternative narrative. British political scientists exhibit a 'marked propensity . . . not to question the fundamentals of the British political process' (Hayward 1991: 104). As Dearlove (1982: 438) concludes:

> New perspectives may have had to burst *through* the more established interpretations, but this does not mean they burst them *apart*. Quite the reverse. New approaches and perspectives were slowly absorbed and accepted precisely because they could be interpreted so as to sustain the credibility of the *core* assumptions integral to the earlier accounts and to the tradition of understanding as a whole.

There is a mainstream. The Westminster model survives in spite of many cracks. We offer an alternative; the governance narrative of British government. Before we present this narrative, however, we fill out the content of our interpretive approach. If the Westminster model, a Whig historiography and a positivist epistemology are inadequate, what should we put in their place? In the rest of this chapter, we concentrate on theoretical questions. In Chapters 3 and 4, we provide the alternative narrative.

A decentred approach

Post-structuralist and postmodern varieties of interpretation differ from hermeneutic ones principally because of their hostility to subjectivity and rationality. We favour a form of interpretation that lies between hermeneutics and post-structuralism. Critics often view post-structuralism and postmodernism as marking a total break with the modern ideas of the subject and truth, that is, with a nihilistic irrationalism (Bloom 1987; Habermas 1987). Foucault and others sometimes lend credence to this view, though they are perhaps better understood as attacking autonomy and foundationalist notions of truth without spending enough time spelling out where that leaves us. In contrast, we will defend, first, the possibility of agency even without autonomy, and, second, an anthropological concept of objectivity based on criteria of comparison.

Context and agency

Forms of explanation about human life commonly revolve around two sets of ideas. Those in the first set analyse the social context in which individuals reason and act using notions such as tradition, institution, structure and paradigm. Those in the second set analyse the processes by which beliefs, practices and institutions change using the notions of reason and agency.

Some interpretive theories assume autonomous subjects who think and act according solely to their own reason and commands. Post-structuralists and postmodernists, such as Foucault, rightly oppose such an idea. However, a rejection of autonomy need not entail a rejection of agency. To deny that subjects can escape from all social influences is not to deny that they can act creatively for reasons that make sense to them. On the contrary, we must allow for agency if only because we cannot separate and distinguish beliefs and actions by reference to their social context alone. Different people adopt different beliefs and perform different actions against the background of the same social structure. Thus, there must be a space in social contexts where individual subjects decide what beliefs to hold and what actions to perform for their own reasons. Individuals can reason creatively in ways that are not fixed, nor even strictly limited by, the social contexts or discourses in which they exist. We agree with the post-structuralists and postmodernists that subjects experience the world in ways that necessarily depend on the influence on them of social contexts. Nonetheless, we still should allow that the subject has the ability to select particular beliefs and actions, including novel ones that might transform the relevant social structure. This view of agency suggests that we see social contexts not as epistemes, languages or discourses, but as traditions. The concepts of episteme, language and discourse typically invoke social structures that fix individual acts and exist independently of them. In contrast, the notion of tradition implies that the relevant social context is one in which subjects are born, which then acts as the background to their later beliefs and actions without fixing them. Tradition allows for the possibility of subjects adapting, developing and even rejecting much of their heritage.

So, we insist on the fact of agency. Doing so is not incompatible with our insistence on the unavoidable nature of tradition. On the contrary, we can combine a rejection of autonomy with a defence of agency by saying individuals always start against a social background that influences them but they then can reason and act in novel ways to alter this background. Here our use of tradition allows for individuals extending and changing the traditions they inherit. Just because individuals inherit a tradition does not imply they cannot go on to change it. Rather, the ability to modify a tradition is an integral feature of our responses to the world. We always confront slightly novel circumstances in which we need to apply tradition anew, and no tradition can stipulate how it is applied.

On traditions

When unpacking the idea of tradition, we must not reify traditions (Bevir 1999a: 174–220). Tradition is a starting point, not something that fixes or limits later actions. Tradition is not an unavoidable influence on all we do, for to assume it was would leave too slight a role for agency. Rather, we think of tradition as an initial influence on people that colours their later actions only if their agency has not led them to change it. Every strand of a tradition is in principle open to change. We should also be wary of essentialists who equate traditions with a fixed set or core of beliefs against which they then assess variations (see, for example, Greenleaf 1983a). No doubt there are circumstances when we can identify core ideas that persist through time. But, alternatively, we might identify a tradition with a group of ideas widely shared by several individuals although no one idea was held by them all. Or we might identify a tradition with a group of ideas that passed from generation to generation, changing a little each time, so no single idea persisted across all generations. Finally, we should be careful not to hypostatise traditions. We must not claim an existence for them independent of the beliefs and actions of individuals. Traditions are not fixed entities. They are not given, sat in a philological zoo, waiting for people to discover them. They are contingent, produced by the actions of individuals. The carriers of a tradition bring it to life. They settle its content and variations by developing their beliefs and practices, adapting it to new circumstances, while passing it on to the next generation. We can only identify the beliefs that make up a tradition by looking at the shared understandings and historical connections that allow us to link its exponents with one another.

In rejecting all reified, essentialist and hypostatised views of traditions, we are saying that we should define them pragmatically depending on the events and actions we want to explain. Political scientists construct traditions in ways appropriate to explaining the particular sets of beliefs and actions in which they are interested. They move back from particular beliefs and actions to traditions made up of linked beliefs and actions handed down from generation to generation. What the political scientist should not do, and many problems with the idea of tradition arise because they do so, is to make this move by comparing the beliefs and actions of the individual with a reified tradition. Just as we rejected an essentialist analysis of tradition, so we must abstain from the temptation to place individuals in a tradition by comparing their beliefs and actions with a checklist of core ideas. Because traditions are not fixed entities, we cannot situate people in one by comparing their beliefs and actions with its allegedly key features. Rather, we must recognise that traditions are contingent products of the ways in which people develop specific beliefs, preferences and actions. We must identify the tradition by looking at the background against which people come to hold their beliefs and by tracing the relevant historical connections.

A pragmatic analysis of tradition suggests that political scientists can locate an individual in various traditions depending on what questions they seek to answer. Because traditions do not exist as given and reified entities, the political scientist's task cannot be to place the individual in one of a finite set of fixed traditions. Rather, they should identify the tradition against which someone believed or did something by tracing the relevant connections through time. The precise content they give to the tradition will depend on the particular beliefs or actions they hope to explain. If they want to explain someone's set of beliefs and actions, they will define the relevant tradition in one way. If they want to explain only one belief or action, they may well define it differently. In this sense, political scientists construct traditions for themselves. They pick out the relevant beliefs and actions of the individuals they are studying by using criteria of relevance drawn from their own interests. Yet this scholarly role is not a matter of concern. Any abstraction by anyone depends on a principle of classification that gets its justification from the purposes underlying his or her research. Political scientists may construct traditions but that does not mean traditions are unacceptably subjective. Whether an account of a tradition is judged objective depends on the adequacy of our understanding of the components and links by which we define that tradition. An account of a tradition must identify a set of connected beliefs and habits that intentionally or unintentionally passed from generation to generation at some time in the past.

The explanatory value of traditions lies in the way in which they show how individuals inherited beliefs and practices from their communities. Thus, if we use a broad definition of a tradition, its explanatory power will be weaker.

If we select monolithic epistemes, then we have to define them as the beliefs and actions shared by everyone in an epoch. So, when we try to explain the beliefs and actions of particular individuals, we will be able to explain only why they held these beliefs, not other, more specific beliefs. The more narrowly we define a tradition, the greater will be its explanatory power. Political scientists select traditions to explain specific features of human life. The value of the selected tradition depends on the explanatory power of the evidence for the conceptual and historical links between the beliefs and actions that make up the tradition. The more exact the account of these links, the more fully we will be able to grasp the nature of the tradition, so the more explanatory work it will be able to do. Historical or temporal links show how the relevant beliefs and practices passed from one generation to another and in so doing explain why the beliefs persisted through time. Conceptual links show us how the relevant beliefs and practices form a coherent set and in so doing explain why they persisted together as a loose-knit whole rather than as isolated beliefs brought together by mere chance.

Explaining change

Our analysis of tradition contrasts with previous ones, which usually involved some form of essentialist fallacy echoing a Platonic or Hegelian legacy. Once we reject such legacies, we will regard traditions as purely contingent entities that people produce through their own actions as agents. So, to grasp the content and nature of a tradition, political scientists have to decentre it. A decentred study of a tradition, practice or institution unpacks the way in which it is created, sustained and modified through the beliefs, preferences and actions of individuals in many arenas. The study of politics, for example, should go beyond the state to explore topics as diverse as drains, telegraph wires, schools and managing risk (Barry *et al.* 1996). It should do so because the discourses and practices that govern society arise out of these micro-practices. We have to redefine tradition in a non-essentialist, decentred manner to avoid any lingering sense of objective reason.

Nonetheless, because the idea of a tradition suggests that subjects can change their heritage for reasons that make sense to them, it also encourages us to move away from the post-structuralist simple rejection of truth or objective reason. We should grapple here with the nature and effects of local reasoning. While a rejection of the autonomous subject prevents a belief in a neutral or universal reason, the fact of agency enables us to accept local reasoning in a way that Foucault often seems reluctant to do. Even philosophers who reject the possibility of pure experience and the existence of necessary truths still usually insist that a concern with consistency is a necessary feature of all webs of belief (Putnam 1981: 155–68; Quine 1960: 59). People organise their beliefs to fit their own notion of best belief. Political scientists cannot understand changes in traditions, mentalities or discourses unless they link them to the reasons people had for making them. Traditions do not contain an inherent logic that fixes their development: there are no compelling causes making individuals change their beliefs and actions. Rather, we argue that people change their beliefs or actions in ways that depend on local reasoning. We cannot portray such changes as either purely arbitrary or as explicable by allegedly objective social facts. Change occurs in response to dilemmas.

On dilemmas

The human capacity for agency implies change originates in the responses or decisions of individuals, rather than in the inner logic of traditions.

Whenever someone adopts a new belief or action they have to accommodate their existing beliefs and practices to make way for the newcomer. To accept a new belief is to pose a dilemma that asks questions of existing traditions.

A dilemma arises for an individual or institution when a new idea stands in opposition to existing beliefs or practices and so forces a reconsideration of these existing beliefs and associated traditions (Bevir 1999a: 221–64). Political scientists can explain change within traditions, therefore, by referring to the relevant dilemmas. Traditions change as individuals make a series of adjustments to them in response to any number of specific dilemmas.

It is important to recognise that we cannot straightforwardly identify dilemmas with allegedly objective pressures in the world. People modify their beliefs or actions in response to new ideas they come to hold as true. They do so irrespective of whether these ideas reflect real pressures, or, to be precise, irrespective of whether they reflect pressures we believe to be real. In explaining change, we cannot privilege our academic accounts of the world. For example, academics might think that globalisation is a myth. However, if the elite of New Labour believe in it, it might well pose a dilemma for the Socialist vision of a Keynesian welfare state (and on the self-fulfilling nature of beliefs see Hall 1993; Hay 2002; and Hay and Rosamund 2002). Similarly, academics might conclude the new public management fragments service delivery, but unless political actors come to share this conclusion, it will not constitute a dilemma that motivates change by state actors. What matters, in other words, is the subjective, or more usually, inter-subjective understandings of political actors, not our academic accounts of real pressures in the world. The academic task is to recover the shared (or inter-subjective dilemmas) of the relevant actors. The task is not to privilege academic accounts, although we can allow that the pressures academics believe to be real often overlap considerably with the actors' views of the relevant dilemmas. Here dilemmas often arise from people's experiences; and reality, as we academics conceive it, can provide a useful guide to the nature of other people's experiences even though their experiences were constructed in webs of belief different to our own. Having said that dilemmas often arise from people's experiences, however, we must add immediately that this need not be the case. Dilemmas can arise from both theoretical and moral reflection and from experiences of worldly pressures. The new belief that poses a dilemma can lie anywhere on an unbroken spectrum passing from views with little theoretical content to complex theoretical constructs only remotely linked to views about the real world.

A related point to make here is that dilemmas do not have given, nor even correct, solutions. Because no set of beliefs can fix its own criteria of application, when people confront a new event or belief individuals necessarily change traditions in what is a creative process. A tradition may appear to tell people how they should extend it, modify it or apply it.

However, it can only provide them with a guide to what they might do. It does not have rules fixing what they must do. A tradition can provide hints about how adherents might respond to a dilemma. However, the only way they have of checking whether their response has been true to the tradition is to ask whether they and others are happy with it. The creative nature of responses to dilemmas leads us into the ubiquity of change. It suggests that even when people think they are merely continuing a settled tradition, they often are developing, modifying and changing beliefs and practices. Change occurs even when people think they are adhering strictly to a tradition they regard as sacrosanct. Traditions and practices could be fixed and static only if we did not encounter novel circumstances. But, of course, we are always meeting new circumstances. The state and political institutions are in a constant state of flux.

Although dilemmas do not require particular solutions, we can understand the solutions at which people happen to arrive by reference to the character of the dilemma and of their existing beliefs. Consider first the influence of the character of the dilemma. To accommodate a new idea, people must develop their existing beliefs to make room for it, and its content will open some ways of doing so and close down others. Consider now the influence of people's existing beliefs on their response to a dilemma. To accommodate a new idea, people have to hook it on to their existing beliefs, and their existing beliefs will present certain hooks and not others. People can integrate a new belief into their existing beliefs only by relating themes in it to themes already present in their beliefs. The process of change thus involves a pushing and pulling of the dilemma and a tradition to bring them together.

Although dilemmas are central to explaining change, we cannot reduce the concept of a dilemma any further. As anti-foundationalists, we should allow that beliefs coalesce in webs, not hierarchic structures, so there cannot be a foundational type of dilemma. For a start, because no belief is immune from revision, dilemmas can afflict any of our moral, philosophical, religious, scientific, historical or other subsets of belief. In addition, because the authority and content of an experience depends on the individual's prior theories, we cannot say, as vulgar Marxists do, that only one area of life produces dilemmas. All areas of our experience can lead us to adopt a new belief. Dilemmas can arise from an experience of the relationships of production, an acquaintance with a philosophical argument or scientific theory, an encounter with another culture, and so on.

Beyond a foundational epistemology

Once we allow for local reasoning, we can meet the charges of relativism and irrationalism so often levelled at postmodernism. All too often postmodernists appear to say no account is better than any other. In sharp contrast, we move beyond postmodern critiques of foundationalism by outlining a distinctive account of objective knowledge (Bevir 1999a: 78–126). We think of political practices or institutions as the contingent products of numerous actions inspired by competing narratives. Political practices do not have an essential core that political scientists can use to understand and explain them. Nonetheless, we can judge the merits of rival accounts of such contingent political objects. For example, a decentred account that showed governance to be a contingent product of actions inspired by competing narratives is superior, in our view, to an account of governance as the embodiment of market rationality, or an account of governance as the inevitable product of social forces such as globalisation.

The obvious question to ask is how can we judge the merits of rival accounts of political practices. Although political scientists do not have access to pure facts that they can use to declare particular interpretations or narratives to be true or false, they can still hang on to the idea of objectivity. Political scientists can retain a concept of objectivity defined by shared facts – as opposed to given facts – and by shared normative rules and practices that set criteria for comparing accounts.

Reed (1992: Chapter 6, 1993) also argues against the fragmenting tendencies and relativism often associated with postmodernism. In the study of organisations, he argues, there is:

> a growing realisation that epistemological uncertainty, theoretical plurality and methodological diversity do not necessarily entail a terminal drift towards a disordered field of study characterised by total disarray over philosophical fundamentals, substantive problematic and conceptual frameworks. Indeed, it is the lines of debates that are initiated and developed by different modes of inquiry that hold the field together as a reasonably coherent intellectual practice. They provide the problematics, frameworks and explanations that, together with the institutional arrangements within which 'organisational analysis' is actively carried on, link together epistemological claims and disciplinary practices in such a way that a coherent field of study can be sustained.
>
> (Reed 1993: 176)

A field of study, Reed explains, is a co-operative intellectual *practice*, with a *tradition* of historically produced norms, rules, conventions and standards of excellence that remain subject to critical debate, and with a *narrative* content that gives meaning to it (paraphrased from Reed 1993: 176). Practice, tradition and narrative provide 'for a negotiated and dynamic set of standards through which rational debate and argument-ation between proponents of rival perspectives or approaches is possible', where 'these standards are historically embedded within social practices, traditions and narratives which provide "embedded reasons" . . . for judging an argument true or false or an action right or wrong' (ibid.: 177).

These criteria are not universal and objective but they are 'shared criteria for assessing . . . knowledge claims', and, in ignoring them, the postmodern critique 'radically underestimated' the 'significant, grounded rationality' that we find in our practices and traditions (ibid.: 177).

In an analogous fashion, we might suggest the continuing debates among students of British government define and redefine the criteria by which we judge the knowledge claims of individual members of that community. Such debates are not self-referential because the knowledge claims can be 'reconfirmed' by encounters with practitioners and users. We translate our concepts into conversations in fieldwork, and these conversations produce data that we interpret to produce narratives that are then judged by the evolving knowledge criteria of our academic community. Reconfirmation occurs here at three distinct points. The first is when we translate our concepts for fieldwork: that is, are they meaningful to practitioners and users and if not, why not? The second is when we reconstruct narratives from the conversations: that is, is the story logical and consistent with the data? And the third is when we redefine and translate our concepts because of the academic community's judgement on the narratives: that is, does the story meet the agreed knowledge criteria? Also, we can appeal to bridging devices, or conversations, to ensure our local concept of objectivity remains open to alternative communities. These devices inform the dialogues which construct objective knowledge in any given community as it adapts to other communities. When we encounter alternative practices, we can begin from points of overlap, and move out to embark on a dialogue in which we might justify ourselves, or redefine our concepts or change our notion of objectivity.

While Reed's naturalised epistemology has its merits, it lacks normative, critical bite. There are no grounds for judging, let alone rejecting, the 'truths' other than the grounds on which our community agrees. To overcome this difficulty, we propose that political scientists conceive of objective knowledge, less as what our community happens to agree on, and more as a normative standard embedded in a practice of criticising and comparing rival accounts of 'agreed facts'. The anti-foundational nature of this practice lies in its appeal, not to given facts, but to those agreed in a particular community or conversation. In addition, and of key importance, the normative, critical bite of our approach lies in conducting the comparison by the rules of intellectual honesty. These rules originate in anti-foundationalism and not in a straightforward acceptance of the norms of the relevant community or conversation.

The first rule of intellectual honesty is: objective behaviour requires a willingness to take criticism seriously. The second rule is: objective behaviour implies a preference for established standards of evidence and reason backed by a preference for a challenge to these standards which themselves rest on impersonal and consistent criteria of evidence and reason. The third rule is: objective behaviour implies a preference for

positive speculative theories, that is, speculative theories postulating exciting new predictions, not speculative theories merely blocking off criticisms
of our existing interpretations. These rules of intellectual honesty provide
criteria for comparing theories or narratives. For a start, because we
should respect established standards of evidence and reason, we will prefer
webs of interpretation that are accurate, comprehensive and consistent. In
addition, because we should favour positive, speculative theories to those
merely blocking criticism, we will prefer webs of interpretation that are
progressive, fruitful and open. Objectivity is, therefore, a product of 'local
reasoning' in that it arises from the critical comparison of narratives within
an academic community, reconfirmed in debate between communities,
where all debates are subject to the provisional rules of intellectual honesty.

Our anti-foundational epistemology differs markedly from the positivism
informing conventional approaches to British government. We cannot
evaluate interpretations either definitively or instantly. Because objectivity
rests on criteria of comparison, not a logic of vindication or refutation, the
narrative we select through the practice of comparison will be that which
best meets our criteria. Our selection of interpretations by comparing them
will be continual; no model can be taken as true and the basis for gaining
better and better knowledge. The task of the political scientist cannot be
endlessly to collect, bit by bit, knowledge of a given empirical reality by
using ever more sophisticated and rigorous comparative and quantitative
techniques. It should be to identify progressive, fruitful and open narratives
that interrogate existing narratives, meet established standards of evidence
and reason, and open exciting new avenues for research and practice.

So, the interpretive approach to the study of British government differs
markedly from the Westminster model with its links to a positivist epistemology. This positivist epistemology suggests we can treat social structures
as given facts from which we can read off the beliefs, interests and actions
of individuals. In contrast our approach regards institutions as enacted by
individuals. 'Objective' position in a structure does not determine the
beliefs and actions of individuals. Rather, their beliefs and actions construct the nature of the relevant organisation or network. Our approach,
therefore, encourages us to decentre government. It encourages us to
explore, using for example, the tools of history and ethnography, the ways
in which the activities of particular individuals make and remake
governmental institutions.

Criticisms of interpretive theory

The question of 'how we know what we know about British government'
admits of many answers. While obviously we believe there is mileage in
our interpretive approach, we want to encourage discussion. So, how do
other political scientists react to interpretive alternatives to positivism? The
most accommodating recognise interpretation as an integral part of social

explanation. A famous example is Max Weber's account of *verstehen* (Weber 1978: vol. 1, 4–22). Weber champions explanations through ideal types that provide satisfactory accounts of action by incorporating the analysis of both meaning (of intentions) and objective (quantified) data. Alternatively some political scientists regard interpretive theory as useful for limited areas of their discipline, such as values and ideologies. Finally, the most hostile political scientists reject interpretive approaches as inappropriate or as superseded by a positive, scientific alternative. Interpretive theorists should allow that objective data could provide useful guides to research and reinforce some conclusions. They also need to respond to the specific criticisms raised by other political scientists.

Two criticisms are prominent and important. First, critics allege that interpretive theories provide inadequate accounts of material reality. Second, they claim such theories provide no basis for criticising social life.

For some critics, interpretive approaches do not allow for the material constraints on social action. Although interpretive theorists must indeed remain implacably opposed to any form of economic reductionism, they can allow for economic influences in several ways. For a start, they might accept that dilemmas often reflect material circumstances. What matters is the subjective beliefs people hold about the world but these beliefs often arise because of pressures in the world. For example, the dilemma of inflation, although variously constructed, was a reasonably accurate perception of a real economic pressure, even if the responses were as varied as the constructions. There is a real world out there, and, while we do not have unmediated access to it, it is a source of pressures. In addition, just because a government acts on a particular view of the world does not mean its view of the world determines the effects of its action. The effects will depend on how others react and their reactions will collectively constitute a relevant material reality. Whether a new deal for the long-term unemployed will lead to them getting jobs depends, for example, on how they react to the opportunities given to them, how employers view them, and the state of the economy.

Other critics complain similarly that interpretive approaches cannot account for the solidity and persistence of institutions. They can, but it demands a different way of thinking about institutions. Interpretive theories deny that institutions have a reified or essential nature. They challenge us to decentre institutions; that is, to analyse the ways in which they are produced, reproduced and changed through the particular and contingent beliefs, preferences and actions of individuals. Even when an institution maintains similar routines while personnel changes, it does so mainly because the successive personnel pass on similar beliefs and preferences. So, we should not say that interpretive theory is lacking on institutions, but rather that it rethinks the nature of institutions. Interpretive theory sees institutions as sedimented products of contingent beliefs and preferences. It is still possible to generalise about institutions so conceived.

Another criticism of interpretive theories suggests they lack critical power. The varieties inspired by hermeneutics and ethnology appear forced to accept the self-understanding of those they study. Yet we can ascribe unconscious or even irrational beliefs to people when interpreting their words. Our thick descriptions are still our interpretations of other people's constructions and the logic of comparing webs of interpretation still applies. Similarly, the varieties of interpretive theory inspired by post-structuralism and postmodernism can lack a notion of truth by which we can condemn beliefs as false. Yet our anthropological approach to objectivity means we can dismiss some beliefs without appealing to a notion of absolute truth. Indeed, because we reject absolute truth, we are compelled to oppose those political ideologies that claim to be based on such a truth. We should deconstruct all those discourses that try to close themselves off, or that dismiss alternatives as unreasonable or absent. Such deconstruction would apply not only to fascism or communism but arguably also to many varieties of liberal universalism (Bevir 2000a).

Of course, to condemn systems of belief as false is not to dismiss them as ideological in the sense of being reflections of a class interest. Because interpretive theory opposes economic reductionism, it must avoid such a concept of ideology. Nonetheless, it can keep the idea of ideology as distorted belief, where distortions are identified with departures from the norms of belief formation (Bevir 1999a: 265–308). Ideologies would thus have a close association to lies, the unconscious and contradictory beliefs. Imagine that politicians say unemployment has risen because of a global recession while believing it did so because of a global recession aggravated by government policy. We could condemn their utterance as ideological, not because it is false, but because it involves deception. Their words hide their true beliefs for political advantage.

Conclusion

Interpretive theory encompasses many approaches, all of which oppose the vague and lukewarm positivism that provides the basis for so much political science. In defiance of positivism, exponents of an interpretive approach take seriously the role of ideas and meanings in individual lives and social practices. Most interpretive theorists argue the meaningful nature of human life makes the model of natural science inappropriate to political studies. Some insist the human sciences must understand the objects they study rather than seek explanations for them (Winch 1958). Others insist the human sciences are explanatory but distinguish the narrative form of explanation from the strictly causal form found in natural science.

Although interpretive approaches all focus on meanings, they often take different views of meaning. Many of the key debates following the rise of post-structuralism and postmodernism concern the nature of the subject and the limits of reason. Traditional varieties of interpretation can come dangerously close to embodying an analysis of the subject as autonomous and an analysis of reason as pure and universal. Post-structuralists and postmodernists rightly criticise such analyses. They prompt us to decentre traditions and practices. Yet postmodern and post-structuralist varieties of interpretation can come dangerously close to denying any scope to the subject and to reason. We have given an account of the future for interpretive theory which lies in steering a course between the two. We postulate a subject who is an agent, but not an autonomous one, and local reasoning that never becomes universal.

During the second half of the twentieth century, most positivist political scientists followed Bentham in asking, is it true? Unfortunately for them, as Greenleaf (1983a: vol. 1, 286) argues:

> The concept of a genuine social science has had its ups and downs, and it still survives, though we are as far from its achievement as we were when Spencer (or Bacon for that matter) first put pen to paper. Indeed it is all the more likely that the continuous attempts made in this direction serve only to demonstrate . . . the inherent futility of the enterprise.

Perhaps we had better take to heart Cowling's (1963: 209) advice:

> political science, . . . and comparative government, when looked at critically dissolve into these two disciplines [philosophy and history]: and if they do not, they have not been looked at critically enough.

The time has come to return to the discipline's historical and philosophical roots. We should follow Coleridge in asking, 'what is the meaning of it?'

Notes

1 Relevant thinkers include Derrida 1976; Foucault 1972, 1986; Lacan 1977; Lyotard 1984; Rorty 1980 and White 1973, 1987.
2 For example, the recent comprehensive review of political science by Goodin and Klingemann 1996 contains but a brief discussion and one which few proponents of postmodernism, post-structuralism or constructivism would recognise. Closer to home the review of British political science by Hayward *et al.* 2000 similarly touches on interpretive approaches only in passing. Hay 2002 provides the best, indeed the only comprehensive, review of the relevant literature. That said, new institutionalists sometimes emphasise historicity, contingency and the influence of ideas in ways that overlap with our interpretive approach. See, for example, Hall 1986; Hall and Taylor 1996; and Hay and Wincott 1998. Also those colleagues with a sociological inclination will be familiar with other recent work that overlaps with our interpretive approach to British government. See, for example, Hay 2002; and Jessop 1990.

3 For brief histories of the discipline see Bevir 2001; Chester 1975; Hayward 1991; Hayward *et al.* 2000; and for the nineteenth century see Collini *et al.* 1983. For other assessments of the political science of British politics see Dearlove 1982; Gamble 1990; Hayward 1986, 1991; Johnson 1989; and Marsh *et al.* 1999.

4 Tivey 1988 provides a useful guide to both the shared ideas in the mainstream literature and the many variations on those shared ideas, thereby removing the need for a lengthy list here. Marsh 1999 also subscribes to the view that there is a mainstream or family of ideas about British government shared by practitioner and academic alike. Gamble 1990: 412 makes the same point with different examples. For sceptical readers, we refer them to those repositories of the disciplines' inherited views – textbooks. For a recent review of several texts 'haunted by the ghost' of the Westminster model see Smith 1999b. See also Epstein 1987, especially the references on pp. 100–4; Harrison 1996; Hennessy 1995; Norton 1983, 1984, 1996; and Porter 1994.

5 See also among many others Lijphart 1984; Parker 1979; Weller 1985: 16, 1989; and Wilson 1994: 190–3.

6 For a brief summary of other critics of the Westminster model see pp. 28–31 below.

7 Although we do not want to return to, and are critical of, earlier versions of the historical and philosophical approach to British government (see, for example, Greenleaf 1983a and b), we are primarily concerned to challenge positivist accounts of the Westminster model. We take positivism to have two main theses: that one can explain human behaviour in terms of allegedly objective social facts about people in a way which makes beliefs or meanings largely irrelevant or unnecessary; and that the relation between antecedent and consequent in political explanation is a causal or necessary one akin to that found in the natural sciences.

8 There was also an important challenge to the Westminster model's focus on central elites; for example, Hechter 1975 and Nairn 1981 looked at British government from the periphery, not the centre.

9 See, for example, Dearlove and Saunders 1984; Jessop 1990a; Kingdom 1991; Leys 1983; Miliband 1969, 1982; Nairn 1981.

10 The more distinguished contributions include Johnson 1977; Mount 1992; and Willetts 1992, all of whom claim Oakeshott 1975 as their intellectual godfather. The Institute for Economic Affairs has published many pamphlets on: marketising public services; pushing back the boundaries of the state; and the defects of British political institutions.

11 See, for example, Aucoin 1995; Hood 1991, 1995; Pollitt 1993; Pollitt and Summa 1997; Rhodes 1997b, 1998; Wright 1994.

3 Governance in Britain

LIBRARY, UNIVERSITY OF CHESTER

Introduction

We must now tell the governance story. The governance literature grapples with the changing role of the state after the varied public sector reforms of the 1980s and 1990s. It explores how the informal authority of networks constitutes, supplements and supplants the formal authority of government and develops a more diverse view of state authority and its relationship to civil society. There are, however, at least seven separate uses of governance relevant to the study of British government: corporate governance, the new public management, good governance, international interdependence, socio-cybernetic systems, the new political economy and networks.

In this chapter, we will review the literature on governance relevant to the study of Britain before summarising the governance narrative. The literature that we review is pervaded by the lukewarm positivism characteristic of British political science. This chapter is a ground-clearing exercise focused on the positivist account of governance. Only in Chapter 4 do we examine how our anti-foundational, interpretive approach leads us to decentre the governance narrative. Now we run through the main uses of the term.

Seven definitions of governance

Governance can be used as a blanket term to represent a change in the nature or meaning of government (Jørgensen 1993; March and Olsen 1989). The relevant changes concern the extent and forms of public intervention, notably the use of markets and quasi-markets to deliver public services. To employ Stoker's (1998a: 18) apt phrase, governance is 'the acceptable face of spending cuts'. Governance understood as the minimal state encapsulates the preference for less government, but it says little else, being an example of political rhetoric.

Governance as corporate governance

One use of the term governance refers to directing and controlling business corporations (see, for example, Cadbury Report 1992: 15). The Chartered

Institute of Public Finance and Accountancy (CIPFA 1994: 6) translated this use for the public sector. It wants to see more efficient governance in the public sector or 'a more commercial style of management' to bring about 'a different culture and climate'. This 'departure from the traditional public service "ethos"' means, however, that public services now must exercise 'extra vigilance and care to ensure that sound systems of corporate governance are both set in place and work in practice'. CIPFA's report applies three principles to public organizations: it recommends openness or the disclosure of information, integrity or straightforward dealing with completeness, and accountability or holding individuals responsible for their actions through a clear division of responsibilities.

Governance as the new public management

Initially the new public management (NPM) had two meanings – corporate management and marketisation. Corporate management means introducing private sector management methods to the public sector through performance measures, managing by result, value for money and closeness to the customer. Marketisation means introducing incentive structures into public service provision through contracting-out, quasi-markets and consumer choice.

NPM is relevant to our discussion of governance because steering is central to the analysis of public management and a synonym for governance. For example, Osborne and Gaebler (1992: 20) distinguish between 'policy decisions (steering) and service delivery (rowing)'. They argue bureaucracy is a bankrupt tool for rowing. In place of bureaucracy, they propose 'entrepreneurial government', which will stress competition, markets, customers and measuring outcomes. This transformation of the public sector involves less government (or less rowing) but more governance (or more steering). Similarly, although Peters (1996: 1) defines governance as 'institutions designed to exercise collective control and influence' – a definition so broad it covers all forms of government – he also uses steering as a synonym for governance (Peters 1995: 3). In effect, like Osborne and Gaebler, Peters (1996) uses governance to describe recent public sector reforms, but, in sharp contrast to Osborne and Gaebler, he does not argue for any one reform. He identifies several variants of reform – the market, participatory, temporary and regulatory states – and discusses their different effects. Governance signals the importance of the new public management (see also OECD 1995).

Governance as good governance

Government reform is a worldwide trend. Indeed, good governance is the latest flavour of the month for international agencies such as the World Bank (1992) where it now shapes lending policy towards third world countries (see also OECD 1996). Leftwich (1993) identifies three strands to good governance: systemic, political and administrative. The systemic use of governance is broader than government covering the 'distribution of both internal and external political and economic power'. The political use of governance refers to 'a state enjoying both legitimacy and authority, derived from a democratic mandate'. The administrative use refers to 'an efficient, open accountable and audited public service' (ibid.: 611). To achieve efficiency in the public services, the World Bank seeks to encourage competition and markets, privatise public enterprise, reform the civil service by reducing overstaffing, introduce budgetary discipline, decentralise administration, and make greater use of non-governmental organizations (Williams and Young 1994: 87). In short, good governance tries to marry NPM to the advocacy of liberal democracy.

Governance as international interdependence

A growing literature covers governance in the fields of international relations and international political economy. Two strands of this literature are directly relevant to the study of British government. These are the ideas of the hollowing-out of the state and of multi-level governance.

The idea of the hollowing-out of the state implies that international interdependencies erode the authority of the state. Thus, Held (1991: 151–7) suggests that four processes are limiting the autonomy of nation states: the internationalisation of production and financial transactions, international organisations, international law and hegemonic powers and power blocs. As a result, the nation state's capacities for governance have weakened. However, 'it remains a pivotal institution' because it is essential to 'suturing' power upwards to the international level and downwards to sub-national agencies (Hirst and Thompson 1995: 409, 423). The state appears as a 'source of constitutional ordering', providing minimum standards in a world of interlocking networks of public powers (ibid.: 435).

Multi-level governance characterises much of the European Union. For example, trans-national policy networks, emerged where: there was a high dependence in the policy sector; policy-making was depoliticised and routinised; supra-national agencies were dependent on other agencies to deliver a service; and there was a need to aggregate interests. In the EU, multi-level governance posits links between the Commission, national ministries and local and regional authorities. It is a specific example of the impact of international interdependencies on the state (see Hooghe 1996).

Governance as a socio-cybernetic system

The socio-cybernetic concept of governance highlights the limits to governing by a central actor. It claims there is no longer a single sovereign authority. Instead there is great variety of actors specific to each policy area. There is interdependence among these social–political–administrative actors. There are shared goals. There are blurred boundaries between public, private and voluntary sectors. There are multiplying and new forms of action, intervention and control. Governance arises out of interactive social-political forms of governing. Thus, Kooiman (1993b: 258) distinguishes between governing or goal-directed interventions and governance, which is the result, or the total effects, of social–political–administrative interventions and interactions. In contrast to the state and the market 'socio-political governance is directed at creating patterns of interaction in which political and traditional hierarchical governing and social self-organization are complementary, in which responsibility and accountability for interventions is spread over public and private actors' (ibid.: 252). Government no longer rules supreme. The political system is increasingly differentiated. Luhmann (1982: xv) claims we live in 'the centreless society', or at least in a polycentric state characterised by multiple centres. The tasks of government are now to enable socio-political interactions, to encourage many and varied arrangements for coping with problems and to distribute services among the several actors. Examples of the new patterns of interaction abound in Britain, where they include self-regulation and co-regulation, public–private partnerships, co-operative management, and joint entrepreneurial ventures.

Governance as the new political economy

The new political economy approach to governance re-examines both the government of the economy and the boundaries between civil society, state and the market economy as they become increasingly blurred. To illustrate the variety of approaches that fall under this broad description, we outline both a positivist and a neo-Marxist account.

For positivists such as Lindberg *et al.* (1991: 3), governance refers to 'the political and economic processes that coordinate activity among economic actors'. They explore the 'transformation of the institutions that govern economic activity' by focusing on the 'emergence and rearrangement' of several institutional forms of governance. They identify six ideal-type mechanisms of governance: markets, obligational networks, hierarchy, monitoring, promotional networks and associations (ibid.: 29). Their discussion of these mechanisms does not focus only on which ones promote economic efficiency under what conditions but also on social control understood as 'struggles over strategic control and power within economic exchange' (ibid.: 5). The state is not just another governance mechanism because it acts as a gatekeeper to sectoral governance and because it can promote or inhibit production and exchange. This positivist approach explores the ways in which the state, understood as both an actor and a structure, constitutes the economy and influences the selection of governance regimes (Lindberg *et al.* 1991).

For neo-Marxists, such as Jessop (1997, 1999), governance is 'the complex art of steering multiple agencies, institutions and systems which are both operationally autonomous from one another and structurally coupled through various forms of reciprocal interdependence'. There has been a 'dramatic intensification of societal complexity' stemming from 'growing functional differentiation of institutional orders within an increasingly global society'. These complexities 'undermine the basis of hierarchical, top-down co-ordination' (Jessop 1997: 95, 1995: 317 and 324; see also Le Galès 1998: 495). The distinctive feature of this approach is allegedly a concern to put 'governance' in a systematic, broader theoretical framework. Jessop (1995: 323) recognises the differences between governance and regulation, contrasting, for example, 'the distinctively Marxist genealogy of the regulation approach' and its well-defined economic problematic and concern to explain the stability of capitalism with the pre-theoretical stage of governance theory and its substantive concern with interorganisational co-ordination. However, Jessop's analysis of governance draws on his strategic-relational approach with its focus on the complex dialectical inter-relationships between structure, agency and strategy. Shorn of much and varied detail, the explanatory heart of this approach to governance lies in the political economy of regulation theory (see Le Galès 1998; Stoker 1998b for variations on this theme). It brings a critical eye to bear on the instrumental concern of governance with solving co-ordination problems, arguing governance is not necessarily more efficient than markets and identifying several strategic dilemmas that make governance prone to fail (Jessop 1997: 118–22).

Governance as networks

The notion of governance is closely linked to the idea of networks. We now review this network literature. In the 1990s, a massive outpouring of work on networks inspired a vigorous debate.[1] In response to the debate, we will ask 'where are we now'. For ease of exposition we will distinguish between networks as interest intermediation and networks as governance (see Börzel 1998).

Networks as interest intermediation

Proponents of networks as interest intermediation see policy networks as a meso-level concept linking the micro-level of analysis, which deals with the role of interests and government in particular policy decisions, to the macro-level of analysis, which explores broader questions about power in modern society. Network analysis stresses continuity in the relations between interest groups and government departments – a process referred to as interest intermediation. Policy networks are sets of resource-dependent organisations. Their relationships are characterised by power-dependence so any organisation is dependent on other organisations for resources, and to achieve their goals organisations have to exchange resources. Actors employ strategies within known rules of the game to regulate the process of exchange. Relationships are a game in which organisations manoeuvre for advantage. Each deploys its resources, whether constitutional-legal, organisational, financial, political or informational, to maximise its influence on outcomes while trying to avoid becoming dependent on the other 'players' (Marsh and Rhodes 1992a).

Theorists of networks as interest intermediation treat them as institutional structures which limit participation in policy-making, define the roles of actors, decide which issues to include and exclude from the policy agenda, shape the behaviour of actors through the rules of the game, privilege certain interests not only by according them access but also by favouring their preferred policy outcomes, and substitute private government for public accountability (see Marsh and Rhodes 1992a; Rhodes 1997a: Chapters 1 and 3). This focus on institutional structures leads various political scientists to construct typologies with lists of the characteristics of different types of policy networks and policy communities (see, for example, Grant *et al.* 1988; Waarden 1992; Wilks and Wright 1987). These typologies typically treat policy network as the generic term. Networks are said to vary along a continuum according to the closeness of their linkages. Policy communities are at one end of the continuum because they have close links; issue networks are at the other end because they have loose links. We illustrate such a typology in Table 3.1.

A policy community has the following characteristics: a limited number of participants with some groups consciously excluded; frequent and high-quality interaction between all members of the community on all matters related to the policy issues; consistency in values, membership and policy outcomes which persist over time; consensus, with the ideology, values and broad policy preferences shared by all participants; and exchange relationships based on all members of the policy community controlling some resources. Thus, the basic interaction is one that involves bargaining between members with resources. There is a balance of power, not necessarily one in which all members equally benefit, but one in which all see themselves as being in a positive-sum game. The structures of the participating groups are hierarchical so leaders can guarantee compliant members. An issue network, in contrast, involves only policy consultation. It has the following characteristics: many participants; fluctuating interaction and access for the various members; the absence of consensus and the presence of conflict; interaction based on consultation rather than negotiation or bargaining; an unequal power relationship in which many participants may have few resources, little access and no alternative. Because these models are ideal types, however, no policy area is likely to conform exactly to them.

There has been much debate about the analysis of policy networks as interest intermediation. For example, Dowding (1995) criticises it on three

Table 3.1 Types of policy network

Dimension	Policy community	Issue network
Membership:		
– Number of participants	Limited number, some groups consciously excluded	Large
– Type of interest	Economic and/or professional interests dominate	Encompasses range of affected interests
Integration:		
– Frequency of interaction	Frequent, high-quality, interaction of all groups on all matters related to policy issue	Contacts fluctuate in frequency and intensity
– Continuity	Membership, values and outcomes persistent over time	Access fluctuates significantly
– Consensus	All participants share basic values and accept the legitimacy of the outcome	A measure of agreement exists, but conflict is ever present
Resources:		
– Distribution of resources within network	All participants have resources; basic relationship is an exchange relationship	Some participants may have resources, but they are limited and basic relationship is consultative
– Distribution of resources within participating organisations	Hierarchical; leaders can deliver members	Varied and variable distribution and capacity to regulate members
Power:	Balanced power among the members. Although one group may dominate, it must be a positive-sum game if community is to persist	Unequal powers, reflecting unequal resources and unequal access

It is a zero-sum game |

grounds. First, he argues that policy network is just a metaphor of no explanatory value. Second, he argues the approach does not go beyond typology to specify causal relationships – for example, between the density of linkages in a network and policy outcomes. Moreover, in as far as there is an implicit explanation, he complains it does not rely on the characteristics of networks to explain actions. Rather, it relies on the properties of actors; on, for example, the resources individuals can deploy, not on their nodal position in the network or some other structural characteristic.

Third, Dowding argues the analysis of games and bargaining is undeveloped and even confused by the distinctions between micro- (or individual), meso- (or network), and macro- (or state) levels of analysis. These distinctions are not needed for 'an analytical theory which produces testable empirical implications under different conditions'. Dowding would have us adopt a deductive, rational actor model that covers theories of bargaining and quantitative network analysis (see, for example, Laumann and Knoke 1987; and for critical comments see Marsh and Smith 2000).

The debate rolls on. Several political scientists criticise Dowding because he focuses on agents rather than exploring how the structure of a network affects the process of bargaining (Marsh 1999: 12–13 and 67–70; Marsh and Smith 2000). Marsh and Smith (2000), for example, argue that network structures shape the preferences of actors so there is a dialectical relationship between structure and agency. They criticise Dowding for taking refuge in intentionalism and methodological individualism and for failing even to recognise the structure–agency problem. They accept that at the micro-level networks are comprised of strategically calculating subjects whose actions shape policy outcomes. However, they continue, the preferences and interests of these actors cannot be assumed. Instead, they must be explained by a meso- or macro-level theory. For Marsh and Smith, the future thus lies in longtitudinal, qualitative and comparative case studies.

Networks as governance

The most recent work on policy networks treats them as the heart of governance. This literature falls into two broad schools that differ in how they seek to explain network behaviour. One school appeals to power-dependence, the other to rational choice. We illustrate the two approaches with respectively the work of the British research programmes on Local Governance and Whitehall, and the work originating at the Max-Planck-Institut für Gesellschaftsforschung.

POWER-DEPENDENCE

The British Economic and Social Research Council's Research Programmes on Local Governance and Whitehall fuelled much recent research in Britain. The Local Governance Programme explored the way in which the system of government beyond Westminster and Whitehall changed from a system of local government into a system of local governance involving complex sets of organisations drawn from the public and private sectors (Stoker 1999b, 2000a). Governance thus appears as a broader term than government. It captures a system in which any permutation of government and the private and voluntary sectors provides services. Complexity arising out of the functional differentiation of the state makes interorganisational linkages a defining characteristic of service delivery. The several agencies must exchange resources if they are to deliver services effectively. All organisations have to exchange resources; they have to employ strategies within known rules of the game to achieve their goals (Rhodes 1999: Chapter 5; Stoker 1998a: 22).

The ESRC Whitehall Programme generalises the governance argument from local government to British government as a whole. It challenges the conventional wisdom of the Westminster model (Rhodes 2000a). Networks are a common form of social co-ordination, and managing interorganisational links is just as important for private sector management as for public sector. Networks are a means for co-ordinating and allocating resources – a governing structure – in the same way as markets and bureaucracies. From this perspective, governance consists of self-organising, interorganisational networks. These networks are characterised, first, by interdependence between organisations. Changes in the role of the state mean the boundaries between the public, private and voluntary sectors are shifting and opaque. Second, there are continuing interactions between network members, caused by the need to exchange resources and to negotiate shared purposes. Third, these interactions resemble a game with actors' behaviour rooted in trust and regulated by rules that are negotiated and agreed by network participants. Finally, the networks have a significant degree of autonomy from the state. Networks are not accountable to the state; they are self-organising. Although the state does not occupy a privileged, sovereign position, it can indirectly and imperfectly steer networks. The key problem confronting government is, therefore, its reduced ability to steer.[2]

THE MAX-PLANCK-INSTITUT AND ACTOR-CENTRED INSTITUTIONALISM[3]

For Renate Mayntz, Fritz Scharpf and their colleagues at the Max-Planck-Institut, policy networks represent a significant change in the structure of government. Networks are specific 'structural arrangements' that deal typically with 'policy problems'. They are a 'relatively stable set of mainly public and private corporate actors'. The links between network actors serve as 'communication channels and for the exchange of information, expertise, trust and other policy resources'. Policy networks have their own 'integrative logic' and the dominant decision rules within them stress bargaining and sounding-out. Like the power-dependence approach, the Max Planck school stresses functional differentiation, the linkages between organisations, and dependence on resources (Kenis and Schneider 1991: 41–3). The Max Planck school also stress the advantages of networks over markets and hierarchies. Networks can avoid not only the negative externalities of markets but also the 'losers' – that is, those who bear the costs of political decisions – produced by hierarchies. They can do so because:

in an increasingly complex and dynamic environment, where hierarchical co-ordination is rendered difficult if not impossible and the
potential for deregulation is limited due to the problems of market
failure, governance becomes more and more feasible only within policy
networks, which provide a framework for efficient non-hierarchical co-
ordination of the interests and actions of public and private corporate
actors which are mutually dependent on their resources.

(Börzel 1998: 16)

To explain how policy networks work, Scharpf (1997: Chapters 2 and
3) combines rational choice theory with the new institutionalism to
produce an actor-centred institutionalism. His basic argument is that
institutions are systems of rules that structure the opportunities for actors,
whether individual or corporate, to realise their preferences. So, 'policy is
the outcome of the interactions of resourceful and boundedly rational
actors whose capabilities, preferences, and perceptions are largely, but not
completely, shaped by the institutionalised norms within which they
interact' (ibid.: 195). Networks are one institutional setting in which public
and private actors come together. They are informal institutions characterised by informally organised, permanent, rule-governed relationships. The
agreed rules build trust and foster communication while also reducing
uncertainty; they are the basis of a non-hierarchic co-ordination. Scharpf
uses game theory to analyse and explain these rule-governed interactions.

The power dependence view and the Max Planck school agree, therefore, that governance as networks is a common and important development
in advanced industrial societies where the relationship between state and
civil society has changed dramatically.

A governance narrative

The positivist literature on policy networks inspires a governance narrative
that challenges the Westminster model. We now outline the main features of
this narrative before, in the next chapter, decentring it in accord with our
anti-foundational, interpretive approach. The governance narrative claims
to capture recent changes in British government in a way the Westminster
model cannot. What is new in British government? To answer this question,
the governance narrative starts with the notion of policy networks or sets of
organisations clustered around a major government function or department.
These groups commonly include the professions, trade unions and big
business. Central departments need the co-operation of such groups to
deliver services. They need their co-operation because British government
rarely delivers services itself. It uses other bodies to do so. Also there are too
many groups to consult so government must aggregate interests. It needs the
legitimated spokespeople for that policy area. The groups in turn need the
money and legislative authority that only government can provide.

Networks

Policy networks are a long-standing feature of British government; they are its silos or velvet drainpipes. Typically, policy networks evolve a consensus about what they are doing, a consensus that serves at least some of the aims of all involved. They have evolved routine ways of deciding issues. They are a form of private government of public services, scathingly dismissed by the New Right as producer groups that use government for their own sectional interests. The Conservative government of Margaret Thatcher sought to reduce their power by using markets to deliver public services, bypassing existing networks and curtailing the 'privileges' of professions, commonly by subjecting them to rigorous financial and management controls. But these corporate management and marketisation reforms had unintended consequences. They fragmented the systems for delivering public services, creating pressures for organisations to co-operate with one another to deliver services. In other words, and paradoxically, marketisation multiplied the networks it aimed to replace. Commonly, packages of organisations now deliver welfare state services. What is new, then, is the spread of networks in British government. Fragmentation not only created new networks; it also increased the membership of existing networks, incorporating both the private and voluntary sectors. What is more, the government swapped direct for indirect controls so central departments are no longer either necessarily or invariably the fulcrum of a network. The government can set the limits to network actions: after all, it still funds the services. But it has also increased its dependence on multifarious networks. Devolution to Scotland, Wales and Northern Ireland simply adds a further layer of complexity that is likely to fuel territorial networks.

If networks are the defining characteristic of governance, how do they differ from the more widely understood notions of markets and hierarchies or bureaucracies? Table 3.2 shows the distinctive features of networks viewed as a mechanism for allocating and co-ordinating resources and public services.

Table 3.2 Markets, hierarchies and networks

	Markets	*Hierarchies*	*Networks*
Basis of relationships	Contract and property rights	Employment relationship	Resource exchange
Degree of dependence	Independent	Dependent	Interdependent
Medium of exchange	Prices	Authority	Trust
Means of conflict resolution and co-ordination	Haggling and the courts	Rules and commands	Diplomacy
Culture	Competition	Subordination	Reciprocity

Clearly networks are a distinctive co-ordinating mechanism notably different from markets and hierarchies and not a hybrid of markets and hierarchies. Of their characteristics, trust is essential because it is the basis of network co-ordination in the same way that commands and price competition are the key mechanisms for bureaucracies and markets respectively (Frances *et al.* 1991: 15; see also Powell 1991). Shared values and norms are the glue that holds the complex set of relationships in a network together. Trust is essential for co-operative behaviour and, therefore, the existence of the network. With the spread of networks there has been a recurrent tension between contracts on the one hand with their stress on competition to get the best price and networks on the other with their stress on co-operative behaviour. Other key characteristics include diplomacy, reciprocity and interdependence (Rhodes 1997b).

So, we start our alternative story about British government with the idea that governance refers to governing with and through networks. As we noted earlier, the term is used as shorthand to capture public sector change; to encapsulate the shift in British government from government (the strong executive) to governance (through networks). It refers to the changing form of the British state and to the ways in which the informal authority of networks constitutes, supplements and supplants the formal authority of the state. Later we will suggest an interpretive approach requires us to decentre governance as networks to examine how networks are constantly recreated through contingent contests over meanings.

Core executive

A recurring debate about the British executive focuses on the relative power of prime minister and cabinet. Although the debate has its critics, political scientists continue to complain of Blair's presidentialism. Their complaint assumes the best way to look at the executive is to look at key positions and their incumbents. Instead of such a positional approach, proponents of the core executive define it by its functions. Instead of asking which position is important, they ask which functions define the innermost part or heart of British government. The core functions of the British executive are to pull together and integrate central government policies and to act as final arbiters of conflicts between different elements of the government machine. Institutions other than prime minister and cabinet, including, for example, the Treasury or the Cabinet Office, can carry out these functions. By defining the core executive in functional terms, they make the key question, 'who does what?'

There is a second strand to the argument favouring a focus on the core executive rather than prime minister and cabinet. The positional approach also assumes that power lies with specific positions and the people who occupy those positions. But power is relational and contingent: it depends on the relative power of other actors and on, as Harold Macmillan succinctly put it, 'events, dear boy, events'. So, ministers typically depend on the prime minister for support in getting funds from the Treasury. In turn, the prime minister depends on his ministers to deliver the party's electoral promises. Both ministers and prime minister depend on the health of the American economy for a stable pound and a growing economy to ensure the needed financial resources are available. Recognising such power-dependence encourages us to focus on the distribution of resources such as money and authority in the core executive and explore the shifting relationships between actors.

The term 'core executive' directs attention to two key questions: 'Who does what?' and 'Who has what resources?' If the answer for several policy areas and several conflicts is that the prime minister co-ordinates policy, resolves conflicts and controls the main resources, we will indeed have prime ministerial government. However, as Wright and Hayward (2000: 33) concluded, core executive co-ordination is modest in practice. It is 'largely negative, based on persistent compartmentalisation, mutual avoidance and friction reduction between powerful bureaux or ministries'. Even 'when co-operative, anchored at the lower levels of the state machine and organised by specific established networks, co-ordination is sustained by a culture of dialogue'. Moreover, co-ordination is 'rarely strategic, so almost all attempts to create proactive strategic capacity for long-term planning . . . have failed'. And, finally, co-ordination is 'intermittent and selective in any one sector, improvised late in the policy process, politicised, issue-oriented and reactive'.

The endless search for effective co-ordination continues in British government. New Labour's reforms attempt to promote co-ordination and strategic oversight to combat both Whitehall's departmentalism and the unintended consequences of managerialism. As Norton (2000: 116–17) argues, 'ministers are like medieval barons in that they preside over their own, sometimes vast, policy territory'. Crucially, 'the ministers fight – or form alliances – with other barons in order to get what they want' and they 'resent interference in their territory by other barons and will fight to defend it'. The core executive is segmented into overlapping games in which all players have some resources with which to play the game and no one actor is pre-eminent in all games.

In sum, power-dependence characterises the links between both barons and the barons and prime minister. Looking at the heart of the machine as if it is a core executive characterised by power dependence reveals the limits to the Westminster model's depiction of a strong executive. Co-ordination is intermittent, selective and sectoral. Reforms to strengthen the core executive almost always reflect the strength of the barons and the core's past weakness, not its current strength. With an almost brutal realism, Wright and Hayward (2000: 34) conclude core executives lack political will, time, information, cohesion and effective instruments. The existing positivist literature analyses core executives by position or functions. In contrast, an interpretive approach suggests the core executive can be understood as diverse and scattered meanings, beliefs and practices.

Hollowing-out

The argument about the strength of the British executive is overstated. It is clear there were always many constraints. With the trend from government to governance, moreover, the constraints have become ever more insistent. The storyline of the past twenty years is one of fragmentation confounding centralisation as a segmented executive seeks to improve horizontal co-ordination among departments and agencies and vertical co-ordination between departments and their networks of organisations. An unintended consequence of this search for central control has been a hollowing-out of the core executive.

The hollowing-out of the state suggests the growth of governance has further undermined the ability of the core executive to act effectively, making it increasingly reliant on diplomacy. In what ways has the capacity of the British core executive been eroded? The state has been hollowed-out from above by for example international interdependence, and from below by for example marketisation and networks, and sideways by agencies. Internally the British core executive was already characterised by baronies, policy networks and intermittent and selective co-ordination. It has been further hollowed out internally by the un-intended consequences of marketisation, which fragmented service delivery, multiplied networks and diversified the membership of those networks. It will not be long before devolution to Scotland, Wales and Northern Ireland imposes further difficulties. Indeed, there may be a demonstration effect that will give added momentum to the demand for regional devolution in England.

Externally the state is also being hollowed out by membership of the EU and other international commitments. Menon and Wright (1998) allow that Britain has 'forged an efficient policy making and co-ordinating machine' because the government speaks and acts with one voice. It has been successful in its 'basic strategy of opening up and liberalising the EU's economy'. However, its 'unjustified reputation' for being at the margins of Europe is justified for EU constitution building and 'an effective and coherent policy making machine becomes ineffective when it is bypassed' for the history-making decisions.

Few would consider the problems of steering an ever-more complex, devolved government machine and being bypassed for constitutional, history-making decisions as evidence of the core executive's ability to act effectively. It is important to distinguish between intervention and control. Indisputably the British centre intervenes often but its interventions do not constitute effective control. Here an interpretive approach points to the diverse meanings with which all sorts of individuals – providers and citizens – respond to government interventions. Their contingent responses help to explain the gap between intervention and control.

The differentiated polity

The Westminster model treats Britain as a unitary state but this term is a black hole in the political science literature. It is a taken-for-granted notion all too often treated as a residual category, used to compare unitary with federal states to highlight the characteristics of the latter. However there are several types of unitary state and Britain differs in that, for Scotland, Wales and Northern Ireland, pre-Union rights, institutional structures and a degree of regional autonomy persisted throughout the post-war period. In other words, administrative structures are not standardised; there is a maze of institutions and a variegated pattern of decentralised functions. To refer to Britain as a differentiated polity is to make it clear that political integration and administrative standardisation have been and are incomplete. As British government grew, typically it became more specialised in both the functions it delivered and the territories it governed. The differentiated polity also covers many of the changes of the 1980s and 1990s that led to significant changes in the functional and territorial specialisation of British government. Recent changes multiplied networks as an unintended consequence of marketisation, increased the degree of international interdependence, and, as a result, reduced or hollowed out the core executive's capacity to steer. These trends reinforce the interpretation that centralisation and control are incomplete. Britain is best viewed as a differentiated polity – an unruly disUnited Kingdom.

Devolution will provide further impetus to the swings of the pendulum from centralisation to governance and back. It may be one of the most significant reforms of the post-war period because it reinforces decentralisation with divided political authority. Devolution to the English regions will not take place in the life of the second Blair parliament. But the new Regional Development Agencies and the promise of regional referendums on whether to introduce elected assemblies have not stilled the clamour of regional voices for devolution. Rather, political decentralisation remains on the political agenda. The civil service may soon confront a patchwork quilt of regional assembles and directly elected mayors in England – as well as the devolved administrations of Scotland, Wales and Northern Ireland – which will need a new machinery of government to manage intergovernmental relations both for domestic matters and for the EU. Diplomatic skill in intergovernmental bargaining will become a prominent part of a civil servant's repertoire. Britain will get a taste of the federal-provincial diplomacy so characteristic of other Westminster systems such as Australia and Canada. In the words of the Head of the Home Civil Service, Sir Richard Wilson (1998) the civil service 'are going to have to learn skills that we haven't learned before'.

In short, the networking skills increasingly needed to manage service delivery will also be at a premium in managing the intergovernmental relations of a devolved Britain. The task is to manage packages – packages of services, packages of organisations and packages of governments. This is not the picture of British government painted by most current versions of the Westminster model. On the contrary, their account of Britain as a unitary state emphasises political integration, centralised authority, a command operating code implemented through bureaucracy and the power of the centre to revoke decentralised powers. The governance narrative, in contrast, emphasises political devolution, fragmentation and interdependence, and decentralisation. Later we will argue an interpretive approach suggests we should decentre the institutions of governance. Even devolved, fragmented and interdependent institutions do not have a given form defining a path-dependent development. Rather they are constantly recreated and modified through contingent contests over meanings by agents inspired by competing traditions.

Conclusion

Any narrative that seeks to redraw the theoretical map of British government will always court the danger of appearing one-sided. The governance narrative counters a view of British government that sees Britain as a unitary state with a strong executive. Obviously the British executive can act decisively. Equally obvious, the centre co-ordinates and implements policies as intended at least some of the time. But current versions of the Westminster model attach too little importance to the sour laws of unintended consequences. Governments fail because they are locked into power-dependent relations and because they must work with and through complex networks of actors and organisations. The governance narrative clearly suggests that to adopt a command operating code builds failure into the design of the policy, no matter that denim sports shirts have replaced suits and gentle words have replaced strident handbagging. Such centralisation will be confounded by fragmentation and interdependence that, in turn, will prompt further bouts of centralisation. The governance narrative identifies several reasons for breaking free of the shackles of the Westminster model.

Devolution is the first step, and it is proving a hard pill to swallow. Devolved governments do their own thing. They elect first ministers the British government does not want to deal with. They adopt policies the British government does not approve of, even policies which embroil the centre in disputes not of its making. Similarly, if at a more dull level, policy networks implement and vary policies in ways the centre dislikes. The Department for Education and Employment battles long and hard with the Treasury for extra money for the education service only to see local authorities spend that money on services other than education. Trusting devolved governments, local authorities and, indeed, any decentralised agency, to deliver the services people want and to be accountable to those whom it serves is a big step for a British central government that habitually intervenes at will. Hands-off is a lesson no government has been willing to heed since 1945 but hands-on controls are no way to manage a differentiated polity.

Vincent Wright (1997: 13) comments that the interactions of state, market and society throw up many contradictions and dilemmas but a distinguishing feature of governing is its 'overarching and integrative function'. It provides 'ballast', 'a semblance of coherence', 'occasional steering ability' but 'above all' it provides 'a degree of legitimacy to governance'. Recent reforms and faulty maps threaten that legitimacy. The analysis of governance seeks to identify the intended and unintended consequences of the reforms of the 1980s and 1990s and so to correct faulty maps. In the next chapter, we will argue that to correct faulty maps, it is not enough to accept the governance narrative. We must also decentre it.

Notes

1 On policy networks in Britain see Dowding 1995, 2001; Frances *et al.* 1991; Hindmoor 1998; Jordan 1990; Le Galès and Thatcher 1995; Marsh 1999: Chapter 1; Marsh and Smith 2000; and Rhodes 1988, 1997a: Chapters 1 and 2, 1999: Chapter 8. For the rest of Europe see Börzel 1998; Bogason and Toonen 1998; Blom-Hansen 1997; Jordan and Schubert 1992; Marin and Mayntz 1991; Kenis and Schneider 1991; and Scharpf 1997.

2 There is a subset of the power-dependence literature that focuses on how to manage networks. The 'governance club' of Walter Kickert, Jan Kooiman and their colleagues at the Erasmus University, Rotterdam illustrates this concern (see Kickert 1993, 1997b; Kickert *et al.* 1997a and b; Klijn *et al.* 1995a; Kooiman 1993a). For a more detailed discussion see Chapter 4.

3 We would like to thank Tanya Börzel (European University Institute, Florence) for her advice in writing the section on the work at the Max-Planck-Institut für Gesellschaftsforschung. Although we were familiar with Fritz Scharpf's earlier work on *politikverflechtung* and the joint decision trap, she drew our attention to his work in the 1990s, most of which is only available in German. For relevant citations see Börzel 1998.

4 Decentring governance

Introduction

The phrase 'the differentiated polity' provides an alternative, or at least amendment, to the Westminster model. Look at any dictionary and it is clear differentiation is a vague term. On the one hand, differentiation refers to functional differences, or growth through specialisation. If we use differentiation in this way, we will offer a positivist account of governance. We will treat governance as a complex set of institutions and institutional linkages defined by their social role or function. We will make any appeal to the contingent beliefs and preferences of agents largely irrelevant. On the other hand, differentiation can refer to differences in meaning. If we understand differentiation in this way, we will offer a decentred account of governance. We will understand the institutions of governance by studying the various contingent meanings informing the actions of the relevant individuals. Clearly, our anti-foundationalist epistemology and interpretive approach push us toward this second understanding of the differentiated polity.

Accounts of governance can and do take a positivist form. However, our interpretive approach prompts us both to shift from the classical Westminster model to governance and to decentre governance, that is, to think about governance in relation to diverse narratives, traditions and dilemmas. Current positivist approaches to governance focus on the objective characteristics of policy networks and the oligopoly of the political market place. They stress topics such as power-dependence, the degrees of independence of networks, the relationship of the size of networks to policy outcomes, and the strategies by which the centre might steer networks.[1] A decentred account of governance would not stress their allegedly objective characteristics. Rather it would focus on the social construction of policy networks through the ability of individuals to create meanings. This chapter develops the contrast between the positivist account of governance that dominated the last chapter and a decentred approach to governance based on the interpretation of meanings.

Decentring governance

Even when positivist accounts of governance abstain from functionalist explanations and language, they typically draw on an institutionalism at odds with our interpretive approach. Typically positivist proponents of governance argue that pressures such as globalisation, inflation and state-overload brought about neo-liberal reforms. Thus, the new public management is seen as a global trend arising from globalisation (see, for example, Dunleavy and Hood 1994; Hood 1991, 1995). However, others argue existing institutions were so embedded that they frustrated neo-liberal reforms (see, for example, Hirst and Thompson 1999). In effect, institutions create the space between policy intentions and their unintended consequences; they explain the difference between the neo-liberal dream of marketisation and the reality of governance as networks. We thoroughly approve of the way positivist critics of globalisation and global governance shift our attention from an allegedly inexorable process fuelled by the pressures of globalisation, capital mobility and competition between states to the ways inherited institutions produce diverse responses to these pressures. However, the concept of an institution used in such accounts is fatally ambiguous. On the one hand, positivists generally reify institutions; that is, institutions are defined as allegedly fixed operating procedures or rules that constrain, arguably even determine, the actions of the relevant agents.[2] On the other hand, such accounts of institutions are sometimes opened to include culture or meanings, which suggests institutions fix neither such meanings nor the actions of the relevant agents. Yet if we open institutions in this way, we cannot treat them as if they were given. Instead, we have to explore how meanings and so actions are created, recreated, and changed in ways that can modify and even transform institutions.

The point at issue is whether we can read off the beliefs, desires and actions of individuals from their institutional locations. If we can, as positivists suggest, then our accounts can reify institutions and it is unnecessary to explore how individuals produce meanings in them. But if we cannot, as anti-foundationalists suggest, then we need to extend our interpretive critique to institutionalism. Here anti-foundationalism implies that neither scholars nor their subjects have pure perceptions or pure reason. Those we study do not have pure experiences or given interests. So, we cannot read off their beliefs, preferences and actions from allegedly objective social facts about them. Rather, they construct their beliefs against the background of a tradition (or episteme or paradigm) and often they do so in response to dilemmas (or problems or anomalies). Institutions do not have a natural or given form. We need to decentre institutions, networks and governance.

A decentred approach to institutions changes our approach to governance in two more ways. For a start, a decentred approach encourages us to examine the ways in which our social life, institutions and policies are created, sustained and modified by individuals. Institutions do not fix the beliefs that spur individual actions. They arise as individuals adapt traditions in response to dilemmas. Because we cannot read off people's beliefs from knowledge of objective social facts about them, we have to explore both how traditions prompt them to adopt certain meanings and how dilemmas prompt them to modify these traditions. When we decentre governance in this way, the idea that it arises from given inputs or pressures becomes difficult to sustain. Political actors construct their understanding of pressures or dilemmas such as inflation and state overload, and so the policies they adopt depend on the traditions on which they draw.

A decentred approach highlights the importance of dilemmas, traditions and political contests for the study of governance. Any existing pattern of governance will have some failings, although different people will have different views about these failings because they are not simply given by experience. Rather they are constructed from interpretations of experience infused with traditions. When people's perceptions of failings conflict with their existing beliefs, they pose dilemmas that push them to reconsider their beliefs and so the intellectual tradition that informs those beliefs. Because people confront these dilemmas in diverse traditions, there arises a political contest over what constitutes the nature of the failings and what should be done about them. Exponents of rival political positions or traditions seek to promote their particular sets of theories and policies, and this political contest leads to a reform of government. So, any reform must be understood as the contingent product of a contest over meanings the contents of which reflect different traditions and dilemmas.

The reformed pattern of government established by this complex process will display new failings, pose new dilemmas and be the subject of competing proposals for reform. There will be a further contest over meanings, a contest in which the dilemmas are often significantly different, and the traditions have been modified as a result of accommodating the previous dilemmas. All such contests take place in the context of laws and norms that prescribe how they should be conducted and sometimes the relevant laws and norms have changed because of simultaneous political contests over their content and relevance. Yet while we can distinguish analytically between a pattern of government and a political contest over its reform, we rarely can do so temporally. Typically, the activity of governing continues during most political contests, and most contests occur partly within local practices of governing. What we have, therefore, is a complex and continuous process of interpretation, conflict and activity that produces an ever-changing pattern of governance.

Meaningful practices

A decentred account of governance represents a shift of topos from institutions to meaningful practices. It begins with an acceptance of the broad picture we have already painted of the core executive, the hollowed-out state and the differentiated polity. However, that picture still objectifies political institutions: at best, it is compatible with the functionalism of positivism as well as an interpretive approach associated with anti-foundationalism. The positivist approach treats networks as social structures from which we can read off the beliefs, interests and actions of individuals. An interpretive approach to governing structures – markets, hierarchies and networks – would not hypostatise them in this way. Rather, it would decentre them to explore the effects of fragmentation of service delivery on the beliefs and preferences, and so practices, of the several participants.

Bang and Sørensen's (1999) bottom-up approach provides an instructive parallel and counterpoint to our concern to decentre governance. Their account of the 'Everyday Maker' examines individuals, their beliefs and actions, as they constantly make and remake local institutions. The study is based on interviews with twenty-five active citizens in the Nørrebro district of Copenhagen. It sought to find out how these citizens engage with government. Bang and Sørensen argue that Denmark has a long tradition of networking. Recent conflicting trends involved political decentralisation through governmental fragmentation, which further blurred the boundaries between public, private and voluntary sectors, and political internationalisation which moved decision making to the EU (ibid.: 11). They describe 'governance as networks' as an ideal type before suggesting that the governance of Denmark now represents a paradoxical mixture of government or hierarchy and governance or networks.

In the context of these conflicting trends, the Everyday Makers of Nørrebro focus on immediate, street-level, concrete policy problems. Their civic engagement is about 'balancing relations of autonomy and dependence between elites and lay-actors in recursive, institutional networks of governance within or without the state or civil society' (ibid.: 3). They find such a balance by adopting such political maxims as: do it yourself, do it where you are, do it for fun but also because you find it necessary, do it *ad hoc* or part-time, think concretely rather than ideologically, show responsibility for and trust in yourself, show responsibility for and trust in others, and look at expertise as an other rather than as an enemy. In their civic engagement, moreover, Everyday Makers display:

> a strong self-relying and capable individuality; a perception of politics as the concrete and direct handling of differences, diversity and dispute in everyday life; a notion of commonality as relating to solving common concerns; an acceptance of certain democratic values and procedures in handling not only of high but also of low politics.
>
> (Ibid.: 3)

For example, Grethe, a grass-roots activist, reflects that she has gained the competence to act out various roles, including those of contractor, board member and leader. There has been an 'explosion' of 'issue networks, policy communities, *ad hoc* policy projects, and user boards, including actors from "within", "without", "above", and "below" government'. The task of the Everyday Maker within these networks is 'to enter in and do work at one point of entry or another' (ibid.: 15). Political activity has shifted from 'formal organizing to more informal networking' (ibid.: 20). Among these networks 'you do in fact miss local government – a visible local government'; local politicians 'become visible at once when there are hullabaloos', but 'in ordinary everyday life, they are conspicuous by their absence' (ibid.: 21). Politics is no longer about left and right. Rather, it is about engaging in what is going on in institutions (ibid.: 23).

There are some instructive contrasts between Bang and Sørensen's concern with lay activists and our decentred, interpretive approach. First, they employ an ideal-typical research method, specifying not only the characteristics of the Everyday Maker but also the maxims that guide their political behaviour. Specific instances are then compared to these ideal-types. Indeed, we suspect that the Everyday Maker represents something of a normative ideal in that her behaviour epitomises the civic engagement that one Danish tradition would like to think characterises their population. An added note of caution is also in order because the Everyday Maker may be an endangered species. Jensen (1998a) has shown how the democratic experiment in Danish social housing is confounded by the fatalism of tenants and the lack of suitable democratic skills. Normative ideals can thus lead the researcher to ignore the fatalist for whom networks will have a different meaning. An interpretive account would not assume the Everyday Maker had fixed characteristics, let alone those of a normative ideal. Rather, it would rely on historical and ethnographic practices to explore the contingent beliefs, preferences and actions of a diverse range of political actors.

Second, Bang and Sørensen's account of networks focuses on the beliefs and actions of only one group of actors, and even for that group it does not provide a suitably thick description. An interpretive account implies micro-analysis but it does not necessarily imply a bottom-up approach. Political scientists should not restrict their interest to any one category of actor. To the Everyday Maker, then, we need to add the street-level bureaucrats, who can make and remake policy, the services users, whose experiences can differ markedly from the expectations of the service provider, and the political and managerial elite who typically seek to steer other actors in the network. Decentred studies of networks would thus build a multifaceted picture of how the several actors understand and construct the relevant networks. There should be no expectation that we will find one monolithic 'true' account. Rather, political scientists construct narratives about how other people understand what they are doing in networks, where these understandings usually both overlap and conflict with one another.

Finally, Bang and Sørensen note but do not explore the traditions and dilemmas which shape the practice of the Everyday Maker, and indeed other actors in the networks. Networks are created and developed against the background of traditions. In addition, networks construct or reconstruct their own traditions. Individuals learn about the network and its constituent organisations through stories of famous events and characters. Local networks with high participation are a long-standing feature of the Danish governmental tradition. The Nørrebro district of Copenhagen is famous even in this tradition for its activism. Recently, for instance, Nørrebro has been the centre of street riots – a rare event in Denmark – over the treatment of immigrants and membership of the EU. Thus, the Everyday Maker acts against the background of local traditions characterised by a particularly strong belief in political activism.

Meaning in governance

We can explore further our decentred account of governance by comparing our answers to the main questions about governance with the answers of institutional and functional accounts. We look at five questions: Is governance new? What is the content of governance? How do we explain changes in governance? How does the centre manage governance networks? Is governance failure inevitable? We answer each question, first, by identifying the limits to the positivist narrative of governance, and, second, by developing an alternative, interpretive account.

Is governance new?

Positivist political scientists sometimes suggest that the emergence of networks is a new phenomenon, marking a new epoch. A sceptic might point out that networks are not new; the main difference is that political scientists now talk about them endlessly. Both points are correct, and misleading. In reply, the political scientist might allow that networks are not new while still insisting that they have multiplied. Precise figures are not available, but fragmenting public services through the increasing use of special-purpose bodies and contracted-out services is obvious and widespread. Moreover, while the dominant narrative of the 1980s and 1990s told the story of how corporate management and marketisation triumphed over bureaucracy, this story ignores the need for negotiation in and between networks. The difficulty here, of course, is that the issue of continuity gets reduced to the pointless and probably impossible task of counting networks, past and present.

Our decentred approach to governance casts a new light on this debate because it treats bureaucracy, markets and networks as meaningful practices created and constantly recreated through particular, contingent actions. In many ways, therefore, networks are an integral part of our social and political life; they are characteristic of bureaucracy and markets as well as governance. For example, the rules and commands of a bureaucracy do not have a fixed form but rather are constantly interpreted and made afresh through the creative activity and interactions of individuals as they confront always slightly novel circumstances. Likewise, the operation of competition in markets depends on the contingent beliefs and interactions of interdependent producers and consumers who rely on trust and diplomacy as well as economic rationality in reaching all sorts of decisions. Once we stop reifying institutions, bureaucracies and markets, we find many of the characteristics allegedly specific to networks are widespread aspects of political structures. Our decentred approach encourages a shift of focus from networks, now recognised as an integral part of social life, to the beliefs held by political actors and to the stories told by political scientists. Governance is new because it signifies an important change in these beliefs and stories. Whether there is more fragmentation or functional differentiation is less important than the search for a new narrative about government that confronts the perceived weaknesses of the bureaucratic and market alternatives. Governance as networks provides a different story and language. In short, an interpretive approach turns the current approaches to networks on their head by insisting that networks are enacted by individuals through the stories they tell one another, and by refusing to treat them as given facts.

What is the content of governance?

One popular positivist explanation for the growth of governance argues that advanced industrial societies grow by a process of functional and institutional specialisation and the fragmentation of policies. Such narratives typically lead to a stipulative definition of governance as, say, self-organising interorganisational networks. In short, positivist political scientists treat networks as objectified structures. For example, a policy network will be seen as an ideal type and the characteristics of this ideal type will be compared with actual changes in government, although no policy network is likely to exhibit all these characteristics.

This view of networks as objectified structures appears in the innumerable typologies that characterise so much of the literature. These typologies characteristically treat network dimensions and characteristics as given. They then try to read off the nature of a particular network, and so the practices of its members, from these given dimensions and characteristics. From an interpretive perspective, such constructs are unacceptably ahistorical. They are static, fixed categories into which we force beliefs, cases and texts. Instances should not be constructed by comparison with the features of an ideal-typical governing structure. It is a commonplace observation that even simple objects are not given to us in pure perceptions but are constructed in part by the theories we hold true of the world.

When we turn our attention to complex political objects, the notion that they are given to us as brute facts verges on the absurd. The facts about networks are not given to us; rather, individuals construct them in the stories they hand down to one another. The study of networks, therefore, is inextricably bound up with interpreting the narratives on which they are based. Probably the best way of illustrating this decentred approach would be to explore the traditions and narratives that inspire political actors. In this way, we could show how governance as networks arises out of the multiple beliefs and preferences that legislators, bureaucrats and others have come to adopt through a process of modifying traditions to meet specific dilemmas. However, the dominance of positivism within political science means little is known about the relevant beliefs and preferences. Later we attempt at times to make good this dearth of knowledge. At other times, however, to show how these narratives reflect different govern-mental traditions, we had no choice but to fall back on academic accounts of the rise and nature of governance as networks. In Britain, we can highlight several traditions, each of which typically inspires a different interpretation of governance. Later we will develop this argument in more detail, but for now, as illustrations only, we briefly outline interpretations of governance as networks from within respectively the Liberal and Socialist traditions.

Henney (1984: 380–1), writing in the Liberal tradition, interprets networks as examples of the corporate state. He equates them with 'the institutionalised exercise of political and economic power' by the various types of local authority, government, the unions and to a lesser extent business. These groups 'undertake deals when it suits them; blame each other when it suits them; and cover up for each other when it suits them'. Their interactions are conducted 'behind closed doors', with each sector existing in a 'cultural cocoon' that rationalises its interests as equivalent to the public interest. The vested interests 'institutionalise irresponsibility'. Producers' interests rule OK, only for Henney it isn't. Thus, he wants to cut local government down to a manageable size by removing some of its functions and by transferring others to the social market. But the problem of networks as producer capture is not easily resolved. Marketisation is the alleged solution but it fragments service delivery structures, creates a motive for actors – whether individuals or organisations – to co-operate and thus multiplies the networks liberal reforms seek to break up. So, belief in the virtues of markets confronts the obvious defects of quasi-markets.

Perri 6, writing in the socialist tradition, interprets networks as a problem of integration. He argues governments typically confront 'wicked problems' that do not fit in with functional government based on central departments and their associated policy networks. Such functional govern-ment is costly, centralised, short term, focuses on cure not prevention, lacks co-ordination, measures the wrong things and is accountable to the wrong

people (Perri 6 1997: 26). He advocates the solution of a holistic government that will span departmental cages. Perri's report, written for a New
Labour 'think-tank', epitomises a long-standing Fabian tradition in the
Labour Party that seeks salvation in administrative engineering. Yet the
problem of integration is not easily resolved. On the one hand, Perri's
reforms have a centralising thrust: they seek to co-ordinate the departmental
cages, a centralising measure, and to impose a new style of management on
other agencies, a central command operating code. But, on the other hand,
a decentralised, diplomatic, negotiating, style is said to characterise network
structures. So, the belief that leaders know best confronts the belief that
decentralised structures need indirect or hands-off management.

We can also provide an illustration of our decentred approach that is
broader than a focus on Anglo-Saxon traditions. Governance has important
implications for other state traditions. Loughlin and Peters (1997: 46)
distinguish between the Anglo-Saxon (no state) tradition, the Germanic
(organicist) tradition, the French (Napoleonic or Jacobin) tradition, and a
Scandinavian tradition that mixes the Anglo-Saxon and the Germanic. In
the Germanic tradition state and civil society are part of one organic
whole. The state is a transcendent entity. Its defining characteristic is that it
is a *rechtsstaat*, that is a legal state vested with exceptional authority but
constrained by its own laws. Civil servants are not just public employees,
but personifications of state authority. In the Anglo-Saxon pluralist
tradition, in contrast, we find a clearer boundary between state and civil
society – there is no legal basis to the state, and civil servants have no
constitutional position. The Jacobin tradition takes the French state to be
the one and indivisible republic, exercising a strong central authority to
contain the antagonistic relations between state and civil society. The
Scandinavian tradition is an 'organicist' one, characterised by *rechtsstaat*,
but it differs from the Germanic tradition in being associated with a
decentralised unitary state and a strong ethos of participation.[3]

These diverse state traditions lead to different interpretations of
governance. For example, local networks with high rates of participation
are common in Denmark. There governance poses the issue of how to keep
the multiplying networks under democratic control given that decentralised
networks are already a feature of the tradition. Similarly, in the Germanic
tradition, the legal framework sets the boundaries to, and guides, official
action. The direct imposition of control is unnecessary. As a result, there is
a high degree of tolerance for the multi-level networks (*politikverflechtung*)
that are so common there and in many other federal systems. In stark
contrast, the Jacobin tradition, with its assumption of conflict between
state and civil society, often portrays networks as a potential threat to state
authority unless they are subject to state control through, for example,
strong mayoral leadership. Obviously we have only illustrated a complex
argument, for this account of state traditions is a broad-brush one that
does not properly allow for their variety and nuances. Nonetheless, even

this illustration seems sufficient to show that, in seeking to interpret and understand the nature of governance, we have to ask whose interpretation of which practice in which tradition.

How do we explain change in networks?

Current explanations of how networks change rely on exogenous, not endogenous, causes. Commonly, they identify four broad categories of change – economic, ideological, knowledge and institutional – all of which are conceived as external to the network (see, for example, Marsh and Rhodes 1992a). An interpretive approach decentres networks by exploring how individual actors enact them. Thus, it encourages us to look for the origins of change in the contingent responses of individuals to dilemmas. By focusing on the individual's responses to dilemmas, we build exogenous change into the heart of networks. As we explained earlier, a dilemma arises for an individual or a group whenever a new idea stands in opposition to their existing beliefs and so forces reconsideration. Because we cannot read off the ideas and actions of individuals from objective social facts about them, we can understand how their beliefs, actions and social practices change only by exploring the ways in which they think about, and respond to, dilemmas. Thus, an analysis of change and developments in governance must take place through a study of dilemmas. We build change into the heart of our account of networks by exploring how individual actors respond to dilemmas to reinterpret and reconstruct practices and the traditions they embody.[4]

Stoker's (1999a) analysis of the new public management (NPM) in British local government shows how dilemmas stemming from inflation and changing beliefs about public spending led to the ideas that informed NPM. However, people's responses to dilemmas are contingent so changes intended to introduce NPM in fact led to local governance. Ideally, of course, we should tell the story through the eyes of public managers but their version of the story is not available to us. So, instead we use Stoker's account of how public managers responded to the dilemma of inflation and reduced public spending.

Inflation had become a major problem for the British economy by the end of the 1970s and it was widely accepted that it had direct and immediate consequences for public spending. Such spending was to be cut. Local authorities are a major vehicle for delivering welfare state services and account for much public spending. They became a prime target for a government committed to lowering inflation by curbing public spending. Management reform was one part of the effort to contain public spending. The new public management's rhetoric told a story of promoting economy, efficiency and effectiveness – the '3Es' – through techniques imported from the private sector. This story contrasted sharply with the established one of the local government officer as a professional with clients. In theory, NPM was to deliver more public services for less money. It was to do so through the '3Es' and through marketisation or the use of market mechanisms such as contracting-out. Yet Stoker shows how the '3Es' and marketisation generated unintended consequences, including fragmentation, loss of accountability, and a decline in the public service ethic. More significant for our argument here, he also identifies important unintended benefits. First, NPM disrupted the system. Second, local authorities were increasingly forced to account for their actions in public. Third, this twin pressure produced a sense of crisis, which helped to create new policy ideas. The delicious irony is that the new ideas were not those of NPM but of local governance. In response to the dilemmas thrown up by NPM, local authorities adopted a wider role of concern for the well-being of the locality, worked in partnership with many actors and agencies, and focused on the outcomes of services delivered through these partnerships. As Stoker concludes:

> It is in some respects ironic that the pressures unleashed by new management have encouraged local authorities to rethink and redefine their role. The vision of the New Management reformers aimed at a more efficient and customer-oriented service delivery by local authorities has been challenged by a broader vision of a new community governance.
>
> (Ibid.: 15)

So, the number of networks multiplied. Their membership grew and it was drawn from more sectors. By both intent and as an unintended consequence of reform, moreover, the capacity of the centre to steer those networks declined.

The response to the dilemma of inflation and public spending cuts can be seen in the language used to talk about the management changes. Mackintosh (1999) argues that NPM contains two economic discourses. The public trading discourse is the language of corporate management and marketisation handed down by the government for years. The public business discourse is a reaction to the perceived limits of NPM. It seeks adaptable, flexible relationships for dealing with several agencies and clients. These changes in management and in language illustrate the contingent nature of the way people responded to the dilemma posed by inflation and the need to curb public spending. There is no objective or rational reason for NPM to evolve into local governance. Individuals can modify the practices they inherit in many ways; there is no one rational, scientific or self-interested response to a dilemma.

How does the centre manage networks?

The current literature on networks is practical, seeking to improve network management. Again the positivist orientation of the literature is clear. It treats networks as objectified structures; as if they are cars and the researcher is the car mechanic, finding the right tool to effect repairs. In reviewing this literature on network management, we will use Kickert *et al.*'s (1997b) distinction between instrumental, interactive and institutional approaches, but we will illustrate the approaches using British examples. We recognise that networking strategies will vary with what political scientists hope to manage – the structure of network relations, the process of consensus building, or the outcome of joint problem-solving – but we do not explore these differences here.

The instrumental approach adopts a top-down perspective on network steering. Although there are limits on the centre's ability to steer, it still attempts to do so. This approach accepts that government occupies a special position and will seek to exercise its legitimate authority but it also recognises the constraints imposed by networks. Thus, government departments are the focal organisation, developing strategies that unilaterally alter the structure of incentives to influence relationships of dependency and so to get effective problem-solving. Perri 6 (1997: 10) provides specific examples of this approach in action. Instead of functional government, which he thinks has failed, he wants what he describes as holistic, preventive, culture changing and outcome-oriented government. One specific example of his approach in practice is the policy initiative on Health Action Zones. This initiative exhorts agencies from the public, private and voluntary sectors to work together to bring better health care to the poor. The instrumental approach assumes, as it does here, that the centre can devise and impose tools that will foster integration in and between policy networks to attain central objectives.

The key problem for the instrumental approach is the costs of steering. A central command operating code, no matter how well disguised, runs the ever-present risk of recalcitrance from key actors and a loss of flexibility in dealing with localised problems. Control deficits are an ever-present, and generally unintended, consequence of the top-down imposition of objectives.

The interaction approach stresses network steering and focuses on the dependence of network actors and on developing goals and strategies through mutual learning. It sees collective action as dependent on co-operation, championing management by negotiation and diplomacy. The key to steering is to recognise the importance of wearing the other person's shoes to understand their objectives and build and keep suitable relations of trust. Stoker's (2000b) review of techniques for steering urban governance, for example, includes indirect management through cultural persuasion, communication and monitoring as well as direct management through financial subsidies and structural reform. Klijn *et al.* (1995: 442) distinguish between game management and network structuring. Indirect management through game management includes selectively favouring some actors in the network, mobilising supporters and their resources, greater expertise in the rules of the game, and managing perceptions to simplify compromise. Ferlie and Pettigrew (1996: 88–9) found that the National Health Service was embedded in a web of interagency alliances that changed the style of NHS management. For example, there was a shift to matrix management styles with chief executive officers being increasingly concerned to build and maintain links and to institutionalise strategic alliances. Painter *et al.* (1997: 238) provide specific advice on game management. They conclude local authorities should conduct an audit of other relevant agencies, draw a strategic map of key relationships, identify which of their resources will help them to influence these other agencies, and identify the constraints on that influence.

The key problem of the interactive approach is the costs of co-operation. The obvious version of this argument is that there are more actors in a network, so it takes longer to agree and such delays often prove costly. Network management is time-consuming, objectives can be blurred, and outcomes can be indeterminate (Ferlie and Pettigrew 1996: 95–6). Decision-making is satisficing, not maximising. In addition, the interaction approach ignores the context of network relations. It pays little attention, for example, to the way in which political control can change the perceptions and strategies of local authorities in their dealings with other local agencies.

The institutional approach to network steering focuses on the institutional backcloth, the rules and structures, against which the interactions in networks take place. Thus, Klijn *et al.* (1995: 442) suggest that networking strategies should concentrate on changing relationships between actors, the distribution of resources, the rules of the game, and values and perceptions. Similarly, Stoker (2000b) itemises new funding arrangements and creating new agencies as two key ways of altering the structure of network relations. For example, for urban governance alone, he lists, as tools for giving specific issues a higher profile and for involving a wider range of actors, urban development corporations, housing action trusts, the Housing Corporation and housing associates, English Partnerships, Training and Enterprise Councils, Local Enterprise companies, the Government Offices for the Regions and the Regional Development Agencies. These tools are seen as ways of promoting incremental changes in incentives, rules and culture so as to promote joint problem-solving.

The institutional approach exhibits three main problems. First, incentives, rules and culture are notoriously resistant to change. Second, networks are often closed; they are rooted in the interests of a few, privileged actors who equate their sectional interest with the public interest. Third, appointments to the special-purpose agencies are often patronage appointments, with these bodies rarely being accountable to elected assemblies. As with the instrumental and the interaction approaches, the institutional approach to network management encounters important problems. We cannot consider any one approach a panacea for central steering in the differentiated polity.

The space we have devoted to the management of networks reflects the preoccupations of the literature on governance. The study of governance focuses on practical, technical, often narrow issues. A decentred account of networks raises broader but none the less practical issues.

For a start, a decentred approach presumes that networks cannot be understood apart from traditions. The individuals whose beliefs, interests and actions constitute a network necessarily acquire the relevant interests and beliefs against the background of traditions. In other words, networks are not objectified structures but rather the products of the contingent actions of the various participants. So there can be no single tool kit for managing networks. If networks are differentially and continuously constructed, there can be no one tool kit for managing them. Rather, a decentred approach claims that practitioners learn by telling, listening to and comparing stories. It suggests, moreover, that one of the most important lessons to be learnt is about the diversity and contingency of traditions. Practitioners can learn to understand how the fate of policies depends on the ways service-deliverers, customers, and others understand them and respond to them from within all sorts of traditions. If they do so, they might be able to avoid some of the unintended consequences of reform. Managing networks is about understanding and responding to the relevant practices, traditions and beliefs. Indeed policy advice can be seen as telling relevant stories (Rein 1976: 266–7).

A decentred approach also questions the way positivist discussions of network management focus on the problems confronted by managers, rather than users or politicians (see Kickert *et al.* 1997b; and O'Toole 1997 where even the research agenda is focused on management issues). The existing literature characteristically seeks to tell managers how to do their job more effectively. But there are several participants in networks – politicians, employees, users – all of whom might seek to exercise control by using diverse strategies for different ends. Each may tell different stories about network management and its difficulties.

Is the failure of governance inevitable?

It is a long-standing theme of the political science literature that markets and hierarchies have their limits. To some, networks are seen as the solution to such problems but there is a growing recognition that networks too have marked problems. The main problems are said to be that they: are closed to outsiders and unrepresentative; are relatively unaccountable for their actions; can serve private interests, not the public interest at both local and national levels of government; are difficult to steer; are inefficient because co-operation causes delay; can be immobilised by conflicts of interest; and are difficult to combine with other governing structures. No governing structure works for all services in all conditions. The issue, therefore, is not the superiority of markets and hierarchy over networks but managing networks in the conditions under which they work best. According to most political scientists, networks work best where the following factors combine: actors need reliable, 'thicker' information; quality cannot be specified or is difficult to define and measure; commodities are difficult to price; professional discretion and expertise are core values; flexibility to meet localised, varied service demands is needed; cross-sector, multi-agency co-operation and production is required; such co-operation confronts disparate organisational cultures; actors perceive the value of co-operative strategies; long-term relationships are needed to reduce uncertainty; monitoring and evaluation incur high political and administrative costs; and implementation involves haggling.[5] One effect of marketisation is that it regularly undermines the effectiveness of the networks it spreads. The government promoted competition and contracting-out. The result was to 'corrode common values and commitments' and 'to create an atmosphere of mistrust' (Flynn *et al.* 1996: 115). Market relations had 'corrosive effects' on 'professional networks which depend on co-operation reciprocity and interdependence' (ibid.: 136–7; see also Lowndes and Skelcher 1998). In short, contracts undermine trust, reciprocity, informality and co-operation.

Our interpretive approach both complements and challenges this analysis of governance failure. A focus on contingent meanings provides us with one way of understanding why all governing structures fail. The workings of any policy or institution depend on the ways all sorts of actors interpret and respond to the relevant instructions. Because these responses are inherently diverse and contingent, depending on the traditions and agency of the relevant individuals, the centre cannot be sure it has adequate prior knowledge of the way a policy or institution will operate. So the unexpected is built into governance. All governing structures are necessarily subject to unintended consequences, which prevent them from realising their stated purpose, even on those remarkably rare occasions when policy-makers share a common purpose.

A decentred approach also draws our attention to the diverse beliefs and preferences of actors in a network and so makes us sceptical of any positivist analysis that takes government intentions as its measuring rod, especially when the aim is to improve the chances of success of government policy. Street-level bureaucrats and citizens can deliberately attempt to undermine policies with which they disagree. From their standpoint, policy failure might be a success! There is no one given yardstick for measuring the success or failure of a policy. Governance failure is itself a constructed category.

Conclusion

As we discussed the five questions about governance and networks, we decentred our earlier account of them. Our initial account of governance was compatible with positivism. We have now outlined an interpretive account. We will not summarise here the advantages of focusing on governance, or the limitations of positivist accounts of networks, or what an interpretive approach can add to our understanding. We save this task for the concluding chapter. Still, we want to stress two points. An interpretive approach concentrates on beliefs and preferences as they arise in the context of traditions and dilemmas and it relies primarily on ethnographic and historical modes of inquiry.

An interpretive approach focuses on the beliefs and preferences of actors. It recovers them through ethnographic studies of individual behaviour in everyday contexts with a stress on the interpretation of the meanings of human action (paraphrased from Hammersley 1991: 1–2; see also Geertz 1973: 20–1).[6] The reference to everyday contexts does imply micro-analysis but it does not imply necessarily a bottom-up approach. The analysis is not restricted to any one category of actor. Thus, following Bulpitt (1983), we can explore the operational code, or rules of statecraft, of central political elites. These elites deploy the skills of statecraft to achieve governing competence and to preserve the centre's autonomy in High Politics, including, for example, foreign, defence and trade policy, although increasingly the term also covers macro-economic policy. The approach invites the historical analysis of the beliefs and actions of elite actors. Equally, the example of the Everyday Maker shows the importance of a bottom-up approach. We know street-level bureaucrats can make and remake policy. We know users' experience of services can differ markedly from the expectations of the service provider. And yet, after over a decade of public sector reforms, there is no study of the beliefs and actions of employees, or even middle-level managers, in response to these allegedly dramatic changes. The ethnography of networks invites us to build a multifaceted picture of how the several actors understood the changes labelled here 'governance'.

While ethnography recovers beliefs and preferences, a historical mode of inquiry enables us to explain them by traditions and dilemmas. Individuals are bearers of traditions even as they enact and remake structures in their everyday lives. So, governing structures can only be understood through the beliefs and actions of individuals and through the traditions passed on from person to person. Historical analysis is the way to uncover the several traditions as they develop in response to dilemmas.

The concepts of tradition and dilemma are prominent in our version of the interpretive approach. In Part II we provide three examples of how the study of traditions and dilemmas can improve our grasp of governance in Britain. We provide an aggregate analysis. So, we will not provide a micro-level account of any particular network; that is, an account of the beliefs of the participants that builds up to an exposition of their changing practices. Instead, we will unpack historical traditions as they have evolved and prompted the rise of present-day British governance. More detailed studies of the evolution of particular networks through contests over meaning are necessary to fill out this aggregate story. We hope our story will be persuasive and inspire such detailed studies.

Notes

1 Rod Rhodes's original analysis of networks was clearly rooted in a positivist epistemology. However, it genuflected in the direction of a more interpretive approach through its reference to Sir Geoffrey Vickers and the idea of appreciative systems (Vickers 1968). The term refers to 'that combination of factual and value judgements which describe the "state of the world" or "reality"' (Rhodes 1999: 83–4). It is the individual decision-maker's map of the world. Constructing maps of how others make sense of the world is a defining characteristic of an interpretive and decentred approach to networks.

2 Institutions are 'collections of standard operating procedures and structures that define and defend interest', for March and Olsen (1984: 738); and, similarly, 'they are formal rules, compliance procedures and standard operating practices that structure relationships between individuals in various units of the polity and the economy', for Hall (1986: 20).

3 In this paragraph we paraphrase Loughlin and Peters 1997: 46–55; see also Dyson 1980.

4 Marsh (1999: 5–9) argues for a multi-dimensional analysis of political change. See also English and Kenny 2000; Gamble 1988, 1994; Hay 1996, 2002; and Kerr 2001, although none of these accounts focus on networks. For analyses of change in networks see Hay and Richards 2000 and Marsh 1999.

5 On the conditions under which networks thrive, see Ferlie and Pettigrew 1996: 96–7; Flynn *et al.* 1996: 139–41; Kramer and Tyler 1996: Chapters 4 and 16; Larson 1992: 98; Lowndes and Skelcher 1998; Powell 1991: 268–74; Rhodes 1997a: Chapter 3; Thompson *et al.* 1991: Introduction and Chapters 21–3; Thompson 1993: 54–60; and Wistow *et al.* 1994.

6 For a similar recognition that the political ethnography of networks is an instructive approach see Heclo and Wildavsky 1974; McPherson and Raab 1988; and Rhodes 1997a: Chapter 9.

Part II

The public sector

On traditions and dilemmas

5 Comparing Britain and Denmark

Introduction

In this part of the book we explore the broad patterns of belief – traditions, ideologies or discourses – that informed the development of British governance. Specifically, we use the notions of tradition and dilemma to analyse three facets of British governance: public sector reform, Thatcherism and joined-up governance. These chapters are linked to one another in two ways. First, they trace a historical process. We start in Chapter 5 with an account of the British governmental tradition that provides the background to public sector reform since 1979. Then in Chapter 6 we analyse the different traditions informing the effects of Thatcherism on British governance. Finally, in Chapter 7, we turn to the beliefs underlying New Labour's move toward joined-up governance.

Second, each of these chapters decentres aspects of its forerunner. We use each chapter to raise issues about the notion of tradition. So we start in Chapter 5 by comparing a broad characterisation of the British governmental tradition with the Danish one. By so comparing traditions, we can identify and highlight some defining characteristics of the British governmental tradition but we elide differences within it. The next step is, therefore, to unpack this broad tradition into some of its constituents. In Chapter 6 we identify the Tory, Liberal, Whig and Socialist traditions, and show how each of them produces a distinct account of Thatcherism. Although this analysis draws out some of the differences in the British governmental tradition, we still do not account for how traditions change. The final step, therefore, is to show how dilemmas prompt people to modify traditions. In Chapter 7 we unpack the Socialist tradition further still by exploring the shift from Old to New Labour's conception of governance. Throughout this part of the book, we progressively unpack the idea of tradition to show there is no one level of analysis suitable for answering all questions. In so doing, we also discuss the issues raised by each illustration, including reifying traditions, essentialism, identifying traditions, and the process of change within traditions.

In this chapter, we compare public sector reform in Britain and Denmark. We begin by contrasting the broad pattern of reform in the two countries.

Then we explore their respective governmental traditions to explain the similarities and differences in the reforms. At this level, our account of governmental traditions overlaps considerably with well-known institutional accounts of government in the two countries. This overlap should not surprise anyone. As we suggested in the last chapter, institutionalism is ambiguous. On the one hand, political scientists' accounts of institutions sometimes include culture or meanings. If institutions are seen as the contingent products of conflicts over meanings, they closely resemble our notion of the practices that embody traditions. So, accounts of institutions, practices and traditions will overlap, as they do in this chapter. On the other hand, however, political scientists often give institutions a reified, fixed form, with versions of path dependency, that fix the behaviour of the agents within them. Because our anti-foundational, interpretive approach opposes reifying institutions, we prefer to talk of practices embodying traditions. In our view, institutionalism is insufficiently aware of, first, the diverse beliefs and actions of the agents who constantly recreate institutions, and, second, the contingent way these beliefs and actions develop through creative responses to dilemmas. So, in Chapter 6 we will unpack the diverse, competing beliefs found in the British governmental tradition, and in Chapter 7 we will explore recent changes in one part of this tradition in response to specific dilemmas.

New public management

At the forefront of governmental reform in the late twentieth century was the new public management (NPM). In this chapter we describe how such reforms differ in Britain and Denmark and explain why. NPM refers to a focus on management, not policy, and on performance appraisal and efficiency. Typically it involves disaggregating public bureaucracies into agencies that deal with one another on a user pay basis, the use of quasi-markets and contracting-out to foster competition, cost-cutting and a style of management that emphasises output targets, limited term contracts, monetary incentives and the freedom to manage (Hood 1991). NPM is often said to be a global phenomenon. However, it rapidly became clear, to paraphrase Aaron Wildavsky, 'if NPM is everything maybe it is nothing'. The label now covers almost all types of public sector reform. So, the differences are of far greater interest than the similarities.

Christensen and Lægreid (1998: 470–1; also citing Kickert 1997b and Olsen and Peters 1996) identify a sharp distinction between Anglo-American and Continental reforms. They conclude, 'NPM is not an integrated and consistent theory, but rather a loose collection of diverse doctrines, principles and measures which are partly in opposition to one another'. In a similar vein, Hood (1995) abandons his early characterisation of NPM, suggesting the case for NPM as a global paradigm was overstated. These several commentators remark that the ideas of NPM are internally contradictory, calling for hierarchic steering and egalitarian empowerment in the same breath. Also, as we will see, the similarities in NPM are superficial, masking significant underlying differences. The trend to NPM is not universal. Rather, traditional public administration persists in places such as the EU Commission and Germany. What is more, the aims and results of NPM differ. In Britain, NPM aimed to create the minimalist state. In Denmark, it aimed to protect the state (Ministry of Finance 1993). The language of NPM obscures differences; for example, NPM covers agencification in Britain but not in Australia, and regional devolution in France but not in Britain. Moreover, terms such as decentralisation are ambiguous since they can refer to deconcentration in an organisation or devolution to sub-national governments. Several of the individual parts of NPM are not new; for example, performance measurement. The distinctiveness of NPM could lie in the package not in the parts, but there is no uniform, agreed package. Finally, the meaning of NPM has changed; for example, in Britain the early focus was on cost cutting and efficiency but later the main concern was for the consumer. So, the label NPM masks far more than it reveals. The important tasks now are to identify and to explain the differences between instances of public sector reform during the 1980s and 1990s. We come not to bury NPM but to highlight national distinctiveness.

We selected the two countries for three reasons: conventionally they are seen as examples of different governmental traditions; both have public sector reform programmes; and there is a body of existing research to re-analyse. Any comparison of public sector reform in Britain and Denmark must specify the dimensions along which these reforms varied. The existing literature suggests there are six key dimensions: privatisation, marketisation, corporate management, regulation, decentralisation and political control. We will define each dimension as we discuss the British and Danish reforms. We will not use the generic term NPM: when corporate management is also known as managerialism and, to heighten confusion, managerialism is also known as NPM, it is perhaps time to drop both managerialism and NPM. We will refer instead to public sector reform, and when necessary, specify the dimension.

Trends in public sector reform in Britain and Denmark[1]

This section does not aim to provide a day-to-day, blow-by-blow account of reform in the two countries. We describe the main trends in Britain and Denmark in the 1990s.

Privatisation

Privatisation refers to the sale of public assets to the private sector. Whether the policy was a success in Britain, and one can argue about both its several objectives and the extent to which they were achieved, there can be no doubt about the scale of the programme. The government sold over fifty major businesses and reduced the state-owned sector of industry by some two-thirds, raising some £64 billion to pay for tax cuts. The scale of privatisation will necessarily decline under New Labour simply because so many public assets have been sold already. However, it is not ruled out on ideological grounds; for example, New Labour sold 60 per cent of the equity in the Commonwealth Development Corporation.

In Denmark there is great support for the welfare state and the Conservative coalition's proposals for privatisation in 1982 'provoked a major public outcry against this ideological crusade' (Jensen 1998b: 57), even though it was limited to vague proposals for contracting-out. The Danes have no tradition of nationalisation and, therefore, have less to sell. In 1997, the state held shares in forty-six companies with an asset value of some £13 billion and had a controlling interest in sixteen (Greve and Jespersen 1998: 12). Of the several sales, that of Tele Denmark was the largest share deal in Danish history but any further large privatisation is unlikely (Jensen 1998b: 57; and for a list of other privatisations see Greve and Jensen 2000: Table 2). Privatisation in Denmark is neither a question of party ideology nor of systematic policy but of pragmatic budgetary calculations. In particular, it is a matter of whether selling the organisation will solve its budgetary problems or make the government's annual budget round easier (Greve 1997; Jensen 1998b: 57).

If privatisation policy is low-key in Denmark, corporatisation, especially creating state-owned enterprises (SOEs), has become a large and distinctive reform. Between 1975 and 1995 SOEs tripled in number (Christensen 1998). The aims underlying SOEs are to give management freedom to manage while politicians remain responsible for general policy, and to make SOEs more competitive both by exposing them to market pressures and by recruiting private sector managers (but see Jensen 1998b: 58 for a discussion of the mix of motives). They cover industries such as gas, air travel, steel, shipping and Copenhagen airport. Some SOEs have been privatised – for example, computing, army clothing and telecommunications – but most remain profitably state owned. The post office, electricity and the underground rail system will be the next significant corporatisations. The degree of autonomy acquired by SOEs varies. The policy remains pragmatic. To employ Jensen's (1998b: 58) graphic aphorism, 'the Conservative government of the 1980s had a privatisation policy without privatisation, the current government privatises . . . without any explicit policy'.

Marketisation

Marketisation refers to the use of market mechanisms in the delivery of public services. The term mainly covers contracting-out (for example, compulsory competitive tendering in local government), quasi-markets in the guise of the purchaser–provider split (for example, in health), and experiments with voucher schemes (for example, education). Previous Conservative governments in Britain forced local and heath authorities to contract out and vigorously marketised public services. New Labour will curb marketisation. The purchaser–provider split in health and nursery vouchers will be abolished. However, there was no promised moratorium on contracting-out. New Labour is no enemy of the private sector and public–private partnerships will continue and expand. For example, the private finance initiative (PFI) in health involves the private sector building hospitals and leasing them back to the public sector for up to sixty years. Some thirty-one hospitals will be so financed. In brief, New Labour believes that marketisation 'has a role to play, again not out of dogmatism but out of pragmatism, because we want the best value for money' (Cm. 4310 1999: 35).

In Denmark, although there has been much urging to contract out, there has only been a small increase in contracting for goods and services to 19 per cent for central government and no increase in local government which remains steady around 10 per cent (Greve and Jensen 2000). Indeed, the centre reduced its capacity to control contracting-out by decentralising more powers to local government. Also contracting-out has a distinct style in Denmark, described by Greve (1997: 1 and 12) as negotiating over the objectives of the policy, not just its implementation, and contracts are 'sites for negotiation' (Greve 1998: 16). There has been no 'grand unambiguous leap from "state" to "market"' (Jensen 1998b: 59). To state the obvious, contracting-out is nothing new: the public sector has used the private sector to provide technical services such as refuse collection and cleaning for decades.

Corporate management

Corporate management stresses hands-on and professional management, setting explicit standards and measures of performance, managing by results, value for money and, more recently, closeness to the consumer. There are many variations on this list, most of which have their roots in a preference for a private sector management style that stresses performance measurement in general and output measurement in particular (see, for example, Hood 1991; Pollitt 1993).

Corporate management has a long history in Britain where the reforms, with marketisation, were used to break the alleged power of the public sector unions. Its first hallmark was the '3Es' of economy, efficiency and effectiveness with economy ever-present. The emphasis later shifted to making services transparent to their consumers through mechanisms such as the Citizen's Charter (see Pollitt 1993). New Labour's policy is pragmatic, with the government supporting initiatives such as Benchmarking, which aims to measure and improve quality, and Investors in People, which sets standards for human resources management. Both initiatives continue the habit of importing private sector management practices into the public sector. New Labour also reinvented the Citizen's Charter as Service First. For example, the government has set up a People's Panel comprising 5,000 people from all walks of life to give their views on improving service delivery (Cabinet Office 1998; Cm. 4310 1999: 25 and 29). It also displays a touching faith in the capacity of information technology to improve the quality and responsiveness of local service delivery (Cm. 4310 1999: Chapter 5). Sir Richard Wilson's Report to the Prime Minister on civil service reform (Cabinet Office 1999c) clearly shows the importance New Labour attaches to getting high levels of performance and value for money from the civil service. Managerialism marches into the new millennium.

Corporate management in Denmark covers management by objectives and performance-related pay (PRP). PRP combines measures of organisational outputs, strategic development and human resources development. The bonuses can amount to 15 per cent of an individual's salary (Jensen 1998b: 61). However, only 5.5 per cent of all state employees have switched to PRP. Similarly, the Public Sector Quality Award (PSQA), introduced in 1997, seeks to improve management processes through critical self-evaluation. It is too soon to assess its impact, although at the moment some 70 per cent of state employees have either superficial or no knowledge of the system (Greve and Jensen 2000).

Before marvelling at the pace of change in the public sector, we need to stress, again, that management by objectives and performance-related pay are not new management tools even in the public sector. There is little new here to warrant talk of a new global paradigm. These techniques are the standard fare of management consultants and business schools the world over. Also, in Denmark, while the reforms may pose challenges for the dominant workplace culture of high job security coupled with centralised pay negotiations and powerful unions, they do not seek to emasculate it. Rather, as Jensen (1998b: 62) argues, the corporate management reforms are Janus-like, facing in two directions at the same time. They seek to reward individual excellence through PRP and yet to encourage collective responsibility in delivering high-quality services.

Regulation

As the boundaries of the state were redrawn in the 1980s, many governments, including the Commission of the European Union, sought to strengthen their ability to regulate and audit institutions, their policies and their implementation of those policies. With the advent of privatisation, governments substituted regulation for ownership, and so multiplied the watchdogs of the new private sector monopolies. The audit explosion refers to all forms of internal and external regulation. It covers management and financial audit and evaluation with related quality assurance mechanisms and 'a distinct mentality of administrative control' which focuses on quantified, external, *ex-post*, expert forms of control (Power 1994: 8–9).

In Britain, the new regulatory bodies include the Office of Electricity Regulation, the Office of Gas Supply, the Office of Water Services and the Office of the Rail Regulator. They differ in size, ranging from the Broadcasting Standards Council with a budget of £0.4 million and a staff of fourteen, through the Office of Telecommunications (Oftel) with a budget of £4.5 million and a staff of 120, to the National Rivers Authority with a budget of £30 million and a staff of 6,500.

New Labour has not legislated to change the system for regulating public utilities. Public statements stress responsiveness to customers and criticise fat-cat salary increases. New Labour has set up a Better Regulation Unit in the Cabinet Office and a task force to improve 'the effectiveness and credibility of regulation by ensuring that it is necessary, fair and affordable, and simple to understand and administer, taking account of the needs of small business and ordinary people'. In short, New Labour has stressed reducing bureaucratic red tape rather than, for example, the effectiveness of the public utility regulators in protecting consumer interests.

The increase in internal regulation is also massive. Hood *et al.* (1998: 62–4) identify 134 such bodies spending £776 million a year in running costs and incurring roughly the same amount in compliance costs. Examples of such bodies range from the National Audit Office, the Prisons Inspectorate, the Parliamentary Commissioner for Administration, the Office of Public Service and the Higher Education Funding Council. If anything, the growth has speeded up under New Labour. Hood *et al.* (2000) identify at least twelve major new organisations created or announced by March 1999. These innovations include the Benefit Fraud Inspectorate (eighty-six staff and £3.4 million), the Best Value regime for local government, which includes two new inspectorates, and the Commission for Health Improvement and the National Institute for Clinical Excellence for the National Health Service. The costs of New Labour's changes are estimated as at least £20 million a year.

Hood *et al.* (2000) also detect a significant shift in regulatory philosophy under New Labour (see Cm. 4310 1999: 37–9). There is a growing awareness of the costs of regulation and of the need for consistency of practice between regulators. For example, the government has set up the Public Audit Forum to share ideas about good practice (ibid.: 37). The most significant trend is toward 'enforced self-regulation'; that is, more formal, external regulation for poor performers but 'light touch inspection regimes' (Blair 1999) for good performers. An early example was the Best Value regime for local government where most local authorities were expected to correct their own failings but poor performers were to be subjected to strong central intervention.

The strict financial climate saw the Treasury become more powerful. The Conservative government introduced several changes in budgeting and financial management to strengthen its control of total spending while ostensibly increasing financial delegation (Thain and Wright 1995). However, financial discretion was an illusion. The brute reality of everyday life was cuts in spending. Financial regulation lies at the core of the reform package in Britain. It remains so under New Labour (Cm. 4310 1999: 36–7). Public expenditure plans are set for three years. Resource accounting seeks to link resources to policy outputs. The Comprehensive Spending Review identified the government's spending priorities. The strategy is to have targets and other measures to ensure that priorities are translated into services. Spending patterns were changed and Public Service Agreements (Cm. 4181 1998; Cm. 4310 1999: 36–7) introduced to impose the necessary discipline. 'As always the Treasury is a powerful and ubiquitous force' (Theakston 1998b; see also Gray and Jenkins 1998 120–3).

In Denmark, there are regulatory bodies for electricity, telecommunications, railways and postal services but only *Telestyrelsen* approximates to an independent utility regulator. There are conflicting trends. For local authorities, there has been a 'campaign' to increase 'municipal liberty' by simplifying the rules used by the centre (Hansen 1997: 57). For central agencies, however, departments introduced new controllers to strengthen internal regulation (Greve and Jespersen 1998: 16–18). Central ministries advertise for controllers and set up new control sections targeted at specific directorates. They introduce new audit tools; for example, six-monthly reports on their current economic position as well as enterprise accounts. Responsibility for national audit was transferred to the parliament, giving it greater independence. Since 1996, ministries have been required by law to produce an annual report and accounts, although whether parties, public and media will use them remains to be seen.

The Ministry of Finance plays an important co-ordinating role, which is not restricted to budget making. No central actor co-ordinates ministries. Public sector reform is negotiated, with the Ministry seeking to steer indirectly. The sheer number of reports testifies to its commitment to reform. But no organisation has the direct controls of ministries. Knudsen (1999) shows that co-ordination, whether through the Council of State, the Meeting of Ministers (or Cabinet), or the various types of cabinet committee depends on 'trust and mutual understanding between the politicians involved, and a high level of information and feeling of personal responsibility among civil servants'. The Ministry of Finance and the Prime Minister's Office (PMO) are key cogs in this informal system. For example, at cabinet level 'the detailed negotiations are conducted – or at least supervised – by the Ministry of Finance and the PMO to control the politically sensitive issues'. But the style is one of indirect, not direct, control.

Decentralisation

Decentralisation encompasses both deconcentration and devolution. Deconcentration refers to the redistribution of administrative responsibilities in central government. Devolution refers to the exercise of political authority by lay, elected institutions within areas defined by community characteristics.

Deconcentration

In Britain, most of the reforms of the 1980s and 1990s sought to deconcentrate managerial authority to bodies such as agencies. Agencification means creating semi-autonomous agencies responsible for operational management. The key aim is to separate operational management by agencies from policy-making by core or central departments, leaving the agency free to manage. It is a classical doctrine of public administration. By January 1998, there were 138 agencies in Britain employing 77 per cent of the civil service (Cm. 3889 1998) and the programme was almost complete. New Labour accepted agencies after early doubts. There is no consensus about the extent of deconcentration to agencies. Day and Klein (1997) conclude that in the NHS policy has migrated from the core department to the agency. However, the chief executives of agencies see everyday life as constant interference by the parent department, the Treasury, and the Cabinet Office (Barker 1997). As one chief executive pointed out, 'I am a civil servant and cannot say no' (Cabinet Office 1994a: 31).

The White Paper on *The Citizen's Charter* (Cm. 1599 1991) was Prime Minister John Major's Big Idea. The key objectives were to improve the quality of public services and provide better value for money. The Citizen's Charter contains six principles: published explicit standards, full and accurate information about running services, choice for the users of services, courteous and helpful service, effective remedies, and efficient and economical delivery of services. Sir Robin Butler (1993: 402) describes the Citizen's Charter as 'the culmination of the movement to output measurement', a movement through which consumer interests have come to dominate producer interests, realising 'people power'. It is a little early for such an assessment. Christopher Pollitt (1993: 187) gets nearer to the mark when he concludes, 'it is not so much a charter for citizen empowerment as managerialism with a human face'. Under New Labour, the ideas and concerns of the Citizen's Charter have reappeared as Service First.

The number of agencies in Britain grew dramatically after 1988. They are, therefore, part of the recent reforms and an example of deconcentration. Although the rationale for agencies in Denmark also stresses separating policy and management, they are a long-standing feature of the Danish administrative landscape.[2] They figure in recent reforms but not as an example of deconcentration.

Devolution

Devolution is a distinctive policy of New Labour (Cm. 3658 1997). It will have many consequences for the public sector in Britain as a whole, not just Scotland. Although it is too early to assess the outcomes, some possible problems are already emerging. Thus, the Scottish civil servants will transfer to the parliament but as staff of the Scottish Executive they will continue to be part of a unified civil service. Obvious tensions exist in such dual loyalties. The government recognises this problem, asserting the 'ultimate loyalty of civil servants will remain to the Crown'. However, 'in practice the loyalty of individual civil servants will be to whichever administration they are serving' and they 'will continue to take their instructions from their departmental ministers' (Personnel Division, Cabinet Office, 'Devolution and the Civil Service', Note 2 1998). The British civil service seems likely to become less unified.

Scotland continues to receive its share of public spending and has the power to vary income tax by 3p in the pound. The Scottish parliament sets the framework for other Scottish public bodies, including elected local government. Scotland is now embedded in a changed and changing set of institutional links. A Joint Ministerial Committee (JMC) consisting of ministers of the British government, Scottish ministers, members of the cabinet of the Welsh Assembly and ministers in the Northern Ireland Executive Committee will provide central co-ordination (Cm. 4444 1999: 9–11). The JMC will consider non-devolved matters that impinge on devolved responsibilities and conversely. For Europe, the JMC will co-ordinate the devolved administrations, which may have offices in Brussels but will 'support and advance the single UK negotiating line' (ibid.: 20–3). The role of the civil service and the ways in which ministerial accountability will work remain unclear.

Before 1972, local government could be described as part of the constitution. No such claim would be made today. British central government has exerted ever-greater control over local authorities, especially their spending. Policy was centralising even if the outcomes were not always as intended. After much procrastination, the New Labour government decided there would no regional assemblies for England. It is also nervous about devolving power to local government because it is determined to keep control over public spending. The centrepiece of the government's White Paper on local government (Cm. 4014 1998) is elected mayors. Yet while it stresses the renewal of democracy, it displays a marked reluctance to empower local authorities.

There is a long-standing practice of using boards in Denmark. These boards come in various guises; for example, boards that integrate experts and the representatives of interest groups with public administration and the boards of directors of specific SOEs. The 1980s and 1990s saw a new variety – user boards. These later boards are used to integrate service users, managers and employees in primary schools, colleges, kindergartens, childcare facilities and homes for the elderly (Jensen 1998b: 63–4; Siim 1998: 11–12). Also parents can set up a self-organised kindergarten or school and agree funding with the local authority. Finally, individuals have been given the right to choose between schools and between hospitals. Such freedom of choice aims both to improve efficiency and to empower customers.

A distinction between clients, users, customers and citizens is helpful (Jensen 1998b: 63; Siim 1998: 11). Clients depend on benefits. Customers shop in markets. Users have formal rights. Citizens have a broad participation role covering both the community and individual services. The British Citizen's Charter claims to empower users but falls short of giving them rights, while marketising public services gives customers only limited opportunities to shop around. The Danish reforms also cover the customer and user roles. But there is nothing in the British reforms remotely comparable to either user boards or self-organised services. As Siim (1998: 12) reports, Danes believe the reforms have increased their efficacy as citizens: 'Danish schools and day care institutions are open and participatory institutions' (see also Greve and Jensen 2000). The contrast between customers and citizens oversimplifies but it captures an important difference between the two countries.

The comprehensive reform of Danish local authorities in the 1970s created 275 municipalities and fourteen counties devolving important functions such as social security and social services. It was widely understood as strengthening local self-government by giving local authorities greater functional authority and fiscal leverage (Kjellberg 1988; Norton 1994). The reforms continued in the 1980s. For example, secondary schools and 3,000 km of roads were transferred to the counties, central state regulations of local authorities were either removed or simplified, and the free commune experiment enabled local authorities to exempt themselves from existing legislation. The other side of the coin was tighter spending controls through specific, conditional grants; for example, towards the operating costs of hospitals. Hansen (1997: 62–3) argues that these changes are not a return to local self-government but rather create a 'new municipality'. There has been a shift from 'the traditional, state-centred form of government to a more multi-centred and local form of governance' (ibid.: 45). The municipalities have added a strong role in policy-making to their pre-eminence in implementation. They 'are no longer limited to local adaptation of concrete measures' but are 'participants in the overall goal setting' (ibid.: 65). In brief, Denmark introduced more pluralist service delivery and sought to strengthen participation in an already decentralised system.

Political control

The effort of ministers to reassert political control over the civil service is a common feature of recent public sector reform (Aucoin 1995: 8–9). In Britain, the Royal Institute of Public Administration (RIPA 1987: 43) concluded there had been 'personalisation not politicisation' in senior appointments under Margaret Thatcher. There may have been no overt party politicisation of the higher civil service, but we lost 'institutional scepticism' (Plowden 1994: 104). The transition to New Labour went smoothly – there was only one 'early retirement'. The Prime Minister wrote to the Head of the Home Civil Service, Sir Robin Butler, congratulating him on the smooth transition from a Conservative to a Labour government. There was no night of the long knives for permanent secretaries. The next Head of the Home Civil Service, Sir Richard Wilson, was recognisably a mandarin.

There was a notable increase in political advisers, especially in the No. 10 Policy Unit, which now includes no civil servants. The aim was the better co-ordination of government policy. Sir Richard Wilson conducted a review of the Cabinet Office that aimed to make it the corporate heart of the civil service and to strengthen cross-departmental co-ordination. Specific innovations included setting up special units, for example, the Performance and Innovation Unit to improve the co-ordination of service delivery, and appointing some 300 task forces to review, for example, the 'wicked issues' that cut across departmental boundaries (Cm. 4310 1999: 20, 57). These changes can be interpreted as centralisation because the informing theme is improving the corporate management of the civil service (ibid.: 20). As Peter Hennessy argues, the No. 10 Unit and the Cabinet Office drive government policy-making. He concludes, 'No. 10 is omnipresent in the serious policy reviews'. The exemplar of the new centralisation is the *Ministerial Code* (Cabinet Office 1997) with its injunction that all major interviews, press releases and policy statements should be cleared with No. 10 (Hennessy 1998: 15).

In Denmark at the end of the 1970s there were eighty-seven agencies (or directorates). However, the distinctive story to be told since then is one of de-agencification and contract steering, both of which seek to strengthen political accountability. Jørgensen and Hansen (1995: 552) suggest that agencies or directorates faced persistent problems over administrative duplication and the policy–administration gap: either the agencies inter-fered in policy-making, or ministers would not limit their interventions to general policy, or both. The result was a loss of political accountability and control. Reform sought to resolve this problem by merging various directorates, departments and ministries.

Contract steering in Denmark aimed to improve operational efficiency and to separate policy from day-to-day management and so increase political control over policy through a results-based contract that defined the objectives, tasks, targets, rights and duties of the agency (Pedersen *et al.* 1997). In 1998, fifty-two agencies had a contract (Greve and Jensen 2000). The contracts are not legally binding and last for two to four years. There are no sanctions for failing to meet targets. The agency gets freedom to manage provided it meets its objectives within its budget. Ministers get a firmer grip on policy by clarifying agency objectives, and they can cancel the contract when they want. By 1998, there were fifty-six such contracts. The Ministry of Finance, chief sponsor of the innovation, judges it a success because clarifying objectives led to improvements in efficiency. Others are less sanguine, complaining, for example, that key performance targets were not included in the contracts (see Appendices in Pedersen *et al.* 1997; Greve and Jespersen 1998: 13). As Greve and Jensen (2000) conclude, 'contracts in the Danish version are used in a "soft version", signalling a governance by contact'.

As the Danish government decentralised, so paradoxically it also centralised. Jørgensen and Hansen (1995: 554 and 561) argue these changes 'can be interpreted as attempts to regain ministerial control: to bridge politics and administration – and to give priority to politics'. The problem confronting the Danish government was lack of accountability and control. Ministers opted for the twin strategies of 'bridging' the politics–administration gap by centralising and of 'buffering' by using management reforms to delimit the scope for ministerial intervention.

Explaining the differences

How do we explain the differences?

There have been several attempts to explain the variations in public sector reform in Western Europe.[3] Hood (1996: 273–82) focuses on 'English awfulness', right-wing party politics, poor economic performance and scaling down big government. He finds none an acceptable explanation of the variations. Naschold (1995: 215–17) argues the successful implementation of public sector 'modernisation' depends on 'path dependency' or 'historical traditions, cultural norms and established practices', on political mobilisation by advocacy coalitions of administrative and political elites, on the institutionalisation of such coalitions, and on influential meta-organisations and institutions that produce knowledge (and on path dependency see Hall and Taylor 1996: 941–2; and Hay and Wincott 1998: 955–6). Naschold does not try to explain why the reforms differ in their aims, measures and outcomes. As a final example, Pollitt and Summa (1997: 13–15) suggest that economic pressures, the nature of the political system, administrative structures and party political doctrine explain variations. They favour an institutional approach, concluding that 'the most convincing explanations . . . appear to rest . . . upon the characteristics of the political and administrative systems already in place'. We want to develop the argument that governmental traditions are central to understanding recent changes. At the level of abstraction at which we are now operating, traditions closely resemble institutions, but this is just the first step in our approach. Later, we will open the black box of an institution, or an established practice, to show how it is constructed and reconstructed out of conflicts over meanings as they arise against the background of distinct traditions and dilemmas.

Governmental traditions

A governmental tradition is a set of inherited beliefs and practices about the institutions and history of government (cf. Davis 1998: 158; Perez-Diaz

1993: 7; Loughlin and Peters 1997: 46). So, we argue British and Danish governmental traditions produce public sector reforms that differ in their aims, measures and outcomes. We distinguish between beliefs about central constitutional structures, about political–bureaucratic relations and about state–civil society relations, especially government-interest group links (adapted from Christensen 1995). Administrative reform in Britain and Denmark differs because of significant differences in these beliefs.

Interpreting traditions

The British tradition[4]

The constitution

The conventional wisdom sees Britain as a unitary state characterised by parliamentary sovereignty, strong cabinet government, ministerial account-ability and majority party control of the executive. At its simplest, parliamentary sovereignty means parliament can make or unmake any law with no fear of legal challenge from the courts. Ministers are accountable to parliament for the actions of their department. Collective accountability means ministers must publicly support cabinet decisions.

Three facets of the constitution are directly relevant to our analysis of public sector reform. First, a defining characteristic of the British govern-mental tradition is its strong executive. Birch (1964: 245) captures this characteristic when he says, 'government should have both the powers and the ability to provide strong leadership'. Second, there are no constitu-tional constraints on that executive beyond those it chooses to accept. Once the government decides on a change, it can force it through. Crick (1964: 16) captures the point concisely:

> The only restraints (on authority) are political. Governments are restrained by what they think the country will stand for come the general election, and they adhere to things like general elections because they *prefer* (whether out of ethics, habit or prudence, or all three) to settle disputes politically rather than despotically and coercively.

Finally, the first-past-the-post, two-party system generally produces working majorities in parliament, which the government of the day can rely on to deliver legislation on its manifesto promises.

Political–bureaucratic relations

Britain developed a constitutional bureaucracy. Namier describes it as:

> an unpolitical civil service whose primary connexion is with the Crown, and which, while subordinated to party governments, is unaffected

by their changes: the two permanent elements, the Crown and the civil service, which not by chance together left the political arena, supply the framework for the free play of parliamentary politics and governments.

(Namier 1974: 14; cited in Parris 1969: 49)

In other words, the British tradition believes in a permanent, politically neutral and anonymous civil service that is discreet to the point of being secretive (compare Birch 1964: 241–2). This civil service, moreover, was to be staffed by generalists, both in function and by educational background. The Conservative government's determination to introduce private sector management skills into the civil service is a modern way of criticising the generalist for a lack of specialist skills. The constitutional setting shapes their role: cabinet responsibility and ministerial accountability to parliament cast them in the generalist-political role of supporting their non-specialist minister. Indeed, the generalist civil servant owes no duty to a higher authority than the minister. Sir Robert Armstrong's *The Duties and Responsibilities of Civil Servants in relation to Ministers. Note by the Head of the Civil Service* (25 February 1985 in Cabinet Office 1994b) restates the constitutional belief that 'the duty of the individual civil servant is first and foremost to the Minister of the Crown who is in charge of the department in which he or she is serving'.

State–civil society relations

Greenleaf (1983a: 15–20) describes the British political tradition as a dialectic between the two opposing tendencies of libertarianism and collectivism. Libertarianism stresses four things: the basic importance of the individual, the limited role of government, the dangers of concentrating power, and the rule of law. Its antithesis, collectivism, stresses the public good, social justice, and the idea of positive government. These strains exist in both political parties. They set the boundaries to political debate.

Norton (1984: Chapter 2) stresses four features of British political culture: empirical problem-solving, allegiant and deferential attitudes to the political system, co-operative decision-making, and individualistic yet trusting relations with compatriots and allies. This combination is 'the civic culture' (see also Kavanagh 1990b: Chapter 4; Rose 1985: Chapter 4). Since 1963, this culture has changed only incrementally: 'although subject to modification, the civic culture remains' (Norton 1984: 33). In short, as Birch (1964: 245) argues, the British political tradition places 'consistency, prudence and leadership' before accountability to parliament and responsiveness to public opinion. As a result, the networks of group integration are exclusionary in membership. Britain is characterised by political oligopoly and a passive political culture.

The Danish tradition[5]

The constitution

Knudsen (1991: 96) identifies the following features of 'the Scandinavian model':

> Homogeneity, continuity, high level of organisation. And at the level of the public sector: a strong state tradition, but combined with a high integration between state and society through strong local governments, and through integration with the organisations, a tradition for consensual democracy, tradition for multi-party systems with strong Social Democratic parties and agrarian parties, high welfare ambitions based on institutional rights linked to citizenship, a public sector with universal bureaucracies, a public administration with a low level of corruption and a comparatively high level of efficiency.

Denmark differs from other Scandinavian countries because of its absolutist heritage. The beliefs in parliamentary sovereignty, the direct accountability of ministers and strong local governments have deep historical roots in the challenge to the monarchy. Denmark also owes its strong bureaucratic and legal tradition to the influence of its neighbour Germany.

There is a large measure of agreement about the main features of the Danish governmental tradition. Three features are important for the analysis of public sector reform.[6] The first feature is a negotiative and consensual style of decision-making that we often associate with multi-party coalitions. For example, although there have been nine changes of government in the 1980s and 1990s, each worked within the overall idiom set by previous coalitions. There are many small negotiable cleavages but few large ideological ones. Second, Denmark has a system of ministerial government 'in which each Cabinet minister is politically and judicially responsible', and so 'helped to make central government administration sectoral and rather alien to co-ordination procedures and bodies'. Hence, 'the staff in the Prime Minister's Office is small in number, the formal power of the Ministry of Finance is limited, and the work procedures of the Cabinet are informal' (OECD 1993: 63; see also Knudsen 1991: 75). There is no centralised authority able to organise the government machine. Each department has close connections to agencies and externally organised interests. However, as we shall see, both the Prime Minister's Office and the Ministry of Finance seek to steer indirectly (Jensen 1998b: 60; Knudsen 1999). Third, under the 1849 Constitution, local authorities have the right 'to manage their own affairs under the control of the state'. They have a high degree of constitutional autonomy, described as 'spectacular' by Knudsen (1991: 74). The National Association of Municipalities and the Association of Danish Counties are of 'major importance' (OECD 1993: 63); they are said to constitute 'the local government world' and to speak for 'the local interest'. These phrases capture their high standing and show that they bargain for local authorities with the central state. The influence of these Associations is long-standing. They were one of the bulwarks against absolute monarchy. Local authorities have a dual role: local self-government and local state administration, including collecting 58 per cent of all taxes. This dual constitutional status persists. Central government must negotiate: it cannot command.

Political–bureaucratic relations

The defining characteristic of a *rechtsstaat* is that it is a legal state vested with exceptional authority but constrained by its own laws. Civil servants are not just public employees, but personifications of state authority. The *rechtsstaat* tradition 'emphasises a relatively sharp distinction between politics and administration, political-hierarchical control of the administration and administrative activities based on universal rule' (Christensen 1995: 19). Knudsen (1991: 37) describes the dominant tradition as 'a highly bureaucratic, rule-bound and hierarchic structure designed to promote objective decision making on the basis of appropriate laws or regulations in obedience to the current government, whatever its political complexion'.

However, this tradition is a product of the nineteenth century. Few Danes today would stress the importance of the *rechtsstaat* tradition, although its influence persists with, for example, some 50 per cent of top civil servants having law degrees. Danes today would point instead to the growth of the welfare state, the attendant need for professional expertise and the autonomy of such professionals. Thus, there has been a marked increase in the numbers of top civil servants with degrees in the social sciences, most notably, economics.

State–civil society relations

Allegedly, two Danes stuck in a lift will instantly create an association (Jensen 1998b: 63). Indisputably, Denmark has much associational politics (OECD 1993: 63). This tradition has deep roots: as Siim says, 'there has been a *participatory* tradition of involving ordinary citizens in politics that goes back to the political and cultural self-organisation of the farmers of the nineteenth century and to the ideas of the workers movement in the twentieth century' (Siim 1998: 13).

A further characteristic of the Scandinavian state tradition is that 'participation in public decision-making is more regularised and formalised, as reflected in concepts like integrated participation in government, political segmentation and corporatist features' (Christensen 1995: 23). Other political scientists describe this tradition as a 'negotiated economy' in which resources are allocated through institutional bargaining'. These negotiations are 'between "independent" agents, where the relevant public authority is usually one of several participants'. Although the resulting agreements are not subject to legal sanctions, they are 'discursive, politically or morally binding'. This negotiated economy has:

> 'shattered' public authority: institutional arrangements have been constituted, consisting of numerous, functionally differentiated and mutually independent institutions, which co-ordinate actions through networks, reach decisions via the negotiating games and extract commitments from one another through politically and morally binding agreements.
>
> (Nielsen and Pedersen 1988: 81, 82 and 97)

Danish political culture is divided, then, between citizen autonomy expressed through associations and the formal organised participation of the negotiated economy. A strong state exists in tension with a strong emphasis on self-organisation and individual rights.

Comparing reforms and traditions

Any straightforward comparison of national traditions runs the danger of ignoring significant complexity and diversity. In any country there will be multiple traditions, so an important question is who articulates which tradition. Thus, for Denmark, such notions as *rechtsstaat*, parliamentary sovereignty, welfare state professionalism and ministerial accountability are open to many interpretations. We accept that, ideally, we should provide a more nuanced account of the several traditions and their proponents. The adage has it that the proof of the pudding is in the eating. We may oversimplify but our broad-brush comparison still begins to demonstrate the value of analysing traditions.

Against a backcloth of fiscal pressure, the British government pushed through public sector reform shaped by a governmental tradition characterised by strong executive leadership, no constitutional limits and two-party politics. In Britain, public sector reform is always political, and since 1979 all governments have sought to cut government spending and to exert effective control over the administrative machine. The Conservative government aimed to reduce public spending by redrawing the boundaries of the state. It evolved a clear set of political ideas informing its various reform packages and selling them to the electorate. It attacked big government, local government and waste. It lauded markets as a way of creating more individual choice. It campaigned for the consumer. Privatisation and marketisation pushed back the boundaries of the state and gave the government more control of financial totals but less control over service delivery. There was an explosion of new regulatory bodies, internal to government as well as for external bodies, and a protracted drive to introduce corporate management, all in an attempt to reinforce political control. The New Labour government has pursued similar reforms though in a more pragmatic manner. The outcomes of all the reforms since 1979 remain open to debate. Public ownership has been reduced dramatically but this has been accompanied by an audit and regulatory explosion. The assertion of political control led to no fall in public spending, although arguably it slowed the rate of increase. Fragmenting service delivery systems multiplied networks and reduced the centre's capacity to steer. The fate of British government was that it suffered many unintended consequences.

The Danish government's response to fiscal stress was a 'revolution in slow motion' (Olsen 1983: 188). The aim was to preserve a popular welfare state by selected reforms aimed at getting better value for money. Public sector reform is difficult to distinguish from any other policy area; it has been characterised by a negotiated consensus and a pragmatism that avoided clear winners and losers. The choice of means was a technical matter, not an ideological one. So, privatisation and marketisation were but two options among many, to be used when there was agreement that they were the best way forward. Other means, such as regulation, were scarcely used at all. The government sought greater control through corporate management reforms and the use of 'flexible' contracts. It also distanced itself from problems by decentralising to local government and to citizens. Devolution was sought and won by the national associations of local authorities but the policy also bears a more cynical interpretation as 'off-loading to the periphery' because responsibilities were handed over without the necessary fiscal resources. The reform orthodoxy of the Ministry of Finance claims the reforms enhanced efficiency because, for example, agencies have clearer goals, but the outcomes remain uncertain and ambiguous. Many changes continue 'the Danish tradition of foggy corporate governance in a different disguise' (Jensen 1998b: 65).

So, there are marked differences in the aims, measures and outcomes of the reforms: differences that can be explained by the different governmental traditions of the two countries.[7] These differences are summarised in Table 5.1.

Comparing divergent trends

The constitution

STRONG EXECUTIVE VS. NEGOTIATED CONSENSUS

The British tradition of majority party government underpinning a strong executive means the government can drive through its reforms, whereas such reforms have to be agreed by a multi-party coalition in Denmark and then negotiated with other affected parties. Privatisation illustrates the difference. Britain had a comprehensive, ideologically driven programme of reform designed to create the minimalist state. Privatisation was the

Table 5.1 Comparing governmental traditions

Tradition	Britain	Denmark
The constitution	(i) Strong executive underpinned by two-party system	(i) Negotiated consensus underpinned by multi-party coalitions
	(ii) Parliamentary sovereignty	(ii) Constitutional state
The bureaucracy	(i) Generalists	(i) Specialists with professional autonomy
	(ii) Individual and collective accountability	(ii) Ministerial autonomy
	(iii) Freedom to manage	(iii) Political control
State–civil society relations	(i) Allegiant-deferential	(i) Participation
	(ii) Exclusive networks	(ii) Inclusive networks
	(iii) Citizen as consumer	(iii) Active citizen

flagship policy. In contrast, privatisation is a pragmatic policy in Denmark. Multiplying SOEs may be distinctive, but it is an intermediate solution to changing the boundaries of the public and private sector; it is a means of preserving the state.

PARLIAMENTARY SOVEREIGNTY VS. CONSTITUTIONAL STATE

Although parliamentary sovereignty is a shared constitutional principle, Britain's uncodified constitution means there are few if any constraints on Britain's strong executive. In Denmark, the historical strength of local government, entrenched in the constitution, means it can effectively resist central government. Moreover, its powers have increased. In Britain, parliamentary sovereignty means local authorities have been subjected to ever-more stringent central controls. Contracting-out is one obvious example. In Britain, it was imposed on local authorities. In Denmark, the national associations of local government effectively defended local government against this policy so it was not imposed. Instead the centre had to rely on example and persuasion and, in effect, there was little or no increase in contracting for goods and services in local government. Besides, although relational contracting is spreading in Britain, on a hard–soft contracting scale, the two countries remain poles apart. The Danish approach is non-ideological and contracting is an invitation to negotiate, although it can still stir the political emotions of both left and right. In Britain contracting was a powerful maxim of the New Right for whom it constituted a tool for creating the minimal state.

The bureaucracy

PARTY VS. MINISTER

British ministers are powerful: as in Denmark, they are individually account-able to parliament. Nonetheless, British ministers are always subject to party discipline and collective cabinet accountability. Public sector reform was, therefore, not at the discretion of individual ministers. It was an ideological, party-driven, co-ordinated change. There was no equivalent to the Danish tradition of independent ministers. The Danish system of ministerial government means effective public sector reform depends on political co-operation between ministers. Each minister can decide on the preferred reforms for her or his ministry. There is no overall control of the reform process. No political–bureaucratic system can work without trust and pragmatism, which are the essential currencies of co-ordination in Denmark.

GENERALISTS VS. PROFESSIONAL AUTONOMY

Generalist civil servants in Britain are political administrators. They fire-fight for ministers to keep them out of trouble in parliament and elsewhere. They draw together and interpret specialist advice for ministers who are rarely experts in their field of responsibility. Historically, they have acted as a source of 'institutional scepticism' about policies but, once the decision is made, their job is believed to be to give ministers what they want. Nowadays they are described as 'can do' civil servants. So, they delivered public sector reform. In contrast, there are no generalist civil servants in Denmark. All are specialists, whether lawyers or the professional experts of the welfare state, and they play a key role in policy formulation and design as well as implementation, providing 'integrated advice' (Ministry of Finance 1998 cited in Jensen *et al.* 1999). So, public sector reform in Denmark is characterised by a 'pragmatic tool orientation' (Greve and Jespersen 1998: 14), a 'technocratic-rational' conception of the reforms (Jensen 1998b: 60); and driven by bureaucrats, not politicians, most notably the Ministry of Finance. For example, SOEs reflect the pragmatic, technocratic Danish tradition because they are neither privatised nor state run; they are an intermediate reform.

FREEDOM TO MANAGE VS. POLITICAL CONTROL

So far, we have emphasised the differences between the two countries but analysing traditions can also identify similarities. For example, parliament-ary sovereignty and ministerial accountability mean both governments face the problem of bureaucratic accountability. Politicians and top bureaucrats in both countries distinguish between policy and management, justifying the reforms with the argument that it gives managers the freedom to manage and to deliver public services efficiently. The obvious contrast is between British agencification and Danish de-agencification. British reforms sought to increase the freedom to manage. Danish reforms sought to increase political control, which undermines the rationale for agencies. However, appearances can mislead. Agency reform in both countries seeks to increase political control of the bureaucracy. Although NPM is sometimes said to take apart bureaucratic hierarchies, several strands clearly aim to reinforce hierarchical control. De-agencification is one such strand; it is an attempt to make hierarchy work. Britain faces the same tension between deconcentration and political control. The (then) Conservative Home Secretary, Michael Howard, sacked Derek Lewis, chief executive of the Prison Service, who complained bitterly about the Home Secretary's extensive interference in operational matters. Lewis alleged that Howard 'invented a new definition of the word "operational" which meant "difficult"'. He commented that Howard's attempt to 'use the distinction between policy and operation was no more than a political fig leaf which was so small as to be grossly indecent' (cited in Barker 1997). Politicians in both countries seek control, whether direct as with de-agencification or indirect as with agency framework documents and contract steering.

State and civil society

At the most general level, the difference between Britain and Denmark in the 1990s is between an allegiant-deferential or passive political tradition and a participative tradition characterised by associational politics. This difference obviously underpins the distinctive decentralising strand in Danish public sector reform. We now unpack this explanation of the differences between the two countries.

EXCLUSIVE VS. INCLUSIVE

Public sector reform in Britain was an attack on collectivism and a reassertion of the libertarian strand in the British governmental tradition. It attacked policy networks, which it castigated as examples of producer and trade union power. Union participation was curbed but many British networks are based on professional interests concerned with allocating resources by networks in welfare state services. They persist and, because of service fragmentation, have multiplied and grown stronger in a localised form. It is hard to identify equivalent trends in Denmark where formal institutionalised participation remains a characteristic of Danish democracy and does not systematically seek to exclude important interests.

CONSUMER VS. CITIZEN

As tourists, we should remain wary of becoming dewy-eyed about Danish associational life.[8] Nonetheless, strengthening the roles of both users and citizens in the delivery of public sector services is distinctive. To British eyes, moreover, it might seem an exciting alternative to New Right market prescriptions. The description 'self-organising' is apt and the consumer reforms in Britain are no parallel. Such reforms are distinctively Scandinavian and there is no reason to associate them with the NPM, which never envisaged democratisation as a means of delivering services let alone improving efficiency.[9] If other reforms were foreign imports interpreted through the lens of Danish political traditions, the citizen reforms are an indigenous product of that tradition.

Interpreting distinctive dilemmas

Differences in traditions, within and between countries, explain the different content of public sector reforms. These competing constructions then help to produce distinctive accounts of the dilemmas raised by the reforms. A dilemma, as we explained earlier, arises for an individual or an institution when a new idea stands in opposition to an existing idea and so forces reconsideration. Public sector reform, as interpreted in the two countries, has thrown up different dilemmas.

In Britain, public sector reform was one of the motors behind the shift from government to governance because it multiplied networks. A central objective of reform was to increase political control but the policy had many unintended consequences. How do you control these networks? This question poses the dilemma of steering. Other phrases used in Britain to describe the same dilemma are joined-up government or holistic governance. Whatever phrase is preferred, the problem is always the same. How do you control independent organisations? The answer cannot be the tools of corporate management, since they focus on control and management in organisations not between them.

In Denmark, the most prominent dilemma posed by public sector reform is how to maintain democracy and accountability. The dilemma occurs in many guises. For a start, there is the democratic dilemma of the grey zone where accountability and market competition conflict to the detriment of the former (Greve 1998; Jensen 1998b). In addition, all sorts of questions arise over the self-organising methods of service delivery introduced by the reforms. What do they cost? Who is excluded? The evidence is contradictory. Danish schools may be open. However, pool steering – a pool of government money for which local actors can bid to do something about 'wicked' issues – has only had variable success. Its effectiveness hinges on the capacity of actors to co-operate and create effective local policy networks. They can only do so if they avoid hard-core social problems and difficult minorities. Consequently, self-organisation is not necessarily open and accountable, nor is it controllable by either local authorities or the central state, and this reduced capacity to steer matters even more when groups are excluded.

Conclusion

Nominally we have been talking throughout this chapter about one topic, the new public management. Yet we have shown that the British and Danish governments introduced markedly different policies under this label. We argued these differences arose out of the differing beliefs about the institutions and history of government of each country. Finally, we argued these differences mean the governments confront distinct dilemmas. So, the next phase of public sector reform will not start at the same point. In Britain, the main problem is co-ordination, though, as we emphasise later, this dilemma is constructed differently in various traditions. In Denmark, the key dilemma is democratising governance through self-organising citizens.

There is one obvious qualification to this bald argument. In both countries, the reforms are in progress, so we will have to wait a while before we are able to consider their outcomes. There is also an important limit, not caution, to our analysis of traditions. A broad notion of tradition allowed us to compare countries, but it runs into the problem of reifying traditions with an attendant loss of explanatory power. When comparing the governmental traditions of Britain and Denmark, we need to be wary of reifying them; that is, of defining them as if they had a given form equivalent to a fixed institution, given rules or an enduring practice. In short, the idea of a tradition can be defined so broadly, can become so abstract, that it becomes indistinguishable from the idea of an institution. There is a tension between an idea of a tradition that permits cross-national comparison and one that allows us to decentre institutions as contingent products of political struggles between agents operating against the background of diverse and evolving webs of belief.

Also, the explanatory value of traditions lies in how they account for the processes by which people pick up beliefs and practices. The broader our definition of a tradition, the less it can explain. For any country, we need to move beyond broad comparisons to explore its multiple traditions. In Denmark, for example, concepts such as *rechtsstaat*, parliamentary sovereignty, welfare state professionalism and ministerial accountability are the objects of many, competing interpretations. The story of public sector reform is told several ways. One such narrative in Denmark is the Ministry of Finance's account of NPM as a strategy of reform. This story stresses orderly change and the key dilemma is weak central co-ordination compared with ministerial autonomy. The 'slow revolution' is an alternative narrative in which international ideas about the public sector and its reform are incrementally adapted to fit the existing traditions of Danish government (Olsen 1983). Yet another narrative focuses on the democratic revolution built around the active citizen. In Britain too we find competing narratives of Thatcherism and NPM, and we will explore these in the next chapter.

An understanding of change must explore such conflicting beliefs as they inspire diverse actions. Ideas about the freedom to manage, as discussed in public sector reform, simply point up conflicts since they bump into beliefs about professional autonomy and ministerial accountability. Individuals set out from within a tradition but they can extend, vary and at times reject that tradition. The different stories, the colliding ideas and the dilemmas posed by conflicting ideas become the wellspring for yet more change. We will explore change in Britain again in Chapter 7.

Notes

1 Rhodes 1997a: Chapters 5–7, 1998a, 2000b; and Bevir and O'Brien 2001 provide accounts of public sector reform in Britain under both Conservative governments and New Labour since May 1997. See also Gray and Jenkins 1998; Hennessy 1998; Riddell 1997 and Theakston 1998a and b. Equivalent accounts in English of Danish public sector reform can be found in Greve 1997, 1998; Greve and Jensen 2000; Greve and Jespersen 1998; Jensen 1998b; Jørgensen and Hansen 1995; Jørgensen 1999. We have also used private information collected by Rod Rhodes in his capacity as Director of the ESRC's Whitehall Programme. For both Britain and Denmark, we concentrate on the 1990s. We have not attempted to be up to date because our concern is to describe and interpret trends, not to provide a micro-study of administrative events.

2 Danish agencies are also known as directorates and distinguished by keeping professional administration within the ministry, albeit with a special status. This contrasts with the Swedish model, which stresses professional autonomy and locates professional administration outside the ministries and the Norwegian model, which oscillates between the two, seeking a balance between professional autonomy and political control (Christensen 1995: 30).

3 See Hood 1996; Naschold 1995; Pollitt and Bouckaert 2000; Pollitt and Summa 1997; Rhodes 1997c: Chapter 5; Wright 1994: 104–8.

4 On the British governmental tradition our main sources are Beer 1965; Birch 1964; and Greenleaf 1983a and b; and, to show that our summary has at least widespread currency, we have drawn on the popular textbooks by Kavanagh 1990b; Norton 1984; and Rose 1985.

5 Our main sources on the Danish governmental tradition are Christensen 1995; Elder *et al.* 1982; Jensen 1998b; Knudsen 1991: Chapter 1, especially 89–97; Knudsen and Rothstein 1994; and OECD 1993.

6 We give a few examples to support this conclusion. Elder *et al.* (1982: Chapter 1) treat Denmark as a consensual democracy characterised by high 'regime legitimacy' and 'widespread support for the principle of parliamentary government'; 'a low level of conflict about the actual exercise of power within that state'; and 'a high degree of concertation in the gestation of public policy'. Christensen (1995: 25) argues 'the Scandinavian state tradition . . . is primarily characterised by homogeneity and consensus, . . . strong cultural norms of collectivity and equality, and specialised arenas'. So, 'the parliamentary principle . . . resulted in both strong executive and legislative powers, and a close, co-operative and consensus-oriented style, characterised by trust and mutual adjustment' (ibid.: 13).

7 We are exploring how traditions shape reforms. Another way of doing so might be to illustrate the inadequacies of accounts of public sector reform that ignore the impact of governmental traditions. See, for example, Anne Drumaux, 'Commentary', in Pedersen *et al.* 1997. She argues for sanctions in contracts, criticises the ministerial power to revoke contracts, insists the Ministry of Finance must continue to advise on and promote the reforms, and wants standardisation of contract procedures. She completely ignores the constitutional position of ministers and the central role of trust and pragmatism in bargaining between ministers. She wants to change the Danish governmental tradition without even recognising that it is a constraint on her proposals! For example, the role of the Ministry of Finance as the pilot of the reforms can be interpreted as an erosion of ministerial government. The underlying message of reform is the urgent need for central co-ordination, not ministerial autonomy. What chance this message will be welcomed by ministers seeking to reassert political control?

8 It is as well to ask what the link is between associations and democracy rather than assuming there is one. It can be argued that associational life presumes social and cultural homogeneity and that some minorities, such as refugees, are excluded. If so, being one of us becomes a prerequisite of associational democracy, it is not open to all and is, therefore, undemocratic.

9 Although we think decentralisation, especially self-organising, was not part of the new public management, it is generally subsumed under this label, for example by the OECD 1995: 8.

6   Narratives of Thatcherism

Introduction

The broad notion of tradition we used to compare Britain and Denmark has limited explanatory value. We now need to unpack it – to decentre it – to identify some of its complex and diverse constituents. In this chapter, therefore, we identify the Tory, Liberal, Whig and Socialist traditions, and show how each underpins distinct analyses of Thatcherism, including its attempts at public sector reform. The rise of governance as networks began with the Thatcher reforms of the public sector, notably marketisation and the new public management (NPM). Our interpretive approach requires us to unpack the conceptual underpinnings of governance by examining the diverse traditions through which Thatcherism and these reforms were enacted. Table 6.1 sketches the four dominant traditions and their account of Thatcherism. In this chapter, we provide a brief summary of each tradition and examples of its narratives of Thatcherism. We then explore the associated problems of essentialism and identifying traditions. These problems highlight the need to analyse change in traditions by exploring dilemmas. We sketch such an analysis of change at the end of this chapter, but flesh it out in an analysis of the Socialist tradition in Chapter 7.

When confronted by the anarchy of political history, we tame it. The complex is made simple. The confusing, myriad events are reduced to chronology. We impose an order on discontinuity and change. It is inconceivable that people and events remain incomprehensible. This threat is removed by the stories – the narratives – we tell one another about what happened. All too often, however, the search for understanding ends by reducing a complex multiplicity of narratives to a monolithic entity. Such is the case with Thatcherism.

We revisit the several accounts of Thatcherism, not to provide a comprehensive explanation of the phenomenon, but to show there is no monolithic, unified notion of Thatcherism – the dominant traditions in British government provide distinctive narratives about it. There is no heritage in the guise of a distinct policy programme, a political hegemony or a leadership style. The heritage of Thatcherism lies instead in the dilemmas it helped to make salient in all the dominant traditions of British government, dilemmas that have changed the ideas of each one. Thatcherism is no more because the main narratives of Thatcherism have been absorbed by the dominant traditions of British government, which changed and continue to be changed as their exponents wrestle with and resolve the dilemmas. Although we speculate future generations will see Thatcher herself as part of the Tory tradition about strong leaders rather than the Liberal tradition about markets, our main concern is to highlight the multiplicity of stories about Thatcherism and the continuing dilemmas created for the dominant traditions.

The next section provides brief examples of several narratives of Thatcherism embedded in various traditions to show there is no essentialist account (see Table 6.1). We show how Thatcherism wrought dramatic change in British government, not because it was a unified phenomenon but because it highlighted the salience of certain dilemmas for every tradition.

Thatcherisms

A comprehensive historical review of each tradition would be unduly long. Our concern is to analyse Thatcherism as it is constructed in different

Table 6.1 Narratives of Thatcherism

Traditions	Tory	Liberal	Whig	Socialist
Themes	Preserving traditional authority	Restoring the markets undermined by state intervention	Evolutionary change	Role of the state in resolving the crises of capitalism
Narratives	Party and electoral survival	Reversing Britain's decline	Strong leadership and distinct ideology give new policy agenda	Failure of the developmental state
Thatcherisms	v.1 One nation (e.g. Gilmour 1992)	v.1 Markets (e.g. Willetts 1992)	v.1 End of consensus (e.g. Kavanagh 1990a)	v.1 Political economy (e.g. Gamble 1988)
	v.2 Statecraft (e.g. Bulpitt 1986)	v.2 Culture (e.g. Skidelsky 1989)	v.2 Leadership (e.g. King 1985)	v.2 Developmental state (e.g. Marquand 1988)

traditions. So, we provide only a summary of each tradition before discussing examples of its narratives of Thatcherism.[1]

The Tory tradition

The Tory tradition is elusive and relentlessly inconsistent (Honderich 1991). All too often its proponents define it more by what it isn't than by what it is. Gilmour (1978: 121–43) argues the Conservative Party is not averse to change (ibid.: 121), not a pressure group (ibid.: 130), and not ideological (ibid.: 132). More positively, 'the fundamental concern of Toryism is the preservation of the nation's unity, of the national institutions, of political and civil liberty' (ibid.: 143). Blake (1985: Chapter 11 and postscript) argues Conservatives are against centralisation, equality and internal splits but, to leaven the mix, they are for the national interest. Gamble (1988: 170–1) describes the British state as the Tory state with the defining characteristics of racial and national superiority, a deferential attitude towards authority, a secrecy surrounding the practice of high politics, an anti-egalitarian ethos and a status hierarchy.

Some strands recur in the Tory tradition. For example, Michael Oakeshott provides the philosophical underpinnings for several raconteurs of Tory narratives. Ian Gilmour (1978: 92–100, 1992: 272–3) adopts Oakeshott's distinction between the state as a civil and an enterprise association. An enterprise association is 'human beings joined in pursuing some common substantive interest, in seeking the satisfaction of some common want or in promoting some common substantive interest'. Persons in a civil association 'are not joined in any undertaking to promote a common interest . . . but in recognition of non-instrumental rules indifferent to any interest', that is, a set of common rules and a common government in pursuing their diverse purposes (Gilmour 1978: 98; see also Mount 1992: 74–5; Willetts 1992: 72–3). So a free society has 'no preconceived purpose, but finds its guide in a principle of continuity . . . and in a principle of consensus' (Gilmour 1978: 97). The Tory tradition favours civil association and only accepts the state as an enterprise association 'when individuals are able to contract out of it when it suits them' (Gilmour 1992: 272). Nonetheless Gilmour (1978: 236) accepts that some state intervention will often be expedient, practical politics, essential to preserving the legitimacy of the state. For all its hedging about the role of the state, the Tory tradition upholds its authority. People are self-interested and hierarchy is necessary to keep order. Scruton (1984: 111) makes the point forcefully: 'the state has the authority, the responsibility, and the despotism of parenthood' (see also Gamble 1988: 170). Strong leaders wield that authority to uphold national unity, to correct social and economic ills and to build popular consent.

We now examine briefly two narratives of Thatcherism, as One Nation Toryism and as statecraft.

One Nation Toryism

This narrative of Thatcherism sees it as a threat to both the Conservative Party and national unity. Gilmour (1992) is scathing about the 'dogma' of Thatcherism. He argues Thatcherism is based on 'a simplistic view of human nature'. He disputes that 'everyone is driven by selfish motives' and that 'everyone pursues his selfish interests in a rational manner' (ibid.: 271). Thatcher is not a 'true Conservative ruler' because she bullied people into conformity with her view of Britain as an enterprise association (ibid.: 273). The economy was not transformed. Markets are not always right. 'The state cannot desert the economic front' (ibid.: 276). 'Much social damage was also done.' 'British society became coarser and more selfish' (ibid.: 278). Gilmour's brand of One Nation Toryism holds that if the state is not interested in its people, they have no reason to be interested in the state (Gilmour 1978: 118). So, the government should '"conserve" the fabric of society and avoid the shocks of violent upheavals' and 'look to the contentment of all our fellow countrymen' (Gilmour 1992: 278).

Statecraft

Bulpitt (1986) developed the Tory narrative of Thatcherism as statecraft. He argues, 'what the Conservatives wanted to achieve in government was a relative autonomy for the centre . . . on those matters which they defined as "high politics" at any particular time' (ibid.: 27). So, the Conservative Party's main bias lies in its statecraft – 'the art of winning elections' or government survival. The main dimensions of statecraft are: a set of governing objectives; political support mechanisms able to build quiescent party relations and win elections; hegemony or winning the elite debate about 'political problems, policies and the general stance of government'; and a governing code or a set of coherent principles underlying policy-related behaviour (ibid.: 21–2). The distinctiveness of Thatcherism does not lie in its ideology or ideas but in its statecraft. Initially it focused on macro-economic management and foreign affairs, but showed no reluctance to extend its definition of high politics and centralise when opposed. The details of Conservative policy are not the focus of analysis. The key point is that the Conservatives sought to achieve governing competence by redefining high politics and increasing the centre's relative autonomy. This statecraft is a long-standing bias of the Conservative Party and 'there is a great similarity between the Conservative party led by Mrs Thatcher and its predecessors under Churchill and Macmillan' (ibid.: 1986: 39).

So, the Tory tradition in whichever narrative guise stresses tradition, authority and continuity, shares the storyline of party and electoral survival, but produces divergent interpretations of Thatcherism. Explaining the differences is easy. Gilmour stresses the break with tradition whereas Bulpitt stresses the continuities. Both share the concern with party survival and electoral success. They differ in their assessments of Thatcher's state-craft. Gilmour is a pessimist, seeing division and damage. Bulpitt (ibid.: 39) is an admirer of Thatcher's ability 'to understand and work with the limitations placed on elite activity'. All of which prompts an ironic conclusion. So often seen as a prime exponent of the Liberal tradition by both friend and foe, Thatcher typifies the Tory tradition with her commitment to strong leadership and her grasp of the arts of statecraft.

The Liberal tradition

The narrative of Thatcherism as the revival of nineteenth-century liberalism, with its faith in free markets, determined to slay the dragon of collectivism, and reverse Britain's decline, both economic and international, is one of the clichés of British government in the late twentieth century. But like so many clichés, it did not become one without containing a large grain of truth. This narrative has its roots in the Liberal tradition's stories about markets and culture.

The story about markets

'New Conservatism' revived the Liberal tradition by stressing freedom, applying the principles of freedom to the economy, and accepting the welfare state on sound Conservative grounds. Thus, Willetts (1992) finds the roots of the New Conservatism in the One Nation Group's (1954) arguments against government intervention and in such philosophers as Friedrich Hayek and Michael Oakeshott. For Willetts (1992: Chapter 6) Adam Smith's 'system of natural liberty' provides the intellectual justification for free markets. Markets tap 'two fundamental human instincts'; the instinct to better oneself and the instinct to exchange. These instincts, when 'protected by a legal order which ensures contracts are kept and property is respected', are 'the source of the wealth of nations'. Big government cannot deliver prosperity, undermines markets and erodes communities. But 'rampant individualism without the ties of duty, loyalty and affiliation is only checked by powerful and intrusive government'. So, Conservatism stands between collectivism and individualism and 'Conservative thought at its best conveys the mutual dependence between the community and the free market. Each is enriched by the other' (ibid.: 182). The Conservative Party's achievement is to reconcile Toryism and individualism. This achievement also belongs to Thatcher. Thatcherism is not the antithesis of conservatism because it too recognises there is more to life than free markets'; it too sought to reconcile 'economic calculation with our moral obligations to our fellow citizens' (ibid.: 47). Also, its distinctiveness does not lie in 'Mrs Thatcher's actual political beliefs – very little of what she said could not have been found in a typical One Nation Group pamphlet of the 1950s' (ibid.: 52). It is distinctive because of Thatcher's 'political qualities'; her energy and conviction; her ability to move between general principles and the practical; and her judgement about which issues to fight (ibid.: 52–3).

So, the Thatcherism narrative in the Liberal tradition restores markets to their allegedly rightful place in Conservatism: it 'is within the mainstream of conservative philosophy' (ibid.: 54). Thatcherism also displayed great political skill. The government stuck to its principles and showed that the commitment to freedom meets people's aspirations and made them prosperous (ibid.: 61). State intervention stultifies. Competition improves performance: 'free markets are . . . the route to prosperity' (ibid.: 136)

The story about culture

The Liberal tradition also seeks to rescue Britain from economic decline and to restore the country's international standing. The origins of Britain's decline lie not only in state intervention undermining markets but also in cultural hostility to capitalism. So, the argument goes, the intellectual and political elite looked down on entrepreneurial behaviour, preferring 'the dream of New Jerusalem' in which there was no unemployment, poverty and ill-health. But their illusion foundered on the 'British disease' of a poorly educated and trained workforce, poor management, low industrial productivity and powerful trade unions. It was a dream that a bankrupted country could not afford and it diverted scarce resources away from much-needed industrial investment and reform (Barnett 1986; and for a study of narratives of decline, see English and Kenny 2000: Chapter 16).

Thatcherism challenged the establishment. Its dream is altogether different. It rejects the permissive society and the radical chic of the 1960s. It is a world of Victorian values – Samuel Smiles, not flower power, rules OK. It emphasises family values, self-reliance and the careful management of money. It dislikes trade unions and big government. It rails against dependence on the welfare state and praises the virtues of self-help and markets. It takes pride in Britain's imperial legacy and seeks to restore Britain's standing in the eyes of the world (see, for example, Gould and Anderson 1987). Cultural change is a prominent strand linking the several essays in Skidelsky (1989). For example, Minogue (1989: 129–30 and 141–2) argues Thatcherism renounces the culture of bourgeois guilt about the working-class and minorities, rejecting 'the three fudging Cs' of caring, compassion and consensus for a culture of individual responsibility. Whether this social Darwinism can reconcile the enterprise culture with social responsibility is open to debate. For example, Thatcher's call to Christian duty does not seem up to the task (Skidelsky 1989: 22) and the electorate does not share Thatcher's values (Crewe 1989: 44).

So the narratives in the Liberal tradition stress markets, and the affinity between markets and a culture of individual responsibility is obvious. Its storyline is to reverse Britain's economic decline through free markets sustained by an enterprise culture.

The Whig tradition

This tradition emphasises the objects that are the historic heart of political science – the study of institutions or the rules, procedures and formal organisations of government, constitutional law and constitutional history. It also has an idealist strand that focuses on the interaction between ideas and institutions.

End of consensus

Much of mainstream social science literature assesses the extent of change in British politics under the Thatcher government. Kavanagh (1990a) uses the theme of 'the end of consensus', and an analysis of the interplay between events, ideas and actors, to argue the political agenda of British government has been substantially rewritten. Consensus refers to agreement between political parties and governing elites about the substance of public policy, the rules of the political game, and the political style for resolving policy differences (ibid.: 6). Thatcher had a distinctive set of New Right inspired policies: using monetary policy to contain inflation; reducing the public sector; freeing the labour market through trade union reform; and restoring the government's authority. These policies would free markets and create the enterprise society. He concludes the government was 'radical and successful' (ibid.: 241) in that it 'reversed the direction of previous post-war administrations' (ibid.: 209). Moreover, its policies, which appeared far-fetched in 1978, such as privatisation, are no longer exceptional (ibid.: 281). In typical balanced, Whig style, Kavanagh opines 'talk of permanent or irreversible changes may be too bold' but 'the Thatcher government has created a new agenda, one which a successor government will find difficult to reverse' (ibid.: 302).

Riddell (1989) casts a more jaundiced eye over the Thatcher record, noting the often large disparity between ministerial rhetoric and achievements (see also Marsh and Rhodes 1992b). He considers Thatcherism as 'essentially an instinct', not an ideology. He argues the Thatcher government provided a much-needed shock to the British economy but it did not reverse the country's economic decline (Riddell 1989: 206). The political agenda changed, the problems of decline became less acute, but there was a large legacy of problems – social division, crime, education and training, the welfare state and regulating the utilities (ibid.: 218). These large areas of political controversy show the limits of the new consensus.

Leadership

King's (1985) elegant and influential essay focuses on Thatcher's style: 'the way in which she personally does the job'. She was a 'very unusual' prime minister because she was in a minority in her own party and she had a policy agenda.

> She . . . had no choice, given her aims and determination, but to lead in an unusually forthright, and assertive manner. Partly this was a matter of her personality; she is a forthright and assertive person. But it was at least as much a matter of the objective situation in which she found herself. She was forced to behave like an outsider for the simple reason she was one.
>
> (Ibid.: 116)

But assertive does not mean she was cavalier; 'not only is she cautious, but she respects power and has an unusually well-developed capacity for weighing it' (ibid.: 118). When confronted by a problem she did not think about organising the work but about who could help her; 'people, not organisations' (ibid.: 122). She 'reaches out for decisions; she reaches out for people. She also reaches out for ideas' (ibid.: 126). She was an actress, aware of her image and skilled in 'the presentation of self, the uses of self'. She was also 'a prodigious listener', 'a prodigious worker', 'a quick and eager learner', and 'considerate and solicitous' to those she trusted (ibid.: 130–1). The political world was divided into goodies and baddies and she deliberately used fear as a weapon against the baddies (ibid.: 132). King is aware of the weaknesses of Thatcher's style – the delays in decision-making, *hubris*, and the enemies she made – but he concludes she added to the repertoire of prime ministerial styles and made the job of prime minister bigger than before. In short, 'she is a formidable personality, and hers is a distinctive prime ministerial style' (ibid.: 133).

Whatever the differences in their assessment of the Thatcher record, these narratives accommodate Thatcherism to the Whig tradition in two ways. First, they identify the constraints on political action and the continuities in policy to domesticate the political convulsions of the 1980s. Thus, Kavanagh (1990a: 15, 18 and 238–41) treats events as a constraint on political leadership; recognises the changes had many causes; and muses how 'disappointment has been a fact of life for British . . . governments'. Nonetheless there has been change and Thatcher is central to his explanation. So, second, these Whig narratives explain change by appeal to the personal power of Thatcher. Kavanagh repeatedly describes her as the 'dominant figure' and as 'a remarkable figure' (ibid.: 243, 272, 276 and 318). King (1985: 137) stresses how she pushed out the frontiers of her authority. Of course, 'we are not claiming that personal leadership is all-important but Mrs Thatcher's personality and policies enabled her to take advantage of the constellation of events and ideas' (see also, among many, Finer 1987; Young 1989).

As ever, Riddell (1989: 216–17) introduces a note of scepticism. He stresses that the changes in macro-economic policy started in the mid-1970s, which, coupled with international developments in the 1980s, would have led to a 'shift away from collectivism towards individualism'. He dislikes the centralising and authoritarian tendencies of the government and is cautious about whether the 'success' of Thatcherism depended on Thatcher. He prefers to describe her government as an example of a 'survivor regime', characterised less by its original policies and more by its determination to implement a rolling agenda of policies built out of its experience of government. More important, whatever the difference of emphasis, the storyline in these narratives assigns great explanatory power to Thatcher's personal qualities and her distinctive policies. Above all, they form part of the Whig tradition. Kavanagh (1990a: 209) makes the point succinctly: 'over the long term continuity is more apparent than discontinuity'.

The Socialist tradition

The Socialist tradition, with its structural explanations focused on economic factors and class and with its critique of capitalism, mounted a prominent challenge to Whig historiography. We have shown that the radical or socialist alternative disputes the factual accuracy of significant parts of the Westminster model and it challenges specific theoretical interpretations. The historical story of the Socialist tradition is often ambivalent about, or even hostile to, that of the Whigs. For example, Marquand (1988: 198) comments:

> The old Whig historians were not wrong in thinking that Britain's peaceful passage to democracy owed much to the hazy compromises which unprobed ambiguities make possible. By the same token, however, once these compromises cease to be taken for granted ... arrangements of this sort are bound to run into trouble. ... Respect for the rules of the game will ebb away. ... In doing so, they have focused attention ... on the hidden presuppositions of club government itself ... And, as a result, these presuppositions have started to come apart at the seams.

The Whig tradition collapses because it confronts a heterogeneous, pluralistic society in which authority has been demystified, cultural values have changed, the political system has lost legitimacy, and territorial politics is in disarray (ibid.: 199–204). However, the Whig tradition is still a common starting point and it exerts a pervasive influence. Hall and Schwarz (1985: 8–12) accept, for example, that Britain has a unique political tradition characterised by stability and continuity, although they stress crises and 'frenzied reconstruction' to counter the focus of other commentators on continuities. They still have to recognise the 'passive transformation' of Britain; the marginalisation of radical movements; the 'peculiarity of the British case'; the 'partial and uneven' transition to collectivism; and the 'underlying persistence' of the British political tradition (ibid.: 26–7).

The Socialist narratives of Thatcherism come in many guises with many differences of emphasis. To show this variety, we provide brief summaries of two influential accounts: Gamble's interpretation of Thatcherism as the political economy of the free market and strong state; and Marquand's account of the failure of the developmental state. Both imply that the social democratic consensus of the post-war period hid the contradictions of modern capitalism. That consensus began to fall apart in the 1970s with Britain's continuing economic decline, world recession, the failure of the Labour government and the revival of the Cold War. The governing elite failed to restructure the British state and to modernise the economy (Nairn 1981). So, the Socialist tradition sees Thatcherism as a response to a crisis of capitalism.

The political economy of Thatcherism

Gamble (1988: Chapter 7) rejects all one-sided explanations of Thatcherism and uses political, economic and ideological arguments to explain the fortunes of Thatcherism in promoting both free markets and a strong state. He builds on the work of Hall (1983) who interprets Thatcherism as replacing the existing social democratic ideology with its own vision, creating 'a new historic bloc' (ibid.: 23). However, this new ideological discourse does not emerge, it is constructed. The Conservative hegemonic project is 'authoritarian populism'. The term is deliberately contradictory to capture the contrast between the free market and the strong state strands in Thatcherism. The populism encompasses, 'the resonant themes of organic Toryism – nation, family, duty, authority, standards, tradition-alism – with the aggressive themes of a revived neoliberalism – self-interest, competitive individualism, anti-statism' (ibid.: 29). The authoritarian covers the 'intensification of state control over every sphere of economic life', 'decline of the institutions of political democracy', and 'curtailment of . . . "formal" liberties' (Hall 1980: 161). So the 1980s are characterised by, for example, centralisation, the 'handbagging' of intermediate institutions, the refusal to consult with interest groups and state coercion. Thatcherism stigmatises the enemy within – for example, big unions, big government – while creating a new historic bloc, from sections of the dominant and dominated classes, which seeks to establish hegemony.

The argument from politics sees Thatcherism as one possible conserv-ative, local response to the problems of economic recession and restructur-ing. Gamble (1988: 222) concludes there is 'no Thatcherite electorate, no Thatcherite party, no Thatcherite consensus' but 'there have been several real and significant changes'. The government did have a distinctive ideology and more than any other post-war government, it had a strategy. It sought 'to build new coalitions of interest, to win the battle of ideas for a radical change of direction and the dismantling of old structures and old priorities' (ibid.: 223). Its statecraft was not confined to winning office. The politics of Thatcherism are part of a broader project to modernise British capitalism. Freeing the economy and strengthening the state were an attempt to create 'the basis for a new and viable regime of accumulation'. This argument from economics reasserted 'the traditional international orientation of British economic policy'. The government gave priority to 'the openness of the British economy over the protection of domestic industry'. This accumulation strategy sought to strengthen the integration of the British economy in the world economy (ibid.: 225). It abandoned the manufacturing industries of the Fordist era for a free market accumulation strategy, which sought to make British companies competitive in the international economy. But for this strategy to succeed, the government also had to reform state and civil society. So, it asserted its authority by reducing government responsibilities, distancing itself from interest groups, and disciplining the public sector. The strong state would change attitudes and behaviour in civil society to support the free market.

Gamble is no apologist for Thatcherism. He has a keen appreciation of its limits, recognising that it has not reversed economic decline; it was a transitional period. But he claims his multifaceted account clears up the two central mysteries of Thatcherism. Thatcherism is not alien to Conservatism because its statecraft of restoring the state's authority and autonomy is part of the central Tory tradition. The gulf between ambition and achievement is explained by the scale of the task. The government knew where it wanted to go but its reforms of state and civil society were not up to that task.

The developmental state

Marquand (1988) tries to answer two overlapping questions. Why did the Keynesian social democratic governing philosophy collapse? What are the main economic and political problems which a successor philosophy must address? He argues the collapse took place because Britain failed to become a developmental state. Britain failed 'to adapt to the waves of technological and institutional innovation sweeping through the world economy' and 'Britain's political authorities ... repeatedly failed to promote more adaptive behaviour' (ibid.: 145). Britain failed to become an adaptive, developmental state because of a 'political culture suffused with the values and assumptions of whiggery, above all with the central Lockean assumption that individual property rights are antecedent to society'.

In such a culture, the whole notion of public power, standing apart from private interests, was bound to be alien. Yet without that notion, it is hard to see how a developmental state, with the capacity to form a view of the direction the economy ought to take, and the will and moral authority to put its views into practice, can come into existence (ibid.: 154).

The Westminster model also inhibited an adaptive response. The basis of this model is parliamentary sovereignty which 'inhibits the open and explicit power-sharing on which negotiated adjustment depends' (ibid.: 176). The British crisis is a crisis of maladaptation coupled with: a loss of

consent and growing distrust between governments and governed; possessive individualism or sectional interests dominating the common interest;
and 'mechanical reform' or change through command, not persuasion
(ibid.: 211–12). In short, Britain failed to adapt because its political culture
was rooted in reductionist individualism.

Although it is not his main concern, Marquand's account of Thatcherism
stresses the congruence between its market liberalism and a British political
culture of possessive individualism and the inability of both to deal with
the crisis of maladaptation (Marquand 1988: 72–81; see also Marquand
1989). In short, the neo-liberal solution deals with the results of state
intervention, political overload and bureaucratic oversupply, not with the
dynamics or causes of these processes. Possessive individualism is the cause
of Britain's maladaptation, so it cannot provide the solution which lies in
common, not individual, purposes and the developmental, not minimal,
state. As a result, Thatcherism contains three paradoxes (Marquand 1988:
81–8, 1989). First, the policies for a free economy conflict with the need
for a strong, interventionist state to engineer the cultural change needed to
sustain that free economy. Second, the wish to arrest national decline
conflicts with the free trade imperatives of liberalism because of the
weakness of the British economy. Third, the attack on intermediate
institutions – the BBC, local government, the universities – undermines the
Tory tradition which sees them as bastions of freedom; markets conflict
with community.

So, the socialist narratives interpret the 'end of consensus' as part of a
crisis of British capitalism stemming from its inability to become a
developmental state. Thatcherism is a local response to this crisis and is
beset by internal contradictions. Free markets are a transitional solution
for the open economy of a medium-sized industrial country operating in a
global economy.

Dilemmas and their effects

There is no essentialist account of Thatcherism. Even the search for a
multi-dimensional explanation is doomed. It is not a question of identifying the several political, economic and ideological variables and determining their relative importance. It is not a question of levels of analysis.
It is more fundamental. The maps, questions and language of each
narrative prefigure and encode different historical stories in distinctive
ways. Historical stories as different as preserving traditional authority,
restoring markets, gradualism and resolving the crises of capitalism
construct the phenomenon of Thatcherism in radically different ways. We
have decentred Thatcherism, showing there is no single notion to be
explained. Thatcherism as statecraft, as economic liberalism, as leadership and as hegemonic project are different notions evoking different
explanations. Thatcherism, then, was not an objective, given social

phenomenon with a single clear identity, but rather several overlapping but different entities constructed from within overlapping but different traditions.

What links the different constructions of Thatcherism is not an agreement about the phenomena to be explained, but rather a recognition of the peculiar salience of certain dilemmas for British government since 1973. Proponents of all the traditions considered here understand Thatcherism as a response to certain dilemmas and feel pushed by Thatcherism to search for solutions to them. The legacy of Thatcherism consists, therefore, not in a monolithic set of institutions, practices or beliefs but rather in the diverse ways in which people inspired by different traditions have responded to these dilemmas.

Four dilemmas occupy centre-stage in our argument. They are welfare dependency, overload, inflation and globalisation. Although the dilemmas arise in all traditions, each tradition constructs the dilemmas differently and accords them different political salience. To recap, Thatcherism as variously constructed highlighted the political salience of the dilemmas for all the traditions. It forced a reconsideration of existing beliefs. So, Thatcherism lives on in the changes made in each tradition in response to the dilemmas. To discuss dilemmas is to focus on these continuing changes, on the diverse impact of Thatcherism, and on how each dilemma contributes to the changes in diverse traditions.

Welfare dependency

The possessive individualism celebrated by the Liberal tradition, as well as in its interpretation of Thatcherism, poses the dilemma of reconciling markets that deliver freedom and prosperity with community. For a conservative, commitment to community is 'the source of individual identity and satisfaction' (Willetts 1992: 69). We have moral obligations stemming from our social roles; we are born into duties. Free markets can destroy communities because they require the free movement of capital and labour. Willetts (ibid.: 92) stresses the need to preserve community to distinguish his brand of conservatism from 'the economic liberal, without a trace of conservatism in him'. But sustaining community and Christian duty also involve meeting the spiralling costs of the welfare state. Care and compassion cost money. The Tory tradition's story about culture claims the welfare state creates welfare dependency, prompting calls for greater individual responsibility and a greater role for the family and self-help. One Nation Tories see the welfare state as a key way of conserving the fabric of society and the state's legitimacy. The invisible line between the nanny state and the caring state generates discontinuities as policy oscillates between penny-pinching cuts, marketising services, privatising benefits and increasing public expenditure on social security and health to the highest levels in the post-war period.

Dependency is a dilemma common to all traditions. Thus, for New Labour, the welfare state now acts as a safety net more than as part of a search for greater social equality (Bevir 2000c). The ideal of moral equality bequeathed to the party by ethical Socialists no longer translates straight-forwardly into rough economic equality. Instead, the traditional ethical Socialist emphasis on the rights of the unemployed and disadvantaged is downplayed. The new story stresses that welfare recipients have duties to society. The Socialist concepts of citizenship and welfare changed and continue to change.

State overload

For all its inadequacies, the overload thesis so popular in the 1970s drew attention to the limits to state authority (see, for example, Brittan 1975; Douglas 1976; King 1975; and for a swingeing critique see Hay 1996: 98–101). One response noted in the narratives on Thatcherism was to attack intermediate institutions such as the trade unions, local government and professional groups and to reassert central authority through the strong state. Several commentators note the market economy depends on the extensive use of state authority to bring about the changes in civil society necessary to sustain that economy, and yet such state intervention undermines markets (Gamble 1988; Hall 1983; Marquand 1988, 1989). Thus, the collectivist and libertarian strands in the British political traditions re-emerge in yet another guise. Too few commentators also note that state authority is itself undermined by markets or, to be precise, marketising public services. The differentiated polity narrative draws attention to ways in which government efforts to reform the state by creating markets and quasi-markets also fragmented the bureaucracy, which was the main government tool for exerting control. Policies are imposed. Implementing agencies rebel. The government depends on them to implement policies but too rarely seeks their compliance through negotiation. The attempt to exert authority, to act as the strong state, founders on the fragmentation and dependence created by state intervention, thus generating difficulties as authority is flouted and intent and outcome diverge, often markedly.

Inflation

Inflation had become a major problem for the British economy by the end of the 1970s when the Labour government, under pressure from the IMF, agreed to introduce strict monetary controls. The problem was often constructed through a monetarist critique of Keynesianism. During the 1980s and 1990s, some proponents of all the dominant traditions came to accept four central tenets of monetarism: the key monetary levers should be interest rates rather than fiscal policy; the supply side of the economy should be considered more significant than demand management; low inflation should be as important a goal of economic policy as low unemployment; and government should develop monetary policy in accord with rule, not discretion, to preserve credibility. This change is central to many accounts of Thatcherism. As important, the emergence of New Labour shows how Socialists confronted the dilemma posed by monetarist ideas for their commitment to full employment and the welfare state. The Labour Party began to emphasise that economic recovery would bring unacceptable inflation unless it took place with a commitment to macro-economic stability and supply-side policies to boost industry. Increasingly it opted for a more positive view of markets. Quasi-market mechanisms as well as privatisation are entrenched on the party's agenda.

Discontinuities appear within the Socialist tradition as the response to inflation leads the Labour Party to distance itself from its legacy and its traditional sources of electoral and financial support. New Labour appears unable to meet the call for redistributive policies from its traditional sources of support while refusing to increase taxes and public expenditure.

Globalisation

We noted earlier the paradox in the Liberal tradition's narrative of Thatcherism between arresting national decline and the free trade imperatives of liberalism. Reasserting national sovereignty is an illusion in a world where trans-national power-sharing is unavoidable. So, the free trade nostrums of neo-liberalism undermine efforts to restore Britain's standing in the world and foreign policy is beset by the discontinuities generated by the clash of global markets and national sovereignty. Within the Socialist tradition, the dilemma is to transform Socialism in one country into line with new economic patterns and new social groups. New technologies globalised key parts of the British economy and changed the interests and expectations of the working class. For example, the British economy could no longer go its own way but had to place itself in the heart of Europe. The European Union and its idea of a social Europe thus became one way of defending and extending the classical welfare state.[2]

Conclusion

The history of the British political tradition cannot be written as the simple triumph of collectivism, a fate bemoaned from Dicey onwards. Rather, dilemmas fuel a process of adjustment that constructs and reconstructs the ideas in each tradition, leading to a history of continuous conflict between evolving traditions. Equally, then, we have rejected the interpretation of Thatcherism as the simple triumph of liberal individualism. We have tried to avoid domesticating Thatcherism by stressing the complex and contradictory ways it was constructed within traditions that provide radically different narratives of it. Thatcherism consisted of competing narratives of what it was. We are all familiar with TINA – there is no alternative. Perhaps, however, a more apt palindrome would be TINT – there is no Thatcherism. Whatever coherence this notion may have had, it has dissipated among the diverse political traditions of Britain. Its impact continues to be felt by each tradition to differing degrees, but it does not form a single narrative. In place of the monolithic, unified phenomenon of British government textbooks, we offer a decentred, non-essentialist account. That said, 'The Queen is dead, long live the Queen' is an apt epitaph because Thatcherism lives on. Its legacy is the diverse way people understood and responded to it. These responses produced distinctive narratives of Thatcherism that highlighted certain dilemmas for each of the dominant traditions. This argument does not seek to belittle the effects of Thatcherism. By changing traditions, Thatcherism changed both the practice of British government and our understanding of that practice.

Governance in general, and public sector reform in particular, clearly illustrate this argument. The rationale for the reforms, especially privatis-ation and marketisation, lay in the Liberal conception of Thatcherism and its 'solution' to the problem of state overload. The policy was explicit. For example, before setting up an agency, the government's Prior Option test required the following questions to be answered: Does the job need to be done at all (e.g. cuts)? Does the government have to be responsible for it (e.g. privatisation)? Does the government have to carry out the task itself (e.g. market testing)? Is the organisation properly structured and focused on the job to be done (e.g. agencification)? In short, these questions require the case be made for keeping a service in the public sector. Initially, agencies were an alternative to privatisation, not a step on the way (see Margaret Thatcher's written answer in HC Deb. 24 October 1988: col. 14), but the Prior Option test meant that an existing agency could still be privatised (see Cm. 2627: 15; and Cabinet Office 1994a: 12 and 13).

One aim of the Thatcher government was to transfer services from the public to the private sector; to shift from hierarchy to markets in the delivery of public services. It was these policies that fragmented public service delivery, multiplied networks and, in part, fuelled the shift to governance. Just as important, these reforms also posed dilemmas for other traditions. There was no going back on privatisation, the sale of council houses or contracting-out. Thus, other traditions had to respond not only to the problem of state overload but also to the neo-liberal 'solution' to it. Our exploration of the ways diverse traditions – Tory, Liberal, Whig and Socialist – accommodated Thatcherism thus provides an account of the broad patterns of belief informing the first wave of British governance.

Even when we split a tradition into its constituent parts, however, we still encounter problems. Trivially, we raise the question of whether there are differences in these more narrowly defined traditions. More signific-antly, we raise the issues of essentialism and how to explain change in traditions. Essentialists equate traditions with an unchanging core idea or ideas and then explore variations. For example, Greenleaf (1983a: 15–20) describes the British political tradition as a dialectic between the two opposing tendencies of libertarianism and collectivism. In doing so, however, he makes these opposing tendencies ahistorical. Although they come into being in the nineteenth century, they then remain static. They act as fixed categories, ideal types, into which he forces individual thinkers and texts, even different parts of the one text or different utterances by the one thinker. As we have seen, tradition is a starting point, not a destination, and so instances cannot be constructed by comparison with the features of a tradition. Traditions do not constitute the beliefs that people come to hold or the actions they perform. So, we need to explore changes in traditions by examining how their adherents responded to specific dilemmas. We cannot simply postulate static Tory, Whig, Liberal and Socialist tradition into which we slot representative political scientists and practitioners. Instead, we need to ask how agents developed, modified, and even transformed such traditions, often while grappling with new circumstances. In the next chapter we will explore the shift in the Socialist tradition from Old to New Labour.

Notes

1 We recognise there is no one-to-one correspondence between author and the traditions as we define them. Our choice of traditions is conventional, see, for example, Barker 1994; and Pearson and Williams 1984. Some authors clearly draw themes from more than one of these traditions as we define them. Equally, the table and our examples are not comprehensive. Thus, for the Socialist tradition, we could discuss its several strands and also distinguish it from the Marxist tradition. Because we will trace the lineage of New Labour's ideas in Chapter 7, and because we are illustrating an argument, not writing a review article on 'Thatcherism', we concentrate on the Socialist tradition. We do not consider Marxist accounts of Thatcherism, although we recognise they were influential: see, for example, Hall and Jacques 1983; Hay 1996: Chapter 7; and Jessop *et al.* 1988.

2 The Socialist tradition is diverse and there are many who are sceptical of the globalisation thesis among their ranks. Because we want to trace the lineage of New Labour's ideas and show how they responded to the dilemmas posed by globalisation, we do not consider the arguments of the sceptics in any detail. The key point is that New Labour has bought into the globalisation thesis, with Anthony Giddens 1998 as the main apologist. For sceptical accounts see Hirst and Thompson 1999; and Hay and Marsh 2000.

7 New Labour's civil service

Introduction

A notion like the Socialist tradition can be too static to explore how specific ideas change through time. If we want to explain the beliefs of New Labour and grasp why they differ from Old Labour, we will have to explore how the Socialist tradition has been adapted.[1] In brief, New Labour's adherence to the Third Way stands as a general response to the dilemmas highlighted by Thatcherism, while its belief in joined-up government stands as a more specific response to the consequences, often unintended, of NPM. Of course, we could construct Tory, Liberal and Whig accounts of New Labour but that is not our purpose. Rather we continue to decentre the notion of tradition. We have moved from a comparison of the British and Danish governmental traditions, through an analysis of several components of the British governmental tradition and now we move to an analysis of the Socialist tradition to unpack yet further the notion of tradition. So, in this chapter we focus on strands in the Socialist tradition, especially the rise to prominence of New Labour's ideas about governance. Throughout we continue to argue that ideas about governance are contingent, contested and variously constructed and by examining change in the Socialist tradition, we continue our exploration of the broad patterns of belief informing British governance.

To simplify and summarise the story, we might say the Thatcherite reforms – marketisation and the new public management – represented the first wave of governance, while New Labour's reforms – the search for joined-up governance – represent a second wave. In this chapter we examine the beliefs, ideology or discourse embedded in the second wave of British governance. To begin, we explain New Labour's concept of the Third Way as a response from within the Socialist tradition to dilemmas such as inflation and state overload. The Third Way thus advocates neither bureaucracy nor markets but rather networks based on trust. We then examine the ways in which New Labour's proposals for modernising government also incorporate responses to dilemmas created by the Thatcherite reforms, notably fragment-ation, steering, accountability and management change. Finally, we offer an evaluation of New Labour's public sector reforms. We highlight problems left unresolved by the second wave of governance.

The Third Way

New Labour has invoked a succession of visions, from the stakeholder society to 'the Third Way', all of which mark its distinctive response to the dilemmas highlighted by Thatcherism. Blair (1998a) declares the Labour Party under his leadership to be 'new in our means, but Labour in our aims'. The same theme is picked up by Gordon Brown, Chancellor of the Exchequer, and Tony Wright, a Labour Member of Parliament, when they express their continuing faith in 'fundamental socialist values' that have 'an enduring quality' even though particular policies have to 'change in the light of new problems, knowledge and circumstances' (Brown and Wright 1995: 13 and 29). The Third Way represents an attempt to keep many strands of the social democratic vision while accepting a need for new policies in response to dilemmas highlighted by Thatcherism.

For much of the post-war era, the Labour Party took an extension of state control to be the primary means of promoting social justice. The state was to create greater equality through progressive taxation and the provision of welfare benefits. By 1980, however, these policies were threatened by a growing concern with inflation and government overload. The New Right understood inflation in the terms of the monetarist critique of Keynesianism. Monetarism encouraged a shift from demand management to supply-side reforms, and the New Right fused advocacy of supply-side reforms with an emphasis on the values of choice and freedom. The state was portrayed as being aloof and unresponsive to individual wants in a way the market was not.

During the 1980s and 1990s, Socialists increasingly came to accept the four tenets of New Right economic theory described earlier (see pp. 120–1), namely that: the key monetary lever should be interest rates, not fiscal policy; the supply side of the economy should be considered more significant than demand management; low inflation should be as important a goal of economic policy as low unemployment; and governments should develop monetary policy in accord with rules, not discretion, to maintain credibility. Labour Party documents now suggested that economic recovery would bring an unacceptable inflation unless pursued with a 'commitment to macroeconomic stability' and 'supply-side policies to boost investment in industry' (Labour Party 1991, 1994). Gordon Brown, as Chancellor of the Exchequer, has expressed New Labour's reluctance either to raise taxes or to boost demand by increasing public expenditure. The government displayed the strength of its commitment to low inflation most dramatically by giving control over interest rates to the Bank of England.

An emphasis on the supply side of the economy has led the Labour Party to modify its stance towards privatisation and marketisation. Mandelson and Liddle tell us New Labour has renounced the statist policies once associated with the Party for a concern with efficiency and good management (Mandelson and Liddle 1996: 27 and 151). In doing so, they tie efficiency and good management to marketisation rather than the traditional bureaucratic model of public service provision. Thus, although the Labour Party remains critical of a blanket assumption of the superiority of the private sector and markets, it has accepted large parts of the supply-side revolution. Even privatisation now has a place in government thinking, as both Blair and Brown pointed out during the 1997 election campaign.

For much of the post-war era, the Labour Party stood for a universal welfare state that entitled all citizens to certain political, social and economic rights. The state, as a moral expression of community, was to provide a guaranteed minimum standard of living to its citizens. For many Socialists, providing universal benefits was also a way of creating virtuous and independent citizens. During the 1980s, however, growing worries about an underclass suggested these Socialists had been too optimistic. Political scientists began to argue that the welfare state had created a class of people who were dependent on benefits and had neither the means nor the incentive to improve their lot. They suggested that providing benefits without matching obligations undermined the individual responsibility of the recipients. The situation makes the underclass immoral, promotes crime, drug-abuse and other evils that corrode the moral fabric of society (Murray 1990, 1994). Once again, the Thatcher governments were the first to address the dilemma posed by a belief in the underclass. They altered the range and conditions of many welfare benefits in ways the Labour Party at first condemned outright.

More recently, New Labour has come to accept much of this analysis of the underclass. It accepts, in Mandelson and Liddle's (1996: 72–3) words, 'the complex web of means-tested benefits weakens incentives' so 'today's welfare state too often traps people in long-term dependency'. Simply by accepting there is an underclass in a condition of welfare dependency, New Labour has committed itself to devising new policies designed less to alleviate poverty than to enable people to break free of the welfare trap. Blair, for example, has made it clear that 'Labour's modern welfare should not just recommend increased benefits but . . . [also] reduce dependency and get rid of disincentives to paid work' (Blair 1994). Thus, the Labour government has put a welfare to work programme at the centre of its agenda (Labour Party 1996).

The welfare to work programme sets up a New Deal between the government and job seekers. The government will provide training, education and places on employment schemes, rather than cash payments. In return, the unemployed have to take up these opportunities or they will lose some of their benefits. The first part of the New Deal to be put into practice was that for young unemployed people. Young people who have been out of work for over six months now have four options: a job with a private or public sector employer, a job in the voluntary sector, a place on an environmental task force or full-time education or training. All the options include a minimum of one day's training a week to provide the recipients with the skills needed to remain in employment. Yet the 'New Deal is not an easy alternative to work', for the young people have 'to take up those opportunities' – 'staying on benefit will no longer be an option' (DfEE 1998). The New Deal has since been extended to lone parents, disabled people and any adult who has been unemployed for more than two years. The government hopes a combination of carrots and sticks will provide the underclass with the chance and incentive to break out of welfare dependency. New Labour is responding to the seeming existence of an underclass by moving from a system of welfare benefits paid by the state to one in which the state provides people with the resources to enter the workforce. As Blair has explained, 'the modern welfare state is not founded on a paternalistic government giving out more benefits but on an enabling government that through work and education helps people to help themselves' (Blair 1996: 209).

By accepting the reality of dilemmas such as inflation and the underclass, Socialists broke with many of the policies associated with the Keynesian welfare state. They implied such policies no longer provided a practical means of realising their ideals. Yet while New Labour thus stands as a response to dilemmas highlighted by Thatcherism, the nature of its response reflects its location within the Socialist tradition. Indeed, the Third Way also stands as a critique of the New Right's response to these dilemmas. It echoes a social account of individuals as existing, and realising themselves, only within community. And it insists that Britain can be economically successful only if we organise our social life in accord with this account of our nature. The Third Way thus represents a critical alternative to the New Right's attempts to deal with social fragmentation and declining economic performance (ibid.: 290–321). New Labour evokes a Third Way in which morally empowered individuals promote social cohesion and thus an economically vibrant nation. The starting point is a belief in moral personhood within community. As Blair argues,

> People are not separate economic actors competing in the market place of life. They are citizens of a community. We are social beings. We develop the moral power of personal responsibility for ourselves and each other . . . People are not just competitive; they are co-operative too. They are not just interested in the welfare of themselves; they are interested in the well being of others.
>
> (Ibid.: 299–300)

New Right doctrines led to an increasingly divided society in large part because they failed to recognise our social nature and so neglected the mutual rights and obligations of individuals within the community. Blair claims, also, that the economic performance of Britain has declined in large part because of the failure of the New Right to allow in its public policies for the social nature of human beings.

Far from simply copying the neo-liberal doctrines of the New Right, therefore, New Labour draws on traditional Socialist ideas to condemn these doctrines. We can detect much the same process in the way New Labour unpacks the Third Way as a vision of public sector reform. Here Socialists traditionally believed in fellowship, enshrined in a bureaucratic state providing universal welfare. The New Right promoted individualism, with social relations based mainly on contracts and the market. New Labour favours a society of stakeholders enabled by a state that forms with them partnerships and networks based on trust (see Table 7.1).

New Labour changed the Party's attitude to delivering public services. It did so by reinterpreting the concerns highlighted by the New Right from within the Socialist tradition. The Old Labour model resembled a top-down, command-style bureaucracy based on centralised rules. The Party became associated with hierarchic patterns of organisation in which co-ordination is secured by administrative orders. The New Right rejected this model, arguing it was inefficient and eroded individual freedom. The Thatcher governments tried to make public services more efficient through privatisation, marketisation and the new public management. Citizens became consumers able to choose between arrays of public services. Although command bureaucracy remains a major way of delivering public services, privatisation, the purchaser–provider split and management techniques from the private sector have become an integral part of British governance.

New Labour does not defend the command bureaucracy associated with Old Labour. Rather, we can identify a shift in the Socialist tradition inspired in part by the New Right's concerns with market efficiency and choice. For example, Mandelson and Liddle (1996: 27) explicitly reject the 'municipal socialism' and 'centralised nationalisation' of the past. They insist New Labour 'does not seek to provide centralised "statist" solutions to every social and economic problem'. Instead New Labour promotes the idea of networks of institutions and individuals acting in partnerships held

Table 7.1 New Labour and governance

	New Labour	Old Labour	New Right
Public philosophy	Stakeholding	Fellowship	Individualism
Service delivery:			
(i) Characteristic organisation	Network	Bureaucracy	Market
(ii) Characteristic relationship	Trust	Command	Competition

together by relations of trust. New Labour's concern with networks based on relations of trust does not exclude either command bureaucracy or quasi-market competition. Rather, New Labour proposes a mix of hierarchies, market and networks, with choices depending on the particular nature of the service under consideration. Government policy is that 'services should be provided through the sector best placed to provide those services most effectively', where 'this can be the public, private or voluntary sector, or partnerships between these sectors' (Cm. 4011 1998). Even a simple service is liable to display a mix of structures, strategies and relationships.

Equally, New Labour embodies a critique of the New Right's model of public service delivery. It suggests the New Right has an exaggerated faith in markets. New Labour, as we have just seen, believes individuals are not just competitive and self-interested but also co-operative and concerned for the welfare of others. So, public services should encourage co-operation while continuing to use market mechanisms when suitable. For example, David Clark (1997), then the Minister for Public Services, explained that policies such as market testing 'will not be pursued blindly as an article of faith' but they 'will continue where they offer best value for money'. New Labour insists markets are not always the best way to deliver public services. They can go against the public interest, reinforce inequalities and entrench privilege. Besides, much of the public sector simply is not amenable to market competition. Indeed, trust and partnerships are essential. Where there is no market, one has to rely on either honest co-operation or specify standards in absurd detail. Far from promoting efficiency, therefore, marketisation can undermine standards of service quality.

New Labour's emphasis on individual choice and involvement overlaps with themes found in the New Right. In promoting customer-focused services, New Labour adopts features of the new public management when it considers them suitable. However, New Labour's model of service delivery does not follow the New Right's vision of the new public management. On the contrary, New Labour argues that many features of this new public management, such as quasi-markets and contracting-out, upheld an unhealthy dichotomy between the public and private sectors: public bodies did not work with private companies but merely contracted services out to them. This argument is used, for example, to justify abolishing the internal market within the National Health Service. The Third Way, in contrast to the vision of the New Right, is supposed to develop networks that enable public and private organisations to collaborate. Examples of such collaboration appear in the partnerships between the public and private sector that are so important to the delivery of the New Deal for the unemployed.

New Labour's networks for public service delivery are supposed to be based on trust. Blair describes such trust as 'the recognition of a mutual purpose for which we work together and in which we all benefit' (Blair

1996: 292). Trust matters because we are interdependent social beings who achieve more by working together than by competing. Quality public services are best achieved through stable, co-operative relationships. Blair talks of building relationships of trust between all actors in society. Trust is promoted between organisations through the Quality Networks programme: organisations should exchange information about their practices to facilitate co-operation. Trust is promoted inside organisations through forms of management that allow individual responsibility and discretion increasingly to replace rigid hierarchies: individuals should be trusted to decide and implement policies without the constraint of strict procedures. Trust is promoted between organisations and individuals through the Service First programme: citizens should trust organisations to provide suitable services, and organisations should trust citizens to use services properly.

So, the Labour government uses networks based on trust to institutionalise its ideals of partnership and an enabling state. Blair (1998b) stated the aims succinctly: 'joined-up problems need joined-up solutions.' This theme runs through the *Modernising Government* White Paper (Cm. 4310 1999; see also Cabinet Office 1999a and 2000). This White Paper says that services must be effective and co-ordinated and the principles of joined-up government apply also to voluntary and private sector organisations. We illustrate New Labour's conception of governance with a detailed examination of its proposals for joined-up government.

Modernising government

New Labour was slow to get under way in modernising the civil service. Initially, a White Paper on 'Better Government' was promised for autumn 1997. But the *Modernising Government* White Paper did not emerge until March 1999. The government has three aims:

- Ensuring that policy-making is more *joined-up and strategic*.
- Making sure that *public service users* are the focus.
- Delivering public services that are *high-quality and efficient*.
                              (Cm. 4310 1999: 6, emphasis in original)

Their programme of reforms has five key commitments:

- **Policy-making:** we will be forward looking in developing policies to deliver results that matter, not simply reacting to short-term pressures.
- **Responsive public services:** we will deliver public services to meet the needs of citizens, not the convenience of service providers.
- **Quality public services:** we will deliver efficient, high-quality public services and will not tolerate mediocrity.
- **Information age government:** we will use new technology to meet the

needs of citizens and business, and not trail behind technological developments.
- **Public service:** we will value public service, not denigrate it.

(Ibid.: 13, emphasis in original)

The easy assessment would be that government policy was pragmatic: we got more of the same. In fact, as we have suggested, the drip, drip style of reform obscured an important shift of emphasis from markets to networks.

The White Paper identifies seven challenges facing the civil service:

- Implementing constitutional reform in a way that preserves a unified civil service and ensures close working between the UK government and the devolved administrations.
- Getting staff in all departments to integrate the EU dimension into policy thinking.
- Focusing work on public services so as to improve their quality, make them more innovative and responsive to users and ensure that they are delivered in an efficient and joined-up way.
- Creating a more innovative and less risk-averse culture in the civil service.
- Improving collaborative working across organisational boundaries.
- Managing the civil service so as to equip it to meet these challenges.
- Thinking ahead strategically to future priorities.

(Ibid.: 56)

The White Paper leads us to pose two questions. Do these reforms address the unintended consequences of the Thatcherite reforms? And will the reforms enable New Labour to meet its stated objectives?[2]

Responding to unintended consequences

The consequences, often unintended, of the Conservative government's public sector reforms throw up several dilemmas for many traditions. These dilemmas include fragmentation, steering, accountability and management change (see also Butler 1997; Rhodes 1997a). New Labour's proposals for modernising government are responses from within the Socialist tradition to these dilemmas.

Fragmentation

One of the most widely debated consequences of the new system is institutional fragmentation. Typically, services are now delivered through a combination of local government, special-purpose bodies, the voluntary sector and the private sector. There are now 5,521 special-purpose bodies that spend at least £39 billion and to which ministers make 70,000 patronage appointments. This sector is larger than local government! The *Modernising Government* White Paper clearly seeks to deal with the issue of fragmentation. It illustrates the dilemma by pointing, for example, to the large number of organisations involved in providing long-term domiciliary care (Cm. 4310 1999: 24). In response to fragmentation, New Labour claims that service delivery depends as never before on linking organisations. So, the White Paper's focus on joined-up government is a direct response to the dilemma of fragmentation.

Steering

Steering is another widely recognised dilemma associated with the Thatcherite reforms. For example, Jenkins (1993: 94) argues that the Conservative government failed adequately to strengthen strategic capacity with their other changes. He claims agencies work in a 'policy vacuum' and steering is 'through a system of crisis management and blame avoidance'. Butler (1993: 404) echoes these same concerns for central policy-making when he writes, 'it is essential that it does not reach the point where individual Departments and their Agencies become simply different unconnected elements in the overall public sector, with . . . no real working mechanisms for policy coordination'.

The former Yorkshire Regional Health Authority (RHA) provides a good example of the limits to the centre's ability to steer. When the parliamentary Committee of Public Accounts (1997) investigated the Yorkshire RHA, it found, to choose one of a litany of sins, the RHA had awarded a contract to Yorkshire Water for clinical waste incineration worth £7.2 million of capital and £2 million a year in revenue. The contract was not let competitively. It was for fifteen years. The Authority did not get NHS Executive approval. The problem was interorganisational; the central NHS Executive could not steer. Government policy is compulsory competitive tendering. EU policy requires all major public sector contracts to be open to member states. But Yorkshire is exempt, it would seem. The centre has rubber levers; pulling the central policy lever does not necessarily mean something happens at the bottom.

Despite several attempts over the years to strengthen central capability, the issue persists. The White Paper's criticism of central departments, its call for a corporate approach, its endeavours to strengthen horizontal policy making and the role of the Cabinet Office all seek to confront the dilemma of the centre's apparent lack of strategic capability. Co-ordination is a central theme of the *Modernising Government* White Paper.

Accountability

The issue of accountability surfaces in many traditions alongside that of fragmentation. The worry is that fragmentation erodes accountability because sheer institutional complexity obscures who is accountable to whom for what. Special-purpose, nominated bodies have multiplied in place of central departments and elected local councils for the delivery of some services. Again, Yorkshire RHA dramatically illustrates the point; the catalogue of misdeeds is eye-catching. The Committee of Public Accounts (1997) was 'concerned' about a further eight instances of 'unacceptable' behaviour that they noted 'with surprise' and 'serious concern', and, on one occasion, even an 'appalled'. They also consider the remedial action 'deeply unsatisfactory'. The report paints a picture of an RHA that embraced the culture of the day, neglected its classical stewardship role, and got away with 'blue murder' for several years. Control was exerted – later, much later. No one was brought to book for the substantial waste of public money. The money was not recovered. Nor can Yorkshire RHA be dismissed as a single, aberrant organisation. It was encouraged to embrace the ethos of the day by the NHS Executive. The Committee of Public Accounts (1994) provides much evidence of the same type and scale of improper behaviour in the Wessex and West Midlands RHAs, out of the (then) fourteen RHAs. The reports show private government in action amid a lack of network accountability.

Confusing accountability with responsiveness compounded the problems of accountability. This confusion matters in two ways. First, responsive service delivery as envisaged by such innovations as the Citizen's Charter supplements, but does not replace, political accountability because the consumer has no powers to hold a government agency to account. Citizens have become consumers of services. The Citizen's Charter is the government's equivalent of the Consumer Association's magazine *Which?* This publication tests such goods as washing machines and television sets and advises consumers on the best buys. Is the Citizen's Charter more effective than *Which?* Probably not. Second, agencification aggravated the accountability gap because the government introduced no new arrangements to preserve the constitutional convention of ministerial responsibility. William Waldegrave (1993: 20) tried to justify this inaction by drawing a distinction between 'responsibility, which can be delegated, and accountability, which remains firmly with the minister'. In this view, creating agencies and the other reforms clarified responsibility but left 'the minister properly accountable for the policies he settles'. The distinction hinges on clear definitions of policy and management and equally clear accounts of the respective roles and responsibilities of ministers, senior civil servants and chief executives. Such clarity does not exist, as the Treasury and Civil Service Committee (1994: 132) pointed out (see also Plowden 1994: 127 and Stewart 1993). Current arrangements allow the minister to take the credit when the policy goes well but to blame the chief executive when things go wrong (see Barker 1997). There is no clear dividing line between policy and operations, a fact that undermines ministerial accountability to parliament since it enables ministers to avoid blame.

In short, the dilemma of accountability gets elided into a dilemma of responsiveness. This elision is a major problem. It is not confined to agencies. The Public Service Committee (1996: Chapters 4 and 5) wanted a more direct line of accountability between parliament, civil servants and the chief executives of agencies. The (then) Conservative government rejected its proposals. New Labour remains largely silent on the topic. The White Paper emphasises 'responsiveness' to citizens as service users. It mentions accountability only when talking about extending the coverage of the Parliamentary Ombudsman, when considering auditing, and to claim that ministerial appointments strengthen accountability (Cm. 4310 1999: 7, 32, 38, 60). Waldegrave's distinction between managerial responsibility and ministerial accountability is alive and well. The White Paper addresses only the former.

Management change

Views differ on the extent to which the senior civil service has acquired more than a veneer of the new managerialism. Departments are 'still managed by people who got there because of their policy skills rather than their management skills' (Watson 1992: 27). Richards (1993: 278) noted how much has remained unchanged: she itemises fast stream recruitment, ministerial accountability, the permanent secretary as sole accounting officer, the policy function, senior appointment procedures, and the delegation of pay and conditions of work to agencies. Theakston (1999: 257–9) concludes the reforms have affected the senior civil service in three main ways. First, 'there is now less group self-confidence'. Second, they are rarely policy initiators; 'they are much less active in pushing their own policy views'. Third, they have a much higher public profile. They are no longer 'statesmen in disguise'. He stresses their role as 'administrative conservators' who guard the institutions, processes and staff of government and the distinctive values and principles of public service. However, the key shift so far has been for senior civil servants to become 'policy managers rather than makers or originators' (Barberis 1996: 42).

Recent public sector reforms, especially corporate management and the '3Es', challenge the culture of Whitehall. Many fear an erosion of public service ethics. With the spread of patronage and one party government for eighteen years, worries grew about standards of conduct. Chapman and O'Toole (1995: 4), for example, defend the traditional British civil service against the 'fashionable pursuit' of management (see below, pp. 147–8). They argue that civil servants must never put private interests before public duty. Management reforms attack the generalist and undermine this notion of public duty. Traditional values are being lost and we must protect them. Business-inspired reforms are no substitute.

Corporate management, open competition and macho-ministers prompted many to ask how we might preserve a public service ethos. This dilemma inspired, for instance, a growing interest in a Civil Service Act. Tony Blair's version of the *Ministerial Code* (Cabinet Office 1997: 21 para. 56) states that ministers have 'a duty to uphold the political impartiality of the Civil Service' and 'to ensure that influence over appointments is not abused for partisan purposes'. The *Modernising Government* White Paper also asserts its commitment to public services and public servants (Cm. 4310 1997: Chapter 6), although it will 'not tolerate mediocrity'. In a speech shortly before his retirement, Sir Richard Wilson (2002) gave us his 'portrait of the profession' in which he reaffirmed the civil service's traditional values of integrity, impartiality and loyalty and made a case for a Civil Service Act.

So, New Labour seeks to balance preserving the public service ethos with public sector reforms. Whether these reforms will include an Act remains unclear.

Will government be modernised?

New Labour represents a response from within the socialist tradition to, first, the dilemmas highlighted by Thatcherism, and, second, the dilemmas thrown up by the often-unintended consequences of NPM. One way of interpreting New Labour's call for modernisation is to see it as recognition of, first, the need to leave behind the hierarchic bureaucracy of Old Labour, and, second, the failings of marketisation and NPM. Modernisation requires the government to overcome the dilemmas we have been discussing. Will the government's proposals resolve them and meet its stated objectives? Few believe so, and four significant issues remain unresolved.

The holy grail of co-ordination

The search for co-ordination lies at the heart of New Labour's reforms. As Kavanagh and Seldon (2000) point out, we have seen prime ministerial centralisation in the guises of institutional innovation with more resources going to No. 10 and the Cabinet Office, and strong political and policy direction as No. 10 seeks a strong grip on the government machine. Such 'power grabs' are 'a reaction to felt weakness, a frustration with the inability to pull effective levers'. However, despite strong pressures for more and pro-active co-ordination throughout Western Europe, the co-ordination activities of the core remain modest (Wright and Hayward 2000). Co-ordination is the philosopher's stone of modern government, ever sought, but always just beyond reach.

There are three dimensions to joining-up: horizontal co-ordination between government departments, vertical co-ordination between depart-ments and service delivery agents; and internal departmental co-ordination. We can illustrate each only briefly. For example, horizontal co-ordination covers: new units such as the Social Exclusion Unit, the Performance

Innovation Unit, the Delivery Unit, the Office of Public Services Reform and Regional Co-ordination Unit and their reports such as the Performance and the Innovation's Units' *Wiring It Up*; new multi-functional departments such as the Department for the Environment, Food and Rural Affairs (DEFRA) and the Department for Work and Pensions (DWP); and inter-departmental central policy initiatives of which the best examples are Public Service Agreements, which seek to marry expenditure to outcomes, and the New Deal welfare to work programme, which brings together the Treasury, DWP and the Department for Education and Skills. Vertical joining-up covers such innovations as the growing number of central–regional–local partnerships; action zones for health, education and employment, which seek to bring together local actors to deal with, for example, inequalities in health provision; and innovative joint policy initiatives such as Surestart, which brings together child care, primary health care and early educational provision to combat child poverty. Internal co-ordination covers such innovations as management boards, comprising not only senior departmental managers but also key external stakeholders.

As New Labour recognises (Mulgan 2001), joined-up government is not without its problems. Thus, horizontal co-ordination runs foul of the departmental interests of the baronies and the short-term-ism of ministers, who are in post for some 18–24 months and want quick results. There is also tension between the two main central co-ordinators – the Cabinet Office and the Treasury. Vertical co-ordination assumes agreement between central government and local actors. Local actors protect their autonomy and feel they do not 'own' the joined-up initiatives. The budgets for joined-up programmes are small. And the new initiatives create their own problems. Thus, there is an epidemic of zones, to the point where the solution to fragmentation seems to have become a part of the problem since the zones add significantly to the many bodies to be co-ordinated. John Denham (1999), then a junior minister in the Department of Health, conceded that 'zones can sometimes make government look more, rather than less complicated to the citizen' and there is the danger of 'initiative overload' because the zones do not join up.[3]

The reforms have a centralising thrust. They seek to co-ordinate departments and local authorities by imposing a new style of management on other agencies. So, although the government does 'not want to run local services from the centre', it 'is not afraid to take action where standards slip' – an obvious instance of a command operating code (Cm. 4310 1999: 35, 37, 45, 53 and 55). Action zones are owned by central government, not local actors. So local agendas are recognised only if they promote the agenda of the centre. Such a code, no matter how well disguised, runs the ever-present risk of recalcitrance from key actors and a loss of flexibility in dealing with localised problems. Gentle pressure relentlessly applied is still a command operating code in a velvet glove. When you are sitting at the top of a pyramid and you cannot see the bottom, control deficits are an ever-present unintended consequence.

'Diplomacy' or management by negotiation is the hands-off alternative to this hands-on management. Network actors commonly adopt a decentralised negotiating style that trades a measure of control for agreement. This style of hands-off management involves setting the framework in which networks work but then keeping an arm's length relationship. At times, central government has shown sympathy for a diplomatic approach to steering. For example, the Department of National Heritage provides the policy framework and policy guidance, prods, for example, the arts network into action by systematic review and scrutiny of its work, uses patronage to put 'one of its own' in key positions, mobilises resources and skills across sectors, regulates the network and its members and provides advice and assistance (Cm. 2811 1995). Such steering is imperfect but just as there are limits to central command, there are limits to independent action by networks. New Labour lacks the trust it seeks to inspire. Any inclination to adopt a diplomatic style, confronts New Labour's fears of the independence it bestows and so it relies on a hands-on command operating code. The White Paper on *Modernising Government* may recognise the need to manage networks but management by negotiation means agreeing the objectives with others not just persuading them that you were right all along, let alone resorting to sanctions when they disagree. New Labour fails to recognise the limits both to central intervention as it tries to balance independence with central control and to networks as a fallible governing structure.

It's the mix that matters

An all-too common feature of government policies, and New Labour is no exception, is that one specific reform or institution is seen as 'the solution'. We argued earlier that all governing structures fail. Bureaucracy and red tape is an old litany. New Labour is clearly conscious of the limits of marketisation. While contracting-out remains, the purchaser–provider split has gone. The public finance initiative stores up problems because, while the Treasury may avoid capital spending, there is an 'affordability gap' – hospital trusts do not have the resources to pay the private sector's charges (Gaffney *et al.* 1999). As with the previous government, the full costs of these policies emerge slowly. We want to suggest there are also limits to networks, which, like all other resource allocation mechanisms, are not cost-free. One clear effect of marketisation is that it multiplies the number of networks while simultaneously undermining their effectiveness. As we argued earlier, contracts undermine trust, reciprocity, informality and co-operation. We are not arguing that joined-up government and networks are unworkable. All governing structures fail. Governments have to find the appropriate mix.

What system of accountability?

The New Labour government, like its Conservative predecessors, conflates responsiveness with accountability. The *Modernising Government* White Paper pays no heed to the question of political accountability as understood in the constitution. The government has no proposals to strengthen ministerial accountability to parliament. The emphasis falls instead on central political control of priorities and managerial control of implementation. *Modernising Government* proposes a technological fix. Devolution apart, political caution pervades the government's distrust of local authorities. For example, any decision about regional assemblies in England is still some way off and hinges not only on a regional referendum but also on the reorganisation of local government within the affected region – a sure-fire recipe for delay (Cm. 5511 2002). Indeed, New Labour's reforms may worsen the problem of accountability. Hogwood *et al.* (2000) show that agencies and special-purpose bodies have multiple constituencies, each of which seeks to hold them to account. There is no system, just disparate, overlapping demands. In zones, the constituent organisations may hold the relevant officials and politicians to account but to whom is the set of organisations accountable? Moreover, as Hood *et al.* (1999) show, joined-up government does not extend to joined-up regulation and no one regulates the regulators. The next generation of Yorkshire RHAs will thrive in these conditions.

Everybody but us

Our final question arising out of New Labour's reforms is whether the administrative elite will be modernised. Speaking in May 1999, on 'The Civil Service in the New Millennium', Sir Richard Wilson, the Head of the Home Civil Service, said:

> I mentioned earlier the pride which the civil service has traditionally taken at its more senior levels in its ability to advise ministers on policy. But we are now beginning to question among ourselves quite how good we were in fact at this skill. Were we talking about devising policies which could be managed effectively to deliver the outcomes which the government of the day wanted? Or were we more concerned with devising policies which the minister could get through his cabinet colleagues and parliament and present successfully to the press? And how often have we in practice gone back later and evaluated the success with which policies have delivered what was claimed for them at the time when they were launched, rather than simply move on to devising the next policy which helps the minister through a difficult moment?

Change is slow. *The Economist* (1999) was quick to point out there were no proposals for evaluating the policy advice and other work of top civil servants. It was too quick to judge. Subsequent reports grasped these nettles (Cm. 4310 1999; Cabinet Office 1999b and c). A report by the Strategic Policy-Making Team, for example, seeks to set the standards for improving policy-making, and it includes peer review (Cabinet Office 1999b: para. 1.4 and 11.4–11.6). However, this review focuses on policy analysis, which tends to be done at grades lower than permanent secretary. In the same vein, Sir Richard Wilson encouraged 'rigorous reviews involving all managers', including permanent secretaries. Some departments now review annually not only the performance of the top civil servants but also of the ministers. It took twenty years of continuous reform before systematic procedures for evaluating the work of top administrators were introduced.

Conclusion

Neo-liberals portray governance as the uniform outcome of policies, such as marketisation and the new public management, that allegedly are the inevitable result of global economic pressures. In contrast, we have defended a decentred theory in which governance appears as a contingent product of contests of beliefs, where the competing beliefs arise within traditions and change in response to dilemmas. Our decentred theory suggests, first, that the outcomes of policies such as marketisation are not uniform but rather reflect regional, national and local circumstances. It suggests, second, that pressures such as state overload are not given as brute facts but constructed as different dilemmas from within various traditions. And it suggests, third, that the policies a state adopts are not necessary responses to given pressures, but rather perceived solutions to one particular conception of these dilemmas, where adopting a set of solutions is a contingent outcome of a political contest.

In this part of the book, we have illustrated our decentred theory through an examination of the broad patterns of belief embedded in British government. First, a comparison of Britain with Denmark showed the outcomes of policies such as marketisation were not uniform. It also provided an account of the broad contours of the British governmental tradition. Second, a study of diverse narratives of Thatcherism showed that the pressures are constructed differently from within different traditions. It also allowed us to identify some of the competing strands within the British governmental tradition. Third, our analysis of New Labour showed how the policies a state adopts reflect the triumph in a political contest of one particular tradition and its understanding of the salient dilemmas. New Labour may share many ideas with Thatcherism about the political economy of the British state but it has a different response to the dilemmas facing the British state. It devised a set of reforms different to those promoted by the Thatcher government. The New Right's concern to roll back the state has been replaced by New Labour's belief that the state can be made to work and a concern to transform the state into an enabling partner. And the New Right's belief in markets and competition within the public sector has been replaced by a broader emphasis on networks based on trust. It should be obvious, moreover, that New Labour's vision of governance replaced that of the New Right in a political contest. The triumph of Blair's vision of New Labour over other strands of social democracy represents the outcome of a contingent, political struggle.

Our decentred analysis emphasises the contingency of outcomes, policies and political contests. It also raises concerns, emphases and questions about the different levels of analysis available to political scientists. To some extent, we have dealt with these concerns as we have gone along. We considered the danger of reifying traditions – of treating them as institutions – if they are defined too broadly: we indicated how this danger prompts us to decentre traditions into some of their components. Also we considered the danger of essentialism if we neglected agency and change within traditions: we indicated how this danger prompts us to explore the way individuals modify traditions in response to dilemmas. Nonetheless, we have throughout concentrated on an aggregate study of the broad patterns of belief embodied in British governance as it is seen and constructed by political movements. We have not offered a decentred analysis of any particular network that deals with civil servants and citizens as well as politicians.

A decentred approach to particular networks would, we believe, reinforce many of our arguments about governance. Our arguments highlight the practices or processes through which patterns of governance are created, recreated and transformed. Instead of invoking the allegedly inevitable, ineluctable consequences of capital mobility and competition between states, we focus on the political contests, and the coercion, that surround the selection and implementation of policy. Moreover, this shift of emphasis surely replaces the straightforward neo-liberal assumption of convergence between states with recognition of continuing diversity. It prompts us to ask whether there is diversity in the design of policies as well as in the consequences. Are the public sectors of different states becoming more similar, or are they becoming more similar in some respects but more diverse in others, or are they even becoming more diverse?

Notes

1 Some commentators locate New Labour not in a Socialist tradition but in a Liberal one (Vincent 1998) or an amalgamation of various traditions (Freeden 1999). However, they do so because they reify traditions and then seek to compare New Labour with such reified traditions. We locate New Labour in the Socialist tradition, because, as we have been at pains to emphasise,

traditions are contingent historical entities not ideal types. For an application of our position to New Labour see Bevir 2000c.

2 We focus on the *Modernising Government* White Paper because it is the defining document of New Labour's reform initiative, which continues to influence civil service reform. There has been a shift of emphasis. Strong leadership (by permanent secretaries) and service delivery are the watchwords of the moment. Nonetheless the main tenets of the White Paper have been reaffirmed on several occasions by Sir Richard Wilson, Head of the Home Civil Service (Wilson 2001, 2002). So joined-up government remains a key plank of reform.

3 Walker (1999) also identifies several other weaknesses in zones. For example they chip away at the competence of local authorities, divert funds from main programmes, cost time and money and, most important, the structural causes of problems like poverty are regional, national and international, not local. The Community Development Programmes of the 1970s taught us this lesson but such criticisms seem to fall into the category of 'inconvenient knowledge', best ignored.

Part III

The civil service

On history and ethnography

8   The roots of governance

Introduction

In Part I, we set out the main features of the notion of governance and of our preferred, interpretive approach. In Part II, we used our approach to analyse the development of British governance, especially the public sector reforms of Margaret Thatcher and Tony Blair. We focused on the beliefs of politicians and the constructions of political movements. In Part III, we turn from politicians to civil servants to provide an alternative angle from which to examine British governance. In doing so, we also provide examples of our preferred modes of inquiry – history and ethnography.

Our interpretation of British governance has concentrated on an aggregate analysis of traditions rather than the beliefs of particular individuals. We explored the broad ideas informing Thatcherism and New Labour rather than unpacking the beliefs of the diverse actors in a particular network. However, our decentred theory highlights the fact that the operation and consequences of public sector reform depend not only on the beliefs of politicians but also on the civil servants who implement them and the citizens who receive them. Just as a decentred theory of a particular network would explore politicians, civil servants and citizens, so we want to expand our interpretation of British governance. We want to turn from the beliefs and traditions of politicians to those of civil servants.

An interpretive approach relies primarily on two modes of inquiry to explore the civil service, namely, ethnography and history.[1] For a start, we use many of the techniques of ethnography to uncover the stories or meanings, the beliefs and practices that are the basic building blocks of our analysis: we study individual behaviour and shared practices in everyday contexts, stressing the interpretation of beliefs or meanings. In addition, we explain these present-day beliefs through the historical analysis of traditions and dilemmas: we identify the ways in which different traditions prompt people to construct governance differently and the specific dilemmas that lead them to modify the traditions they inherit. In the next chapter, we provide a brief ethnographic study. It helps us to begin to understand how civil servants constructed governance under Thatcherism and New Labour.

In this chapter, we unpack the historical roots of contemporary beliefs about the civil service and its reform. First, we identify the competing traditions that inform the main constructions of the civil service. As in the chapter on Thatcherism, we concentrate on the Tory, Liberal, Whig and Socialist traditions. Then we draw back from these competing traditions to describe the shared framework of understanding within which present-day debates take place. As in our comparison of Britain and Denmark, we present an abstract British tradition within which the various, competing strands typically take their own place. Most of the competing narratives of civil service reform in the twentieth century draw, though to varying degrees and with distinctive emphases, on nineteenth-century and inter-war year accounts of the origins and development of the British civil service. They embody the broadly shared themes of British exceptionalism, the generalist civil servant, collectivism, gradualism, elitism, local-self-government and efficiency.

Present-day narratives of reform

The leading narratives about the civil service reflect the same political traditions we summarised in Chapter 6 while discussing Thatcherism. Here we want only briefly to explore the distinctiveness of the Tory, Liberal, Whig and Socialist stories about civil service reform (see Table 8.1). Then we want to concentrate on their shared intellectual heritage in ideas surrounding the nineteenth-century administrative revolution. Although we begin with academic accounts to illustrate each tradition, we also show that practitioners share these traditions by drawing also on official reports and other primary texts about the civil service, such as lectures, interviews, memoirs, autobiographies and biographies. Strictly speaking, of course, we

Table 8.1 Narratives of civil service reform

Tradition	Tory	Liberal	Whig	Socialist
Narrative of reform	Preserving traditional roles and relationships	Regulating the minimalist state	Pragmatic change	Bureaucratic expertise
Examples				
(a) Academic	Chapman 1970	Fry 1995	Hennessy 1989	Kellner and Crowther-Hunt 1980
(b) Practitioner	Gilmour 1992	Hoskyns 1983	Bancroft 1983	Garrett 1972
(c) Official report	Anderson 1946	Efficiency Unit 1988	Cm. 2627 1994	Cmnd 3638 1968

should compile thick descriptions of civil service reform using the accounts or texts of participants, not academic commentaries. In this case, however, there is no clear-cut distinction between academic commentators and elite actors. So, for example, Lord Crowther-Hunt – then known as Dr Norman Hunt – was both a member of the Fulton Committee and a Fellow of Exeter College, Oxford University. Subsequently, he became a political adviser to Prime Minister Harold Wilson, whom he advised on implementing the recommendations of the Fulton Committee. Individuals can be academics, authors of official documents and political actors all at once or at different times in their lives. So, for each tradition we show that academics and elite actors share an image of the system.

The Tory tradition

Chapman and O'Toole (1995: 4) praise 'the traditions of a non-partisan bureaucracy, an actuality which allowed the civil service to come close to practising the virtues of Plato's guardians and Weber's ideal-type of bureaucracy'. They defend 'the virtues of the traditional British civil service, with its emphasis on accountability, and its almost vocational approach to motivation' against the 'fashionable pursuit of apparently new approaches to management'. The notions of accountability to parliament through the minister and of public duty lie at the heart of their critique. They argue that civil servants must display integrity, never putting private interests before public duty, objectivity and impartiality (ibid.: 5–7). To be a civil servant was an 'esteemed opportunity to serve the state in an honourable capacity' (Part 1990: 20). Edward Bridges is the peak of this tradition. Recent management reforms, many Tories argue, attack the generalist. They are leading to the 'demise of public duty'. Agencies fragment the civil service. Civil servants are no longer socialised into its shared traditions. The principles of the Citizen's Charter replace the public service ethos. The Civil Service Code stands as a testament to how far this process has gone; it represents a warning that we will lose the traditional values unless we protect them. Business-like methods are no substitute for old values.

The recurrent Tory belief in preserving established roles and relationships could not be clearer. Chapman's debt to the Tory tradition appears throughout his work (see Chapman 1970: Chapter 7). His biography of Edward Bridges (Chapman 1988) extols the virtues of the generalist civil servant. His general administrative history (Chapman and Greenaway 1980) is, as Gowan (1987) caustically comments, an 'indispensable introduction to the facts and basic sources of late nineteenth and early twentieth century administrative history' that ignores the way in which reform served to sustain aristocratic privilege. With the Tory admiration of the generalist goes a covert acceptance of elitism.

High Tories may well ask, with Lord Salisbury, 'why do we need change, things are quite bad enough as they are'. Or they may say, with Samuel

Johnson, 'if the changes we fear be thus irresistible, what remains but to acquiesce with silence, as in the other insurmountable distresses of humanity? It remains that we retard what we cannot repel, that we palliate what we cannot cure.' For Ian Gilmour (1992: 185) the principal function of the civil service is, similarly, 'to draw attention from long experience to the flaws of instant panaceas'. Writing about the Thatcher governments, he expresses regret that civil servants 'saw that the way to live with ideology was to appear to share it' so they 'executed ordained error without demur'. They neither retarded nor palliated. They did not resist reforms with a vigour nourished by a proper confidence in the old values of the British constitution.

The Anderson Committee, which began work in November 1942, was a cabinet committee that inquired into the fitness of the machinery of government for the extended role of the state after the war. It was a cabinet committee, which ensured the review lay in the hands of ministers and civil servants rather than outsiders. In effect, the committee carried out a 'survey for practitioners by practitioners' (Lee 1977: 18). Anderson submitted his report to the Prime Minister in May 1945. It was never published (but see Anderson 1946). The following passage captures the tone of the exercise:

> The Ministerial Committee was paralleled by a small official committee of three senior civil servants chosen by Anderson himself for their special qualities of judgement. This collated the views of people who were referred to as 'great and wise men' and gave ministers the benefit of their advice in confidence.
>
> (PRO/T222/71:OM 290/01 cited in
> Chapman and Greenaway 1980: 129)

The following passage similarly captures the tone and scope of the review's conclusions:

> While I emphasise the departmental responsibility of ministers as a necessary and vital principle, I at the same time stress the importance, as a practical matter, of adequate machinery for making a reality of collective responsibility. As a means to this end, I would rely on the institution . . . of a permanent but flexible system of cabinet committees.
>
> (Anderson 1946: 156)

As Lee (1977: 151) concludes, the Anderson Committee was a 'special mixture of ambiguity in definition and ambivalence in discussion'. Turbulent times produced not a radical review, but a return to the eternal verities of the insiders of British government. The committee sought to perpetuate such Tory themes and symbols as the generalist civil servant acting as Platonic guardian of an imagined, national good.

The Liberal tradition

In what is probably the most comprehensive history of the British civil service to date, Geoffrey Fry (1969, 1981, 1985, 1993, 1995) has mounted a sustained critique of the generalist administrative class, taking his inspiration from the Liberal tradition. In his first book, he argued the all-rounder tradition was 'more appropriate to the service of a Regulatory State than that charged with administering the Welfare State and managing the economy'. He proposed the merger of the administrative and executive classes, better management, the more extensive use of specialists, and greater exchange of staff with both the rest of the public sector and crucially the private sector. He was an early and perceptive critic of the Fulton Committee 1968, claiming that its proposals were unimaginative and unrealistic when all about him said the report was radical – and his judgement was the sounder. He is one of the few academic admirers of Margaret Thatcher's administrative revolution and the economic liberalism that underpinned it (Fry 1995). Although he recognises there was never a neat divide in the Conservative Party between statism and economic liberalism (Fry 1995: 11–34), he sees the latter as having been depressed by the twin effects of the Keynesian revolution in economics and public expectations about public expenditure and the role of the state. No matter that Enoch Powell could say that 'a "hatred of bureaucracy" was a common and continuing feature of Conservatism'. Until Margaret Thatcher's election, there was, at least to the more ardent neo-liberals, little difference between, say, Edward Heath and the Fabian reforming agenda – both were technocratic and problem-solving. The Thatcher reforms had twin roots in the economic liberalism of the Institute of Economic Affairs (see Niskanen *et al.* 1973) and a concern with bureaucratic inefficiency (see Chapman 1978). Thus, began the era of corporate management, agencification and, most notably, marketisation. The key question became 'what public services must we keep?' The policies of privatisation and contracting-out redrew the boundary between the public and private sectors. 'Reformism gave way to revolution' as the government sought to create 'the minimalist state'. Some claim the changes wrought were as great as those of the Northcote–Trevelyan era.

Fry's Liberal intellectual lineage is spelt out in his own account of the growth of government (Fry 1979) as well as in his account of the career civil service since 1979 (Fry 1985, 1995). He is a successor to Dicey in his arguments against collectivism. He draws on critics of the generalist, whether they are from the left or the right, and on a long line of liberal thinkers and business leaders who railed against bureaucratic inefficiency.

The dilemma of bureaucratic inefficiency was widely shared, most importantly by Margaret Thatcher (1993: 45–9). Sir John Hoskyns (1983) was one of several business leaders seconded to Whitehall. On leaving, he reflected in writing on his experiences. In doing so, he criticised the failure of government to agree and define objectives. He complained about the small world of Westminster and Whitehall, and especially about a civil service closed to outsiders, lacking in confidence and energy, and serving political masters with whom it does not agree. He challenged the convention of political neutrality as leading to passionless detachment instead of radically minded officials, and to the low quality of much policy work. His main proposal for change is to break the civil service monopoly of top jobs and to appoint business outsiders on seven-year contracts. In a similar vein, Leslie Chapman (1978), a former regional director in the (then) Ministry of Public Building and Works, castigated the civil service for waste, inefficiency and inadequate management. His solutions included a new investigative audit department and better, accountable management. During the 1979 election campaign, he advised Margaret Thatcher on efficiency within the civil service (Metcalfe and Richards 1991: 5–6). Although Chapman was widely tipped to become Thatcher's adviser on efficiency in government, that mantle eventually fell on Sir Derek Rayner, joint managing director of Marks & Spencer.

The recurrent Liberal concerns with business-like efficiency, setting clear policy objectives and recruiting better managers, pervade various official reports of the last two decades. The Efficiency Unit (1988: 3–5) argues, for example, that 'senior management is dominated by people whose skills are in policy formation and who have relatively little experience of managing or working where services are actually delivered'. It strongly believes that 'developments towards more clearly defined and budgeted management are positive and helpful'. It accepts that senior civil servants must respond to ministerial priorities but argues the civil service is 'too big and too diverse to manage as a single entity'. So, it recommends setting up agencies 'to carry out the executive functions of government within a policy and resources framework set by a department'. Senior management will have the freedom to manage. So, there will now be 'a quite different way of conducting the business of government'; a central civil service consisting of core departments servicing ministers and agencies at arm's length with clearly defined responsibilities for service delivery.

The Whig tradition

There is no finer sight in present-day British political science than Peter Hennessy in full flight, pricking the pretensions of the great and the good with his witty stories. His monumental study of *Whitehall* (1989) is full of such delightful vignettes. Hennessy's core thesis is that, for all his admiration of the higher civil servants as individuals, as a class they have let Britain down. We have inherited a nineteenth-century bureaucracy, which, for all its modifications and refinements, remains ill-suited to twentieth-century government, and especially to the task of translating political wishes into practical reality (ibid.: 722). He is even prepared to criticise such eternal verities as the generalist and its apogee, Lord Bridges. Although Hennessy has a 'sneaking admiration' for Bridges' talents, he accuses him of missing a great opportunity to reshape his profession (ibid.: 140). Hennessy calls for the civil service to shake off its Northcote–Trevelyan heritage and to 'unfreeze its labour market' by subjecting all senior posts to open competition.

Hennessy can display an admirable ironic detachment about 'the good chap theory of government', that is, a good chap knows what a good chap is expected to do and will never push things too far. He believes the civil service played a part in Britain's decline, and he is willing to produce a long list of reforms. Nonetheless, part of him is also seduced by a good chap's decency and reasonableness. Hennessy wants to work with the Westminster model of representative democracy, not to transform it. He wants to use 'wherever possible, traditional and familiar institutions for new purposes'. He wants reforms that 'go with the grain of Westminster and Whitehall and their traditions'. Arguably, he seeks only to ameliorate rather than to cure the ills he diagnoses. Hennessy thus exhibits a Whiggish empathy with the evolving British constitution: he dances a dance to the ghosts of time, typifying the Whig tradition's celebration of gradual reform and evolution.

There was a time in the early 1980s when it seemed as if the Conservative maelstrom would sweep aside the traditional civil service. Lord Bancroft (1983: 8), a former Head of the Home Civil Service, reflected on these changes in true Whig style:

> I am reminded that Abbot Bower of Inchcolm, commenting on the legislative enthusiasm of James I of Scotland in the Parliament of 1426, applied what he thought an apt quotation: 'to enact new laws with facility, and to change the old with facility, is marvellous damaging to good order'. He was quoting Aristotle. We are heirs to a long inheritance.

Lord Bancroft, again like a true Whig, contrasts his argument 'for organic institutional change, planned at a digestible rate' with a defence of the status quo. Indeed, he explicitly criticises 'the overnight fever of a new department here and a new agency there, in order to accommodate a transient personal whim or political tantrum' (Bancroft 1983; see also Bancroft 1984; the concluding remarks in Dale 1941: Appendix C; and Sisson 1959: 153). Like Hennessy and other Whigs, he wants gradual evolution through sympathetic reforms that work with, and so perpetuate, all that is salutary in Britain's constitution and political practice.

The White Paper, *The Civil Service: Continuity and Change* (Cm. 2627 1994) reflects on a decade of change, and, in true Whig fashion, seeks to consolidate the changes in the broader heritage and pattern of historical development. The White Paper's summary of the role and functions of the civil service claims the civil service has 'a high reputation, nationally and internationally, for its standards of integrity, impartiality and loyal service to the Government of the day'. It suggests, 'the particular standards that bind the civil service together are integrity, impartiality, objectivity, selection and promotion on merit and accountability through Ministers to Parliament'. Although recent reforms delegated management responsibility to agencies, the government acknowledges 'the need to ensure that the defining principles and standards of the civil service are not relaxed'. The White Paper instances the new, unified Management Code (1993), which lays down the relevant standards, and promises a statutory code or a new Civil Service Act. The proposed reforms are meagre. The White Paper even phrases its proposals for open competition for top jobs cautiously:

> Departments and agencies will always consider advertising openly at these (senior management) levels when a vacancy occurs, and then will use open competition wherever it is necessary and justifiable in the interests of providing a strong field or introducing new blood.

Such words hardly herald an open season on top posts in the civil service. Equally, the White Paper remains silent on measuring and improving the work of permanent secretaries. The White Paper's title is an accurate reflection of its contents.

The Socialist tradition

A summary of the contents page of Kellner and Crowther-Hunt (1980) suffices to illustrate the recurring themes of a Socialist analysis of the civil service. They start with an attack on the cult of the generalist and then blame the power of the civil service for frustrating the reforms of the Fulton Committee. Next they turn their attention to recruiting and training the civil service, denouncing its Oxbridge bias, before finally criticising the power of officials in their dealings with ministers, parliament's ineffective scrutiny of the executive and the cult of secrecy. They see the civil service as 'the biggest pressure group'. And they call for 'the kind of professionalism demanded by the Fulton Committee', that is, a bureaucracy of trained managers and experts.

This Socialist or Fabian lineage in the reform of the civil service is so obvious it hardly needs documenting. It emerges in the Webbs' preference for expertise and efficiency in the bureaucracy (Bevir 2002). It runs through Robson (1937), Greaves (1947), Balogh (1959), 'The Administrators' (1964), Fulton (Cmnd 3638 1968), and Garrett (1972) as well as Kellner and Crowther-Hunt (1980). All of these examples of the Fabian tradition develop a consistent set of themes, notably, the need to end Oxbridge elitism by open recruitment, promoting greater professionalism by wider use of experts, a stress on better planning for economic policy-making, and a call for greater democratic control of the bureaucracy. Thus, the Fulton Committee in its infamous, but hugely enjoyable, first chapter weighs into the civil service because 'the structures and practices of the Service have not kept up with changing tasks'. They add, 'we have found no instance where reform has run ahead too rapidly'. The Fulton Committee considers the effects of the 'philosophy of the amateur' as 'most damaging'. It argues that dividing the service into classes 'prevents the best use of individual talent' since specialist classes 'get neither the full responsibilities and corresponding authority, nor the opportunities, they ought to have'. It suggests that 'too few civil servants are skilled managers', 'there is not enough contact between the Service and the rest of the community', and personnel management is inadequate (Cmnd 3638 1968: 11–13). Yet for some the report did not go far enough!

There may have been disagreement about the best way forward, but academics and practitioners had a shared belief that reform was overdue. As Sir Philip Allen (Permanent Secretary, Home Office, and a member of the Fulton Committee) observed:

> An opportunity had been missed of reforming the Civil Service after the war. We simply went back to the old order of things. The Norman Brooks and co were weighed down with work. The Civil Service was not in a very happy position in the post-war period until the 1962 changes at the Treasury, which meant for the first time people had spare capacity to think about these things. Norman Brook had an impossible task as Head of the Home Civil Service and Secretary of the Cabinet.
>
> (Interview, cited in Fry 1993: 2)

So, Tories, Liberals, Whigs and Socialists take notably different views of civil service reform. As a consequence, they typically adopt different proposals for the future. The Tory tradition inspires a wish to return to the ideals of public service. The Liberal tradition prompts an espousal of marketisation. The Whig tradition encourages a belief in the need for consolidation. And the Socialist tradition has recently become associated with calls for joined-up government. The exponents of each tradition consequently engage in heated debate with one another. The Socialist tradition is critical of New Right reforms. John Garrett, businessman, management consultant, Labour MP and a member of the Fulton Committee's Management Consultancy Group, denies, for example, that government services are inherently inefficient and lauds the civil service's ideal of public service. For the Socialists, there is no shared hatred of bureaucracy.

Although we have not decentred these traditions, we hope it is clear, in turn, that there are also significant differences and debates going on within each. We should also stress that these traditions have changed significantly over time as their exponents have grappled with various dilemmas. For example, New Labour's pragmatic approach to marketisation and its advocacy of networks reflect developments within the Socialist tradition inspired by dilemmas such as state overload. We conclude, therefore, there is no one narrative of civil service reform but a set of overlapping and diverging images.

The shared heritage

Civil service reform appears as a set of overlapping and diverging narratives. In what follows, we want to explore the sources of the overlapping beliefs that characterise many of these narratives. We want to pull back from current political debates to look at the widely shared themes that inform the positions of the disputants. The seven themes are exceptionalism, the generalist, collectivism, gradualism, elitism, local self-government and efficiency.

British exceptionalism

Almost all historians agree that Britain in her state-building period neither possessed nor developed a civil service, as we now understand that term. Indeed, 'a modern civil service was established only in the nineteenth century, when "state-building" . . . had already come to a final stage' (Fischer and Lundgreen 1975: 459; see also Jacoby 1973: 165–6). Fischer and Lundgreen (1975: 466) identify three 'crucial' periods of innovation. From 1080 to 1230, in the Anglo-Norman period, there arose the centralised feudal state governed by the King and his household. From 1470 to 1560, the Yorkist to mid-Tudor period, we witness the establishment of government departments as separate institutions run by great officers of the King who recruited personnel by patronage. And from 1780 to 1870, during the Victorian era, there emerges the modern government machine with departments responsible to parliament, staffed by non-political servants, recruited by open competition. Across continental Western Europe, in contrast, a modern civil service is seen as playing a key role in state-building.[2] Narratives of bureaucratic development in Britain, therefore, present themselves as understanding an exceptional case. Why did a modern civil service not emerge in Britain until the late nineteenth century? Narratives of British history fall back on various inter-related explanations for the late development of a central bureaucracy, including geography, the lack of a large standing army, a uniform institutional structure, social mobility, local self-government and the separation of the state from civil society. We will briefly explain each one.

To begin with geography, Britain is an island and this simple fact encourages historians to think about secure borders. Namier suggests, for example:

The historical development of England is based upon the fact that her frontiers against Europe are drawn by Nature, and cannot be the subject of dispute; that she is a unit sufficiently small for coherent government to have been established and maintained even under very primitive conditions; that since 1066 she has never suffered serious invasion; . . . In short, a great deal of what is peculiar in English history is due to the obvious fact that Great Britain is an island.

> (Namier 1961: 6–7; see also Barker 1944: 30; and Finer 1946: 1290–1)

A second related account of British exceptionalism makes much of England not having had a standing army, so that the monarch had less need for high taxation, direct coercive ability and bureaucratic control. Thus, England

has not known, as France and Prussia have known, the effects of military exigency in producing an organized administration to cope with the task of providing not only recruits and taxes, but also the general system of internal control which a great army needs as its basis.

> (Barker 1944: 29–30)[3]

Instead, England looked outwards to the colonies and developed a powerful navy.

A third factor said to sustain British exceptionalism is England's uniform institutional structure. Thomas (1978: 47–9) argues that England 'achieved national identity at a very early stage'. This unity was a product of the development of common law, the triumph of vernacular English, a nation-wide customs system, a unified coinage, national weights and measures, 'national representative institutions, organised, not as a meeting of "estates", but on a territorial basis', the absence of provincial assemblies, and the growth of London as the capital of the economy and the home of parliament.

British exceptionalism is also said to have its roots in comparatively high social mobility and in the balance of social forces in parliament. Moore (1969: Chapter 1) stresses the role of the enclosure movement and the rise of industry in the violent destruction of the peasantry in England. He also emphasises the importance of political structures such as parliament:

Perhaps the most important legacy of a violent past was the strengthening of parliament at the expense of the king. The fact that Parliament existed meant that there was a flexible institution, which constituted an arena into which the new social elements could be drawn as their demands arose and an institutional mechanism for settling peacefully conflicts of interest among these groups.

(Ibid.: 29)

In this way, landed society absorbed the new social groups into its ranks. In short, the gentry kept the balance of social forces in parliament and by its presence in the county.[4]

A further strand in British exceptionalism is the English gentry's strong habit of local self-government. Thomas (1978: 45 and citations) suggests that 'until the eighteenth century England was notorious for her political instability'. The price of stability was allowing the gentry a large measure of local self-government. By the late eighteenth century England had developed 'a system of remarkably weak central control, remarkably autonomous local bodies, and remarkably small units of local government':

> Thus power in local matters (the power which affected men most immediately in the nineteenth century) rested to an extraordinary degree upon the unreformed corporations, parish vestries and justices of the peace – upon small town merchants, farmers and the gentry and parochial clergy. There were some 25,000 petty instruments of government largely independent of each other and of the central authority in England and Wales . . . This system of local government . . . had come to seem . . . part of the natural and eternal order of things.
>
> (MacDonagh 1977: 12–13)[5]

The separation of the state from civil society in England is the final reason historians give for British exceptionalism. Dyson (1980: 43) in particular argues that Britain paid 'little or no attention . . . to the state as a political concept'. Other historians suggest that it is scarcely surprising, therefore, that Adam Smith's separation of state, economy and civil society – each governed by its own laws – appeared in Britain (Braun 1975: 296). At the end of the eighteenth century, the British polity, we are constantly told, was characterised by a diffusion of authority and the limited power of the state:

> The power of the state . . . was effectively limited by the universally accepted principle that all administration was essentially the mere fulfilment of duties imposed by common or statute law. Such a principle left little or no room for the imposition of direct administrative control by the central government over local authorities . . . The eighteenth century was an era of almost complete autonomy for the local institutions of the country. Their duty was to carry out the law and not to obey the commands of the central executive.
>
> (Keir 1961: 312; see also Chester 1981: 66)

Because our broad concept of governance covers the changing relationship between state and civil society, it is important to stress that the narrative, shared by academics and practitioners alike, is one in which British government, not state, was built on a separation of state and civil society that made Britain an aberrant case. The consequences of this exceptionalism for the British civil service are clear. Parris pungently summarises the point:

> The 'permanent civil service' prior to that time (1780–1850) differed from its modern counterpart in three significant ways. It was not permanent, it was not civil, and it was not a service.
>
> (Parris 1969: 22)

British exceptionalism lies at the heart of all those narratives of British government that stress continuity, the capacity of British institutions to evolve and cope with crises and the practical wisdom of England's constitution.[6]

The generalist civil servant

Ancient Toryism with its 'Gothic administration' (Finer 1952a: 333) may have died hard, but it did buckle and eventually crumple under the continuous onslaught of what might be described as pragmatic collectivism.[7] Almost without exception, narratives of the modern civil service begin with the Northcote–Trevelyan Report (1854). This Report is said to have instituted both constitutional bureaucracy and the generalist civil servant. As noted earlier, a constitutional bureaucracy consists of an unpolitical, permanent civil service, subordinated to party governments, that provides the framework for parliamentary politics and governments.

For many administrative historians, the Northcote–Trevelyan reforms replaced recruitment by patronage with open competition and promotion by merit. They created the neutral, anonymous civil servant. They did not. The subordination of permanent officials to a minister responsible to parliament can be traced to the early years of the nineteenth century (Kitson-Clark 1973: 69; see also Taylor 1927 [1836]: Chapter II; and Finer 1956: 377–96). The convention has its roots in parliament's ascendancy over the Crown (see Chester 1981: 93–4 and 120–2). A rejection of the concept of the state for the notion that sovereignty is vested in the Crown-in-parliament personalises government by conferring powers on the '"over-life-size" role of ministers' (Dyson 1980: 40–1). As a result, public servants are no longer 'closet statesmen' (Kitson-Clark 1973: 87; see also Finer 1952a).

For many administrative historians, the Northcote–Trevelyan Report also created the generalist civil servant. Once again, however, it did not, although it was an important harbinger of this figure. The principles underlying entry to the higher civil service stressed, in Macaulay's words, that men who have been engaged, up to one or two and twenty, in studies which have no immediate connexion with the business of any profession, and of which the effect is merely to open, to invigorate, and to enrich the mind, will generally be found, in the business of every profession, superior to men who have, at eighteen or nineteen, devoted themselves to the special studies of their calling.

(Macaulay quoted in Parris 1969: 287)

Jowett similarly said, a 'knowledge of Latin and Greek is, perhaps, upon the whole, the best test of regular previous education' (Benjamin Jowett, cited in Fry 1969: 70).[8] So, the preference for the all-rounder prevailed over a preference for relevance from the first competitive examinations.

Although the speed of change must not be overstated, the place given to the generalist civil servant reached its height between the two world wars when first Sir Warren Fisher and then Sir Edward Bridges was Head of the Home Civil Service. During the inter-war years there was created that 'blend of intimacy and informality which has characterised the higher echelons of Whitehall' (Chapman and Greenaway 1980: 113; see also Beloff 1975; Chapman 1988 and O'Halpin 1989).

Bridges best captures the theme of the generalist. He appeals to a 'departmental philosophy', which is 'the essence of a civil servant's work' being the 'slow accretion and accumulation of experience'. A departmental philosophy contains knowledge about what worked and what did not work, what aroused public criticism and what did not. It is thus 'the duty of the civil servant to give his minister the fullest benefit of the storehouse of departmental experience; and to let the waves of the practical philosophy wash against ideas put forward by his ministerial masters'. Here Bridges identifies four 'skills or qualities' needed by civil servants. First, they must have 'long experience of a particular field'. Second, there are the specialised skills of the administrator,

> perhaps it should be called an art – the man or woman . . . who will be a good adviser in any field because he or she knows how and where to go to find reliable knowledge, can assess the expertise of others at its true worth, can spot the strong and weak points in any situation at short notice, and can advise on how to handle a complex situation.

Third, the civil servant should possess the qualities associated with the academic world: 'the capacity and determination to study difficult subjects intensively and objectively, with the same disinterested desire to find the truth at all costs'. And, finally, the civil servant must 'combine the capacity for taking a somewhat coldly judicial attitude with the warmer qualities essential to managing large numbers of staff'. (All quotes in this section are from the reprinted version of Bridges 1950: 50, 51, 52 and 55–7.) Hence, administration was, for Bridges, not a science but an art, and recruits would acquire the relevant qualities by learning on the job. What the administrator needed was 'a general understanding of the main principles of organisation' or 'a kind of rarefied common sense'. The departmental secretary was a 'general manager', comparable to 'the conductor of an orchestra'. The analogy was with rowing. You cannot become a good oarsman by studying diagrams and angles. You learn to row 'from the mere fact of rowing in a good crew behind a really good oarsman, for the good style and rhythm proved as catching as measles'. (The quotes in this section are from Bridges 1956: 6, 14 and 23.)

The Fulton Committee (1968) was to rant famously about this cult of the amateur with its subordination of the specialist to the generalist (see also Macleod 1988). Similarly, Thomas Balogh, a special economic adviser to Harold Wilson, complained that the Treasury, and the civil service, lacked a proper professionalism, being characterised by a pervasive 'dilettantism' (Balogh 1959). Some critics, including Balogh, have even blamed Britain's relative decline on the weaknesses of a higher civil service skilled in policy advice but with little skill in either planning or working with industry (see Chapman 1963; and for a survey of the argument see Gamble 1994). The image of the generalist pervades many narratives about the British civil service, both narratives that laud the image, as did Bridges, and narratives that berate it, as did the Fulton Committee.

Collectivism

Dicey's (1914: 62–9) defence of individualism against collectivism established the dominant terms for understanding the administrative revolution of the nineteenth century for at least a generation. He divided the nineteenty century into three periods. The period from 1800 to 1830 was, he argued, an era of legislative quiescence or an era of old Toryism. Even so, it saw the reports of various commissions into public accounts that sought to abolish sinecures, increase efficiency and introduce public servants paid for out of funds voted by parliament. Perhaps more important, the foundations for nineteenth-century reform were laid with the emergence of the cabinet, Treasury control and the growing separation of politics and administration. The period from 1825 to 1870 was typified by the Benthamite spirit of inquiry and the Northcote–Trevelyan Report, which sought to improve the quality of civil service personnel by abolishing patronage and introducing entry by open competition and promotion by merit. Dicey called the period from 1865 to 1900 the era of collectivism. It witnessed both the extension of open competition – starting with the 1870 Order in Council – and the unification of the service.

There are several weaknesses in Dicey's interpretation of nineteenth-century administrative history. For a start, from 1865 to 1900 may perhaps more accurately be seen as 'a period of consolidation and co-ordination'

(Cohen 1965: 21; MacLeod 1988: 9; Drewry and Butcher 1991: 34–7). Administrative growth followed no grand plan but rather trod a wary path between the ideal of *laissez-faire* and a more pragmatic collectivism. In addition, Dicey provoked a spirited debate about the nature and influence of Bentham's ideas. While MacDonagh rejects both the influence of Benthamite ideas on legislation in the period from 1830 to 1870 and Dicey's conclusion of increased central control between 1865 and 1900, Hart (1965: 39–61) criticises MacDonagh for generalising from the single case study of the control of emigration as well as for identifying Benthamism with *laissez-faire*. Parris too criticises the identification of Benthamism with *laissez-faire*, emphasising that Bentham's commitment to the principle of utility did not preclude an extension of state intervention, requiring only that the merits of any government action be judged by its results. So, there is no necessary contradiction between Benthamite ideas and intervention. As Alan Ryan (1972: 61) argues, 'there is no such thing as *the* utilitarian view of bureaucracy, either in the advocacy of more rather than less government or in pressing the claims of expertise against those of public opinion – and vice versa'.

Given such disagreements, the temptation must be to agree with Thomas that 'the influence of Benthamism or Evangelicalism upon the middle classes remains uncertain' (Thomas 1978: 77). Nonetheless, we surely cannot ignore the influence of Dicey on that interpretation of British government during the nineteenth century that sees it as the gradual triumph of collectivism (Greenleaf 1983a and b, 1987). Dicey helped to establish the idea of a pragmatic collectivism as a powerful theme found in many narratives of administrative history and civil service reform.

Throughout the twentieth century, there have been several attempts to control and promote or to roll back the collectivism that Dicey helped to place so squarely on the administrative agenda. While we already have explored some of the narratives on rolling back the state, as typified by Thatcherism, there were many earlier clarion calls for an administrative revolution and managerial rationalism (Fry 1981). As Harris (1990: 86) observes, planning came in many guises and from many sources, but all shared the belief that the market mechanism could not rescue British industry. For example, Sidney Webb's ill-judged praise of the Soviet Union occurred because he believed that planned production for community consumption would rationalise the economy for the social good (Bevir 2002). It would abolish mass unemployment, with the devastating alternation of commercial booms and slumps. Even the Conservative government of Macmillan adopted an indicative style of planning embodied in the National Economic Development Council (NEDC) on which government, trade unions and employers sat down to discuss the state of the British economy. This tripartism characterised economic policy-making for much of the 1960s and 1970s and was more about information, advice and persuasion than planning (Lowe 1999: Chapters 4 and 5; Lowe and

Rollings 2000). Wilson's National Plan was an abortive experiment but his government too sought to solve economic problems through institutional reform of the civil service, local government and various welfare state services (Cronin 2001). Heath too continued this approach (Cmnd 4506 1970), creating giant central departments and introducing an intimidating battery of acronyms such as PAR (Programme Analysis and Review) and CPRS (Central Policy Review Staff). For Harris (1990: 111), all these changes can be summed up as 'the final triumph of managerial rationality' of which the planning experiments were but one variant.

Gradualism

A Tory view of the nineteenth century sees the adaptability and responsiveness of government as taking place without effort. In the words of Judith Hart, 'all will turn out for the best if we just drift in an Oakeshottian boat' (Hart 1965: 39). Oliver MacDonagh's model of administrative change exemplifies this Tory interpretation. He not only draws attention to various socio-economic factors but also stresses the impact of the internal dynamics of government, especially the civil service, in fostering administrative growth (MacDonagh 1973 [1958], 1961, 1977). MacDonagh argues that the 'peculiar concatenation of circumstances' of the nineteenth century provided 'very powerful impulses' for change. These circumstances included the social problems created by industrialisation and urbanisation, developments in technical and scientific knowledge which provided solutions to these problems, the widespread influence of humanitarian sentiments and intense public pressure to deal with the problems, and the recognition that it was the responsibility of government to introduce legislation to deal with them (MacDonagh 1973: 12–13). The combination of these circumstances triggered a recurrent legislative–administrative process, termed a 'model' by MacDonagh. The process begins with the exposure of an intolerable social evil, which generates public pressure for legislation. Although the affected interests dilute the legislation as it is enacted and enforced, a precedent for intervention is established. The legislation proves to be ineffective, so executive officers are appointed to remedy the defects. The executive officers then demand both fresh legislation and a superintending central body. Now the perceived solution no longer lies in legislation or increasing numbers of staff, but in growing expertise and closing legislative loopholes by continuous review and experiment. The executive officers demand and obtain broad administrative discretion, which, allied to systematic inquiry, leads to a dynamic approach to administration and increased intervention.

Several historians have challenged the accuracy of MacDonagh's model. Parris (1973: 43–52) concludes from a study of ten branches of administration, not including the emigration service, that 'not one has been found where there is even a reasonable degree of fit between model and reality'. Dunkley challenges MacDonagh's view that the emigration service developed through its own internal momentum, claiming that 'development was more fortuitous than logical, self-generating, or inevitable' (Dunkley 1980: 379). Hart (1965: 49–50) suggests that MacDonagh's claim that ' "intolerability" was the master card' in stimulating action against social evils is tautologous. There was 'no agreement' about what was 'intolerable' and the thesis 'is so elastic that it can never be proved false'.

MacDonagh sees nineteenth-century administration as 'creative and self-generating'; as an 'independent historical process in operation' (MacDonagh 1973: 7, 20 and 355; see also MacDonagh 1961: 16, 346–7 and 348). Even if his model has proved controversial, a related theme of gradualism pervades many narratives in British administrative history. Hart (1965: 59–61), for example, criticises his argument not because of its gradualism but because it underplays human agency – 'there were men behind the abstractions'.

Elitism

Historians have taken diverse positions on the class interests served by the Northcote–Trevelyan reforms. Kingsley (1944: 60ff.) portrays them as a product of pressure from a rising, educated middle class in search of jobs.[9] Hart (1972: 63–81) dismisses this claim, showing there was no shortage of jobs. MacDonagh (1977: 202) argues civil service reform 'was promoted by the middle class', but with the objective of a 'further loosening of the aristocratic hold on government' (see also MacDonagh 1973: 21). Mueller (1984: Chapters 3 and 5), in contrast, argues the report sought to protect both the aristocracy and the gentry. Gowan similarly observes (1987: 19–20) the gentry were a part of the middle class that 'had long mingled with the aristocracy, . . . had places . . . as poor scholars at the top public schools and Oxbridge, . . . entered the church, the bar and the army'. So, he dismisses as 'preposterous' MacDonagh's claim that the reforms sought to overthrow the old order.

These historical disagreements about the class interests served by the reforms obscure a broad agreement about their elitism. Almost all historians portray the reforms as little more than a shift of power within an elite composed of aristocracy, gentry and the upper levels of the middle classes. As Gladstone said at the time:

> I do not hesitate to say that one of the great recommendations of the changes in my eyes would be its tendency to strengthen and multiply the ties between the higher classes and the possession of administrative power. . . . I have a strong impression that the aristocracy of this country are even superior in natural gifts, on the average, to the mass; but it is plain that with their acquired advantages, their *insensible*

education, irrespective of book-learning, they have an immense superiority. This applies in its degrees to all those who may be called gentlemen by birth and training; and it must be remembered that an essential part of any such plan as is now under discussion is the separation of *work*, wherever it can be made, into mechanical and intellectual, a separation which will open to the highly educated class a career and give them a command over all the higher parts of the civil service, which up to this time they have never enjoyed.

(W.W. Gladstone to Lord John Russell, January 1853,
reproduced in Cromwell 1977: 139–40, emphasis in original)

While historians might debate the extent to which the administrative reforms of the nineteenth century were technocratic, concerned with efficiency, and beneficial to the middle class at the expense of the aristocracy, they all understand them as keeping a strongly elitist favour. As MacDonagh concedes in his reassessment of the Northcote–Trevelyan Report:

there is a good reason to suspect that nothing less was aimed at than the exclusive preservation of the vital sphere of civil administration for the educated upper and upper middle-classes, while there was still time to beat the oncoming democracy to the gun.

(MacDonagh 1977: 206; see also Gowan 1987: 33;
Mueller 1984: Chapter 5)

The reforms sought not only to preserve the privileges of the gentry, but also to forge a link between the higher civil service and the humanities provided at Oxbridge. They protected an exclusive elite in the, initially incipient, guise of the generalist civil servant. We should not be surprised, therefore, that issues about recruiting to the higher civil service, the privileged position of Oxbridge, and the dominance of the humanities play a large part in present-day debates about reform.

Local self-government

If historians take diverse positions on the nineteenth-century administrative revolution, there is an awesome consensus about local self-government. Mackenzie (1961: 5) observes that 'in some sense or other local self-government is now part of the English constitution', although nothing was heard of this tradition before 1832. Its classical expression can be found in Joshua Toulmin Smith's views, which were a conservative reaction to the pragmatic collectivism of the nineteenth century:

Centralisation is the foul dragon that is ever gnawing at the root of Yggdrasil, the great World-tree of freedom; Local self-government is the true Urda's spring, whose pure waters alone keep freshened forever, the strength and growth of Yggdrasil.

(Smith 1849)

But in less florid terms, local self-government occupied a prominent position in the Whig and Liberal pantheons. For John Stuart Mill (1910: 346), it was also a bulwark against centralisation and bureaucratisation. 'It is,' he said, 'but a small portion of the public business of a country which can be well done, or safely attempted, by the central authorities.'[10] Freedom exercised locally strengthens freedoms in the larger community, promoting a democratic climate, the notion of give-and-take, and appreciation for the viewpoints of others. It also performs some specific tasks: it is a training ground for politicians; it provides an education in citizenship for the populace; and it is a mechanism for holding government to account. This Whig view persists to this day and is widely shared among both academics and elite actors. Thus:

> Local representative institutions are designed to meet the fundamental requirements of participation, discussion and education. They do provide, on the largest scale, an opportunity for the citizen to share in public discussions and administration, they do provide the machinery of discussion and vote to elicit his [sic] consent, they do provide in the only possible way for the political education of the people.
>
> (Wilson 1948: 21)[11]

However, the Second World War had some important effects on the way elite actors perceived local government. 'For the first time in many centuries, local authorities ceased to be the main intermediaries of power between citizen and the state' (Harris 1990: 90). Although accepted as the main agents for delivering the welfare state, local self-government was seen through increasingly jaundiced eyes. As Anthony Crosland (former Labour Secretary of State for Education) said:

> All governments and Ministers are a bit schizophrenic about their relationship with local authorities. On the one hand they genuinely believe the ringing phrases they use about how local government should have more power and freedom. . . . On the other hand a Labour government hates it when Tory councils pursue education or housing policies of which it disapproves and exactly the same is true of a Tory government with Labour councils.
>
> (Cited in Boyle *et al.* 1971: 171)

Local government was no longer seen as a bulwark of the constitution. For the New Right, local government was the home of producer interests. Conflict between the Thatcher government and local authorities was described as 'a squalid and politically corrupt process' (Jack Straw, Labour opposition front bench spokesperson, *Hansard*, 25 February 1985). But changing views about local government were not the prerogative of the New Right. The watershed event is the reorganisation of local government in 1974. It was initiated by Labour, enacted by the Conservatives and implemented by Labour and so cannot be seen as a partisan reform. Such notions as community, local identity and historic roots were supplanted by the view that local government was about the efficient delivery of services. Even under New Labour the debate remains mainly about the best way of delivering services.

If ideas about local self-government have been replaced by ideas about functional efficiency, there is a counterweight to this late twentieth-century orthodoxy in devolution to Scotland and Wales. As one senior civil servant remarked, 'we have a knack of taking decisions under anaesthetic, and it hasn't worn off yet'; a cute way of noting that devolution stands for dramatic change. His next, if more prosaic, observation that 'the first meeting of the Joint Ministerial Committee [to co-ordinate the devolved administrations] was an extraordinary constitutional event which nobody remarked on' reinforces the observation that devolution may come to be an informing principle of the British constitution. Indeed, it may come to occupy the place previously reserved for local self-government.

Efficiency

Efficiency is not a neutral term. It is invariably linked with many other political values. So, the search for efficiency is a theme found in narratives that equate efficiency with scientific expertise as well as those that condemn bureaucracy as inefficient when compared with markets and private sector styles of management.

The leading Fabian, Sidney Webb, identified socialism with the efficient organisation of society conceived as co-operative and co-ordinated organisation with state activity (Bevir 2002). The Fabians, he implied, should act as positivist experts, providing information and policies to diverse politicians. Although Webb believed in liberal democracy, he suspected that it would bring a welcome move away from political conflict towards a rule by an administrative and managerial elite. He had a strong faith in experts as a source of neutral compelling advice, although he always restricted their role to providing advice and implementing policies. Decision-making had to remain the provenance of elected representatives. Contemporaries such as Graham Wallas (Qualter 1980: 99 and 162), and inter-war Fabians such as Greaves (1947), shared Webb's strong faith in a science of public administration.

Thomas (1978: 18 and 53) recognises this concern with efficiency in the thought of the Webbs and others. However, she suggests the British approach to public administration was less concerned with economic efficiency than with the problem of red tape, or with the means becoming more important than the end.[12] As she shows, Muir (1910) included the sins of red tape, mystery mongering and gentlemanly malingering as examples of bureaucratic inefficiency. In a similar vein, Sir Stephen Demetriadi launched an energetic attack on the civil service for trying to meet the 'extraordinary demands (of war) with ordinary machinery rotating at ordinary speed'. He was the John Hoskyns of his day, that is, a businessman who became a temporary civil servant, in his case, working in the Ministry of Pensions. On leaving the civil service, he called for the introduction of business methods in government departments (Demetriadi 1921; see also Bunbury 1928). Yet, of course, these complaints by Muir, Demetriadi and others only concerned the role of bureaucracy in ensuring efficiency. They did not question the validity or extent of the quest for efficiency. It is impossible adequately to tell the story of civil service reform in the 1980s and 1990s without referring to a similar concern to promote efficiency, albeit through internal management and importing business skills.

Common themes

Aspects of our seven themes permeate all four of the dominant traditions. The Tory tradition clearly draws on the ideas of exceptionalism, the generalist, elitism and local self-government. The Liberal tradition emphasises efficiency and its opposition to collectivism. It even shares hostility to elitism and to the generalist with the Socialist tradition. The Whig tradition emphasises English exceptionalism and gradualism, while encompassing the managerial rationalism associated with collectivism and the search for efficiency. The Socialist tradition stresses collectivism and the need for reform though not necessarily gradualism. The antipathy to elitism, especially Oxbridge elitism, recently got a public airing from the Blair government. Clearly, these four traditions differ markedly over, for example, the value of the generalist tradition, the case for bureaucracy and the extent and desirability of change. Equally, however, they share a set of overlapping themes, notably the beliefs in exceptionalism and efficiency. For example, former Conservative Prime Minister Edward Heath (1998: 314–17; and Cmnd 4506 1970) argues the case for strategic management and the use of business methods in a way that is barely distinguishable from the Fulton Committee and the Fabians. The links between the traditions, roots and reforms are illustrated in Table 8.2. We must stress one point about this table. All traditions draw on all roots to differing degrees. The table is only a summary device that illustrates the strongest, not exclusive, links.

The historical links between yesterday and today can be obvious. The shift from Sidney Webb's belief in expertise to Tony Blair's call for evidence-based policy-making, for example, is relatively small. Similarly, the Whig tradition lives on in the pronouncements of too many civil

Table 8.2 The roots of reform: summary

Traditions	Roots	Reforms
Tory	Exceptionalism Generalist Elitism Local self-government	Restore local self-government
Liberal	Efficiency Anti-collectivism Anti-elitism Managers not generalists	Marketise public services
Whig	Exceptionalism Gradualism Generalists as managers Efficiency	Return to the organic constitution
Socialist	Collectivism Anti-elitism Anti-generalist Reform, not gradualism	Partnerships and joined-up government

servants and official reports to need detailed comment here. The lineage of the Tory narrative, in contrast, can seem rather more obscure. For Fry (1995: 6), for example, the classical High Tory account of nineteenth-century British government is that of Sir Lewis Namier, and yet Chapman never refers to his work. Yet the presence of a tradition does not depend on citing shared authorities or even an explicit list of core beliefs or a specific lineage. Beliefs and their antecedents can be taken for granted – they can be the unspoken assumptions on which authors build their narratives. The economic liberal strand within the Conservative Party was swamped for much of the post-war period. Nonetheless, it lived on in the speeches of Enoch Powell (Shepherd 1996: 122–4) and the pamphlets of the One Nation Group (Powell and Maude 1954; and more generally Lowe 1999).

We can point to the longevity of these four traditions while also allowing that they have changed in response to dilemmas. Earlier, for instance, we showed how the Liberal and Socialist traditions had responded to the dilemmas of inflation and state overload. The case of civil service reform is a specific part of this more general process. The story of the Tory traditions accommodation to collectivism has been told often (Beer 1965; Greenleaf 1983a and b). Whether Toryism has yet reached an accommodation with Thatcherism's attack on so many of the ideas it venerated, including local self-government, remains unclear. Just as Butskellism and tripartism relegated the liberal strand of the Conservative Party to the sidelines in the 1950s and 1960s, so today the High Tory view of British government has been submerged by the neo-liberal one. Eloquent voices such as Ian

Gilmour and Roger Scruton have been left to express their High Tory protests from the sidelines of the Conservative Party at the start of the twenty-first century.

Thatcherism responded to the dilemmas of inflation and state overload by rejecting government intervention and tripartism but keeping an equally firm commitment to managerial rationality – planning became strategic policy-making, targets became clear objectives and performance measures. The Thatcher reforms challenged the Socialist belief in bureaucracy while endorsing its belief in greater efficiency. Arguably the New Right has a vested interest in state failure. New Labour's programme of reform distinctively assumes that it is possible to make the state work. As we saw earlier, New Labour constructed the dilemma of state-overload differently from the New Right. It rejected not only Old Labour's top-down, command-style bureaucracy based on centralised rules but also the New Right's commitment to rolling back the state by using markets. New Labour's reforms seek to transform the state into an enabling partner by promoting the idea of networks of institutions and individuals acting in partnership and held together by relations of trust.

Conclusion

To understand governance, we must recognise that people socialised in different traditions with varying beliefs construct markedly different meanings of the term. In this chapter we have taken one specific aspect of governance, civil service reform, and tried to identify not only present-day views on the subject but also the historical roots of those ideas. We have identified four competing but overlapping traditions. We have also shown that although no one tradition dominated, academics, practitioners and official reports share a set of themes that occur across diverse traditions. For example, the era from 1964 to 1976 was one of managerial rationalism permeated with Fabian ideas whereas neo-liberal ideas characterised the 1980s. We have shown that the shared themes have their roots in various accounts of the nineteenth-century administrative revolution, although each tradition has its own distinctive mix of ideas because of the way it understands and evaluates the details of these themes. We conclude that analysing the way traditions change is essential to understanding present-day notions of governance whether defined as civil service reform, or as public sector reform, or as networks or as the boundary between state and civil society. However, although we have peppered our account with quotes from practitioners and official reports, it remains a broad canvas. Indeed, as in our account of various narratives of Thatcherism, we are in danger of taking an essentialist view of the relevant traditions. In the next chapter, therefore, we want both to explore recent changes in the beliefs of civil servants and to decentre the story of governance further. We do so through the ethnographic technique of interviews with permanent secretaries.

Notes

1 To invoke a historical mode of inquiry is not to postulate a single historical method. Rather, we are pointing to the need to explain current beliefs and actions by locating them against the background of the past. There are, of course, many different views of how this might best be done. For an extended defence of our view, conducted in debate with some of the alternatives, see Bevir 1999a.

2 Among many see Alford and Friedland 1985: 185–98; Barker 1944: Chapter 1; H. Finer 1946: 1290; S. Finer 1980; Heady 1984: 128–33; Kamenka 1989: 89; Nash 1969; Page 1990; Rueschemeyer and Evans 1985; Skocpol 1979, 1985; and Tilly 1975b.

3 See also H. Finer 1946: 1290; S. Finer 1975b: 109–24; Namier 1961: 6–7.

4 See: H. Finer 1946: 1290; and also Anderson 1974; Barker 1944: 30; Dowse and Hughes 1986: Chapter 5; Fischer and Lundgreen 1975: 464–5; Moore 1969: Chapter 1.

5 See also Barker 1944: 33; Chester 1981: Part I; Finer 1946: 1290 and 1292; Fischer and Lundgreen 1975: 558–9; Greenleaf 1987: Chapter 2; Thomas 1978: 67–8 and 77; and Sidney and Beatrice Webb 1963: 309.

6 There was also a vigorous debate within English Marxism about the 'peculiarities' of the English. See Anderson 1992 [1964]; Nairn 1981 [1977]; Thompson 1978 [1965]. For a social democratic 'take' on the debate see Hutton 1996; and Marquand 1988.

7 Relevant surveys of this revolution include: Chapman and Greenaway 1980; Chester 1981; Cohen 1965; MacDonagh 1977; Parris 1969; Smellie 1950. Useful collections of articles include: Cromwell 1977; Stansky 1973; and Sutherland 1972. Useful bibliographies are: Cromwell 1966 and Sutherland 1970.

8 At the time, Jowett was Fellow and Tutor at Balliol College, Oxford, and, along with Macauley, was instrumental in persuading Trevelyan and Northcote to recommend competitive examinations for entry to the civil service. His proposals for the examinations were appended to the report and do include 'relevant' subjects.

9 For a summary of the Northcote–Trevelyan Report see Chapman and Greenaway 1980: 36–53; and Cm. 3638 1968, Committee on the Civil Service (Fulton), Appendix 3: 108–31. For summaries of nineteenth-century views on the Report see Rhodes 1973; and Hughes 1949.

10 At one time local government was thought to have become a 'political anachronism' with the demise of the Whigs around 1900 (Blaas 1978). More recently, however, Whiggish themes, including local government, have been traced in later Liberal and Socialist thought (Burrow 1981, 1988; Stapleton 1991). Perhaps the moral is that we should not reify traditions as if they have discrete and fixed positions and never interact or impact upon each other's trajectories.

11 See Sharpe 1981; Smith 1969; and Whalen 1969.

12 Thomas (1978: Chapter 5) also discusses the power of the official, focusing on Lord Hewart's (1929) claim that delegated legislation gave the executive in general and civil servants in particular too much power.

9 The meaning of governance

To understand British governance, we need to unpack the dominant traditions and to explore the ways these traditions change in response to dilemmas. In the previous chapter, we unpacked the main traditions through which the civil service enacts governance. In this chapter, we examine the changing beliefs of civil servants through an ethnographic study of the permanent secretaries. We explore how the dilemmas posed by public sector reform have impacted on the broad set of themes we described in the last chapter – exceptionalism, the generalist, collectivism, gradualism, elitism, local self-government and efficiency. We argue the civil servants both construct and respond to dilemmas such as the demand for efficient management by drawing on these themes. More particularly, we argue the civil servants domesticate the successive waves of governance by reading them in terms of their traditional concerns with the generalist and efficiency. Although the beliefs and practices of civil servants have changed, the changes have been refracted through familiar prisms.

This chapter also serves a methodological role in our overall argument. So far, we have concentrated on providing an aggregate analysis of British political traditions. One of the dangers of this focus is that we neglect the differences in the beliefs of the individuals lumped together in a tradition. The theory informing our interpretive approach stresses individual agency. Our approach calls for a decentred analysis; that is, we need to highlight the diversity of a tradition by unpacking the actual and contingent beliefs and actions of its individual adherents. So in this chapter we provide 'thick descriptions' of the world of two permanent secretaries by means of an ethnographic form of inquiry. Ethnographers reconstruct the meanings of social actors by recovering other people's stories from practices, actions, texts, interviews and speeches (see, for example, Geertz 1973: Chapter 1; Taylor 1971: 32–3). Thus we follow Hammersley and Atkinson (1983: 2) in making the basic claim for the ethnographic method that 'it captures the meaning of everyday human activities' and encourages the researcher to get out there and see what actors are thinking and doing. It generates descriptive accounts valuable in their own right (ibid.: 237). It is exploratory – 'unstructured soaking' (Fenno 1990: 57) – and encourages fresh lines of thought. Ethnography or non-participant observation encompasses many ways of collecting qualitative data about beliefs and actions – for example, diary analysis, 'shadowing', elite interviewing, participant accounts.[1] This chapter is based on lengthy semi-structured elite interviews.[2] It is worth stressing that our approach differs from conventional accounts of the civil service in two ways. First, there is a noteworthy literature solely on the permanent secretaries that assumes we can read off the beliefs of top civil servants from their institutional position and socio-economic background (see, for example, Barberis 1996, which also contains a comprehensive bibliography; Harris and Garcia 1966; Richards 1997; Theakston and Fry 1989; Theakston 1999, 2000). Clearly we do not think that beliefs can be so determined. Rather, we would urge political scientists to study the texts – the writings, lectures, interview transcripts and actions – of civil servants to identify their beliefs. Second, conventional accounts offer the reader the author's analysis substantiated by short quotes from civil servants selected to support the argument (see, for example, Garrett 1972; Kellner and Crowther-Hunt 1980).[3]

Who are the permanent secretaries?

The Thatcher, Major and Blair governments all sought to improve the managerial efficiency of the service and to make recruitment more open and competitive. Change has been afoot for two decades. The number of civil servants fell dramatically. Most civil servants now work in agencies. Management is the order of the day. Nonetheless, statistically the top civil servant remains instantly recognisable (see Table 9.1). In Theakston's (2000) terms the permanent secretaries are civil service 'lifers'. They are

Table 9.1 Permanent secretaries, 1970–98

	1970	*1980*	*1990*	*1998*
Oxbridge	15 88.2%	14 66.6%	15 75.0%	13 65.0%
Average age	56.2	56.4	55.5	53.9
Average prior Whitehall service	29.6 years	30.8 years	31.5 years	29.4 years
Private Office experience	10 58.8%	16 76.2%	19 95.0%	15 75.0%
Treasury experience	8 47.1%	7 33.3%	8 40.0%	9 45.0%
Cabinet Office (and related units)	6 35.3%	10 47.6%	10 50.0%	8 40.0%
Stint in No. 10 Office	0	4 19.0%	5 25.0%	2 10.0%
Total	17	21	20	20

white, over 50, with an Oxbridge degree in the humanities. They have worked in the civil service for 25 to 30 years, serving in a central as well as a functional ministry; and they will retire at 60 after 5 to 10 years in the top job. Also, of course, they are male – between 1970 and 1998 there were only five female permanent secretaries with two in post.

What do permanent secretaries do?

There are many answers to the question of what top civil servants do. Yet another run through the literature would be tedious for all concerned, so we provide a brief survey of academic accounts of how their job changed in the 1980s and 1990s. This survey provides a context against which we can assess how the civil servants themselves see the changes. It does so, moreover, by relating these changes to the themes of efficiency and the generalist discussed earlier.

Permanent secretaries sit at the top of a hierarchy where three main tasks come together: political advice to ministers, management of their departments and diplomacy or managing external relations. It is a singular combination. Warren Fisher or Edward Bridges would instantly recognise the job's ingredients – they define the generalist. It is arguable whether, and by how much, the balance between these tasks has changed and continues to change because of the search for efficiency.

Advising

Advising the minister cannot be reduced to giving policy advice. Indisputably some permanent secretaries bring cerebral, analytical qualities to policy-making in their department. But both minister and permanent secretary live in a complex political environment, and the permanent secretary must help the minister to manage that environment. Thus, advice is often a matter of support and fire-fighting, not policy, and at times it can extend to the grey area of party politics. Ministers now draw on several sources of policy advice, including political advisers, think tanks and consultants. The civil service in general no longer has a monopoly. Even inside the civil service, advice can come from any member of the senior civil service with the right expertise, not just the permanent secretary (Cm. 2627 1994: 38), who may not even see the advice going to the minister. As Barberis (1996: 42) concludes, the permanent secretaries are now 'policy managers rather than makers or originators'.

Managing

In the 1980s permanent secretaries picked up the technical skills needed to cope with management reforms. Both Conservative and Labour governments want the department to implement their policies effectively. The permanent secretary must get on with the job of ensuring the department 'delivers', a phrase which covers both organising the department and managing its human resources. However, this does not mean operational management, for the day-to-day running of the department is increasingly and extensively delegated. The focus is strategic management often to meet the challenge of fragmentation. Many departments are large, with one or more agencies. There is no simple hierarchy. The permanent secretary is more like the Chair of the Board – a facilitator and a co-ordinator – who seeks to impose some coherence on a complex organisation with many policies. Views differ on the extent to which permanent secretaries have acquired more than a veneer of the new managerialism. One observer maintains that departments are 'still managed by people who got there because of their policy skills rather than their management skills' (Watson 1992: 27). Conversely, Sir Richard Wilson (1998), looking back, observes that 'twenty years ago senior civil servants only had to take an interest in legislation, policy advice and bonding with ministers' but 'wave after wave of initiatives battered Permanent Secretaries until . . . we found ways of . . . bringing our management up to date'.

Diplomacy

Diplomacy, or external representation as it is sometimes called, is used by academics and civil servants alike to cover all the external relations of the department, whether with other central departments, other public agencies (including local authorities), parliament, the media or the EU. Permanent secretaries are the public figureheads of their departments. As Sir Douglas Wass observed, 'finesse and diplomacy are an essential ingredient in public service' (Hennessy 1989: 150). Similarly, Part (1990: 66 and 69) commenting on the Department of Education's negotiations with local education authorities, recalled, 'we felt that there must be more in common between the Home Civil Service and the Diplomatic Service than we had at first supposed'. Departments have always had to square policies with the Treasury and other affected departments and agencies, including No. 10. There have been legendary turf wars between departments when diplomacy failed, while the search by No. 10 to strengthen 'central capability' has been never-ending. All departments sit in the centre of a veritable spider's web of links.

In providing these brief descriptions of the permanent secretary's main tasks, we make their work seem more orderly than is the case. It is hard to communicate the pressures of handling crises and the speed with which tasks come and go. Time is of the essence and the attention span is short. The main activity is talking, reacting to whatever just landed on the desk, whoever entered the room or rang. Equally, although it is commonplace to note the personalisation of appointments and the preference for can-do civil servants who are policy managers not policy-makers, for example, not all permanent secretaries display the fashionable managerial traits. For all their commonality of background, they remain a mixed breed.

Traditions and dilemmas

Ethnographic techniques enable us to recover beliefs and actions. Tradition and dilemma provide the conceptual tools with which to explain the beliefs and actions we thus recover. So, to explain the changing beliefs of the permanent secretaries, we need to understand how the traditions of the civil service shaped their responses to the changes in their world. In Chapter 8 we identified several themes about the civil service common to British governmental traditions. Two of these themes are particularly relevant now; namely, those of the generalist and of efficiency. The generalist theme may be, as Chapman and O'Toole (1995) believe, a national treasure to be preserved at all costs, but it is a modern invention. Also, like any practice, it is not fixed in stone. It is modified as it is handed down from generation to generation and in response to the dilemmas that confront the civil servants of the day. So, in the 1980s and the 1990s, civil servants had to resolve the dilemmas 'the new public management' posed for the tradition of the generalist. They had to adapt their traditions to the demand for greater efficiency and for a reduced role for the state. In the process, however, their beliefs inevitably shaped the reforms.

In saying that the themes of the generalist and of efficiency have deep roots, we do not want to suggest that the beliefs of different eras are identical. The Conservative belief that markets will deliver efficient services is clearly a distinctive turn. Similarly, New Labour's advocacy of joined-up government, with its emphasis on networks and trust, is distinctive. These shifts have an impact on higher civil servants. Their tasks remain a mix of policy, management and diplomacy, but the content of each and the balance between them shifts. Continuities arise in part because civil servants construct the changes from within traditions. Top civil servants do not resist change. After all it is deeply ingrained in most civil servants that, after a dialogue, they will do what ministers say. Besides, there would be no point in resisting familiar reforms already being introduced in some departments. To higher civil servants, the reforms represent not a transformation of their role, but attempts to contain costs and spending and to adjust the balance between policy, management and diplomacy. In the extracts that follow we show how the permanent secretaries understood the reforms; how new ideas were incorporated into, and adapted by, existing traditions.

The interviews

Background and recruitment

Sir Robin Mountfield

> I'm a scouser born and bred. My father left school at 16, became an apprentice clerk in the Mersey Docks and Harbour Board and ended up as its General Manager.

The school [Merchant Taylors' Crosby], although it sounds like a public school, was a direct grant school. Like about 85 per cent of the pupils, I was on an 11+ local authority scholarship. Historically, it was the local grammar school for the poor children of the neighbourhood and I feel it reneged on its history by going independent in the 1970s.

Until I was 16 I did not want to go to university. It was quite a late decision to have a crack at university. [I won] an open scholarship [to Magdalen, Oxford]. There was the entrance exam and Alan Taylor interviewed me, among others, and terrified me stiff. Most of us read history. It's magical, but as an institution I am deeply sceptical of it, of the grip it has on British society. All three of my kids went there from their comprehensive school and I'm proud of that but they all came away with the same thing, a love of the place and a loathing of the institution. I didn't get a first, I should have done but I didn't. I worked too scrupulously hard. I worked myself into a rut. I think that's the truth. I got a competent 2:1.

By that time I had acquired a rather toffee-nosed view that I wanted to go into public service in some sense. I applied for a job at the Bank of England, which I recollect offered me £573 a year. I was interviewed by Sir Anthony Abell, a former Indian civil servant who had been Private Secretary to the Viceroy. Anyway I turned that down in favour of a job in the civil service, which paid £726. For that I was interviewed by his brother Sir George Abell, a former Governor of Sarawak.

The selection procedure was what was called Method Two, the two-day interview method, very much the same as the present-day selection board procedure. I've quite a lot of respect for it. It's still a respectable method. If anything it's too thorough by modern standards. It's too much effort into making sure we don't take any square pegs in. I went to the Ministry of Power (1961), not knowing anything about the Ministry of Power at all.

Sir Richard Mottram

[I was born] in Birmingham in an owner-occupied, semi-detached house. My father was, he's dead, an unqualified accountant – office manager. We were modest middle-class people, I suppose. I went to a state primary school. Birmingham had the 11+, and I went to a King Edward's school, King Edward VI Camp Hill School, not the one that was then a direct grant school and was for all the really clever children plus those with money. I pottered along and I got the usual complement of 'O'-levels and managed to fail an 'A'-level, which is good going really [laughs]. I suppose only at the end of my school career, it finally dawned on the school, and it possibly dawned on me, that in some areas I was quite clever, particularly when I got scholarship-level history.

I went from there to Keele University. Nobody in my parents' families, I think, had ever been to university before me. I suppose, in the case of my parents, it was a question of money. My generation was different because my parents were slightly better off and actually it didn't cost you any money. I went to university on a full grant. You could virtually live off it.

[The school] would pick out the brightest people and would prepare them for Oxford or Cambridge. It never crossed my mind even to think about it. Keele was very, very good. It was a very supportive environment. My degree was a combination of modern history, comparative government and economics, plus effectively one paper in international institutions. I was stronger on modern history and on politics than economics. I got a very good degree, triple honours first.

I suppose when I had been there for about three years, because it was a four-year course, I began vaguely to turn my mind to earning a living. So, how did I get into the civil service? I can answer this very readily really. First, I was quite interested in it because I had looked at it a little bit. Somewhere at home I've probably got an essay I wrote about the higher civil service. Because Keele was a caring institution, they had a very active careers service so you talked to them. One of my tutors said to me had I ever thought of joining the Foreign Office? He said if you wanted to you could put in for a familiarisation visit. So I put in, and the Foreign Office did not want me, well couldn't fit me in rather, to be fair to them. So I was offered a familiarisation visit in the home civil service. I said, yeah, I'll take that, so they said defence. The experience of a week in the MoD [Ministry of Defence] hadn't wholly put me off but it was pretty sort of eye-opening. So that was how I ended up doing it. I didn't do it because I thought well this is high status, well paid, you get a pension after forty years, or whatever. The general view was not many people from non-Oxbridge got in but it wasn't unknown, it wasn't impossible. So I suppose I was aware it was an elite thing.

The examination bit was quite hard, but I did reasonably well in that. The two-day thing was quite enjoyable actually, and not impossible. The final selection board I didn't particularly go for, I found that a bit nerve-racking, but I discovered afterwards that actually you never get marked down.

Socialisation and career

Sir Robin Mountfield

The working day seems in retrospect quite leisurely. I suspect about 9.30 to 6.00 probably. I was quite shy in those days and I remember addressing my first assistant secretary as 'Sir'. He was a Yorkshire man and very embarrassed: 'mustn't do that lad' [in mock Yorkshire accent]. I had a lovely man as my first principal, Jock Cairns, who had entered the civil service as a boy clerk and been commissioned into the paras, parachuted into Arnhem. He got away, and came back in as still, I think, a clerk, and by the age of 40 had fought his way up 'class by class' to be a principal which was hard going in those days. These days he might have been a permanent secretary if he'd survived. He acted as a kind of patron and taught me several lessons – to be intellectually rigorous, brisk, businesslike, get a job done, but also remember there are human beings around you. The civil service was a much richer mix in that period after the war and actually we turned much more inward looking in the 60s and 70s and indeed the 80s too.

I spent a couple of years kicking around as an AP [Assistant Principal, Ministry of Power 1961–63] and became private secretary to the permanent secretary, which I suppose was when it began to become quite serious. The permanent secretary was Dennis Proctor. Proctor was private secretary of the Chancellor during the first part of the war. He was unusual for that time. He resigned from the service as Deputy Secretary in the Treasury after the war and went to set up the London end of the Maersk shipping company. Bridges, who was Head of the Home Civil Service, coaxed him back in with the promise of an eventual permanent secretaryship – re-entering the civil service was almost unknown at that time. In between times he had become chairman of the Tate Gallery trustees and uniquely for a civil servant was allowed to retain that position. He had many friends in the art world. By this time Bridges had retired, and his successor Norman Brook didn't rate Proctor so highly. He tried to buy him off from the promise of permanent secretaryship by offering him the post of the High Commissioner to Pakistan, which he refused. He eventually got made permanent secretary at the Ministry of Power.

So Proctor and I became friends and we kept in frequent touch until he died in the 80s. There is one interesting thing I must tell you about him. Six months before the '64 election he was convinced that the Labour Party were to win through. He set in hand a secret exercise to prepare a plan for steel nationalisation, which was known to be in Labour's manifesto. That was quite contrary to all the usual practices; these days it would be frowned on very severely to do serious resource-using work in preparation for a change in government. Eight or ten people worked on it, but things didn't leak in those days. On the Saturday after the election, he called me in from home to open the secret combination cupboard, which contained the secret plan because he couldn't work the combination. He took me to lunch at his club, the Reform, and he got into his battered Triumph Herald and drove into Downing Street and delivered that plan to Fred Lee as he came out having been appointed Minister of Power. And that was actually the plan that was implemented. It was a rotten plan incidentally.

The Ministry of Power was a fascinating little department. Quite small, about 1,000 people, and had some very exceptional people. It was quite a centre of excellence in its time. The fast streamers had a career expectation that if it all went well you would reach Grade 5. I regarded myself as having a reasonable career expectation of getting to assistant secretary in the long run. Until much later, probably ten years later, I had no serious concept that I would get much further.

It was a much less pressured existence. It was a much slower existence. If you did a note of a meeting you would write in manuscript, you would send it down to the typing pool at Basingstoke and the typed version would come back on an onion skin, you would correct the onion skin and it would be sent back to Basingstoke for retyping. It would come back again in corrected form. If it was OK you sent it back to a different pool to be duplicated. So, the whole process would take at least three full days. These days people come out of meetings, type it on to the machine themselves – it's out in half an hour. I think that the amount of responsibility taken early on now is much greater than it was in those days. That's my view, a subjective impression, quite difficult to prove, but I think people take on much more immediate responsibility now in their 20s than they did in those days, which is a good thing.

There was no formal process of staff management. One day, just before we got married, the Director Establishments said, 'Well I gather you're getting married, we'd better give you a pay rise'. So, I was put into Proctor's office, which carried an allowance. At that time training was becoming a more serious business. There was a three-week induction course for assistant principals, after about a year, where I met a lot of friends. In the middle of my time with Proctor, we went on a five months' course at the Centre for Administrative Studies, which was the forerunner of the [Civil Service] College. I made a lot of life-long friendships there. I don't know how it happened but actually about a quarter of them became permanent secretaries or senior ambassadors. That was also the origins of the Mandarins Cricket Club – though cricket was never my thing!

After that I became a Principal [Petroleum Division, Ministry of Power, 1965–8, Steel Division 1968–72], and life became more serious. Still, with few exceptions, until I became a permanent secretary, I did not regularly take work home at any stage in my career. Of course it was difficult in the first two or three months in a new job where obviously you had to, or if you had a crisis or whatever, but I did not routinely do it.

[This job as Principal] was the last time I really got worked up about something I thought was going wrong and I worried a lot about it and made myself ill. At some stage within a year or two after that something changed subconsciously inside me and I've never worried about a job since. Somehow I have distanced myself. Somewhere in that process I matured or whatever, or detached myself, or allowed myself to cut off. I suppose it was a sort of release of pressure or separation of the kind doctors use to deal with their patients. But the involvement and excitement if anything grows.

[In 1972] I went into the private office [private secretary to Tom [now Lord] Boardman, Minister for Industry]. I didn't enjoy that life very much – I think the private office experience has an exaggerated importance in our system and I think it encourages a fascination with levers of power and not with substance or purpose. I've never particularly enjoyed that frenetic high policy courtier world near ministers.

In 1980 they promoted me to under-secretary when I was 40. Carey [Sir Peter Carey, permanent secretary, Department of Trade and Industry (DTI)] became a close friend and patron. It was not a world record but at that time it was pretty early to run the Vehicle Division. It was the first time I had been in charge of a division where you were really in charge of a significant number of people, about fifty I suppose. It was a very active area of industrial policy at the time. If you remember BL [British Leyland] was in crisis and the issue of closure was very much on the cards. And I'm not sure I made myself very popular arguing for it to be given a chance to turn itself around [which to a considerable extent it did].

After the 1992 election Peter Gregson [permanent secretary, DTI] asked me to move to the Treasury. I'd never liked the Treasury, but it was put to me that if I had remaining hope of advancement I ought to do that and in the end after taking a lot of soundings all around the place, I decided to do it. So I moved after eight years as a deputy secretary in DTI for a job on the same level in the Treasury, on the expenditure side. I found the expenditure side rather an arid, negative area of work, not really my cup of tea. After about a year, by which time it was clear I wasn't enjoying it, Terry Burns [permanent secretary] asked me if I would like to go on and head the civil service management side of the Treasury, which I did. I rather enjoyed that, though it was quite new territory for me. It was a time of enormous change in the civil service; we were deeply involved with the *Continuity and Change* White Papers. At the same time, the Treasury's Fundamental Expenditure Review was going on and I was arguing the Treasury should get out of civil service management work and pass it over to the relatively new Office of Public Service and Science (OPSS) in the Cabinet Office, and that was agreed. That was a time of big reductions in the senior civil service: we cut 25 per cent of the top 3,000 posts over two years, largely by early retirement, which puts a new gloss on 'jobs for life'. I genuinely thought I was writing my own civil service death warrant by recommending the abolition of my own job. However, by happy coincidence, Richard Mottram moved at the same time from OPSS to Defence, and it was my good fortune to take over from him as permanent secretary at the same time as the Treasury's civil service work moved to the OPSS. So, I spent a happy and rewarding final four years as permanent secretary, first of OPSS, which then lost Science and gained a few other things including Michael Heseltine and became the OPS, and, when that merged fully into the Cabinet Office, I was permanent secretary of that for my final year.

That was a pretty full four years, managing the department and putting a lot of effort into modernising its systems – finance, personnel, IT, a major relocation and so on. But there was also the privatisation of four of the OPS agencies, and, after the 1997 election, the *Freedom of Information* White Paper, a review of the Government Information Service after the post-election accusations of politicisation – that was the only time I was immortalised, because it became known publicly as the Mountfield Report – the Cabinet Office merger, the *Modernising Government* White Paper, the Millennium Bug preparations. About 70 hours a week on average, but overall a very exciting and fulfilling time.

Sir Richard Mottram

Day one at the MoD [September 1968], I worked in naval personnel. You had this apprenticeship where you worked with a principal. There was a mentor as well: someone who looked after you because you were the elite. The personnel management was quite good. You were given tasks that were development tasks, which were highly supervised by senior people. So I suppose you learnt quite quickly. I went off and did some training courses. This was post-Fulton. We did lots of courses, including the long course, the good old long course, which lasted nearly a year.

You were seen as an important resource, so the line managers paid a lot of attention. I mean I would talk regularly to my line managers, and they gave you feedback about what you were doing and you picked up some important lessons. I worked with this extremely eccentric person in the first job I had. It was a different world to the one we now have. We used to start at 10 and finish at 7. Once a week he would get me round to his office. He'd say to me, 'well what have you done during the week?' I would describe all the various pieces of paper I'd sent out and all the processes I'd engaged in and so on and so forth. He would say, 'no, I didn't ask you that, I asked you what you had done'. You know, this was quite an unusual thing in the civil service, I think (laughs). What have you done? How have you changed things? I was thinking gosh, wow.

You were socialised into the idea of a profession, which had things it stood for, and what the job was about, and what you were there to do. If I thought back to my early days in the naval bit of the Ministry of Defence, you were there to be on the side of the navy, to make something of the navy, to ensure it was well run, and the people were well treated, and there was a tradition that went back sort of 300 years and you were aware of that tradition. You were still working in a building where that tradition was everywhere.

Here was the civil service where, according to the critics, everybody was supposed to be Oxbridge classics, but I joined it without any great stress or strain or difficulty, and people were always nice to me, and I was thinking, 'hang on, I'm not Oxbridge classics', and most of the people who worked with me in the MoD, well none of my contemporaries, were Oxbridge classics. From day one, I thought 'well we're all a bit of a mix here, you know, what's the problem?'

The codes were of three kinds. There was a code about personal behaviour, so you know you've got to turn up on time and you have to be sober and so on. You have to understand the nature of what you were there to do and the values of the thing. The values were transmitted to you, by a process I couldn't now describe, of watching what went on and getting an idea of what was what and what was not what. Thirdly, you learned the limits to how you were expected to handle issues. A lot of it was done on paper, you know, they'd alter a draft and they would patiently explain to you what they wanted, and you'd say, 'shall we say this', and they'd say, 'not quite, say this'. So you'd realise that what you were being taught was that you were always operating within the framework of the acceptable.

Now, what is the framework of the acceptable? First, you were supposed to be working within the parameters of the government. They are about the constitutional position and the powers and prerogatives of ministers and the need for structured decision making. Secondly, in an organisation like the MoD, you were in a relationship with the military who are tough people who know what they want; they expected other people to be able to deliver. Your job was sometimes to deliver what they wanted. Sometimes it was to persuade them that what they wanted wasn't right. Sometimes it was to tell them, 'I'm sorry you can't have it'. You had ultimately to be tough-minded. If you weren't thought necessarily to be part of the dominant culture, far from this doing any harm, it paid off as long as the behaviour you were exhibiting was within the acceptable bounds or limits. If you were coming from somewhere different, but the somewhere different was considered to be constructive to the organis-ation, that was OK. If in meetings you stood up for yourself and you questioned others and you pushed the boundaries of things, this was considered to be a plus.

I went to work in the private office of the Secretary of State for Defence [1971] – a quite interesting, exciting period; it was Lord

Carrington. You would go in on some of the less important meetings, and you were doing a lot of sorting out of the paperwork, and I used to write a few of his draft speeches, and so on. But you know this was in quite a big office and you were the number three sort of person. So the number one and the number two did the big stuff. Nevertheless, the thing is now you're at the top of the organisation looking down, you're interfacing with the rest of the organisation. You're dealing with the permanent secretary and so on. It's all very exciting. It's also quite nerve-racking. You might make a mistake, and you often did, and the pace is quite fast, you've got to be really nimble. I did that and that is the sort of classic rite of passage for the elite. You have to do that job and if you do it reasonably well, it's a tick.

If you looked at my career path, you would see that, generally speaking, I was moving to the areas of the department that were always the most demanding. I was basically moving to different high prestige, highly demanding jobs. You had to deliver, and you had to deliver personally, and you had to deliver as part of a team, and you had to orchestrate a group of people, and these certainly were very stressful situations.

I wanted to get out of the naval area. In fact, I did it really quite well and got quite a good reputation. I'd had enough of it. I wanted to go and do international policy and be sent abroad, so they sent me to the Cabinet Office [laughs]! The Ministry of Defence had two jobs potentially in the Cabinet Office, apart from the intelligence bit. For a long time they provided the private secretary to the secretary of the cabinet and that was a really elite job. We had a principal job in the Cabinet secretariat dealing with defence and overseas policy. This was a key job for the department. It was a key development job. If you got that job, and you did it satisfactorily, this gave you a tick.

[In 1979] I moved to be private secretary to the permanent secretary – Frank Cooper – where I spent two and a half years. This again was a classic career move for a civil servant. This was a top job. You were sitting next door to the great man. You saw how he worked. You underpinned what he did. You were on the inside and you could see how top people worked. So you saw another network. There was a network of permanent secretaries, as there still is, and a lot of mutual loyalty amongst them, and there was a sort of parallel network of private secretaries. You were all in the same boat together, you worked together, and you got to know each other. It was quite funny. You might meet once a year at a party or something and you'd finally put faces to the voices.

The private secretary is really quite important in checking things out, as a sounding board, in an intelligence role, and in reporting what's going on and who thinks what. But there is a great danger you get above yourself and you want to be something different. You weren't sitting there to create policy yourself, but you were in the mind of the person in charge, and you were there to report back faithfully what he was thinking. You could anticipate to an extent how he might react to things, but you had to be very careful about that because some people take on the airs and graces of the boss and guess wrong and think they are the person. You don't want to be that. Your role is to help facilitate the decision-making process. You are not meant to get in the way, have your own views about everything, send everything back, and cause trouble. You're meant to lubricate the wheels.

Then what happened was, and this is a sort of piece of good fortune in career terms, the private secretary to the secretary of state fell vacant. John Nott appointed me but resigned soon after, replaced by Michael Heseltine. He had this absolute rule that he chose his private secretary, thank you very much. He was, therefore, pretty iffy about taking me but eventually he said 'oh well, all right, I'll try him'. He had realised as a junior minister, which is absolutely right, that the system uses ministers for the development of civil servants. He thought this was a bit odd as civil servants were there to serve ministers but actually he was just part of the training machine. So, he said he would take me on the basis that, for all the time he was there, I would be his private secretary. The system was a bit nervous. I said fine by me. And it turned out very well from my point of view since he was a very interesting person to work with and he and I always got on well. So I suppose I did that job for 3½ years [1982–6] which is probably a record!

It was exciting with Heseltine. Defence was big politics, and we had the one or two spectacular things like Ponting, and we had his [Heseltine's] resignation. So these were quite seminal things. Throughout all of that I was in constant touch with him. I mean it wasn't seven days a week, but you were always available. He worked extremely hard. I worked quite hard. It was interesting, it was exciting, it was absolutely at the forefront of what the government was doing. Heseltine is a very dynamic person, full of ideas, very tenacious, knows what he wants, has high standards and so on, but actually very loyal to people around him and he gets a lot of loyalty from them. I don't want to sound anti-Ponting, you know, he had been a friend of mine. But what he did was indefensible, unforgivable. Clive Ponting was supporting the secretary of state and the private office on the subject of the sinking of the *Belgrano*. They were sensitive issues and Heseltine wanted to do the right thing by the public interest. Ponting had been placed in this tremendous position of trust at the heart of this process, working to the permanent secretary, working to the secretary of state, and he betrayed it. It was such a gross breach of trust. Neither of us could accept it. He'd betrayed us.[4]

I was promoted and became the deputy under-secretary that dealt with policy, which was the best, the elite policy job at the Ministry of

Defence [1989–92]. Obviously I had been marked out. I did the defence review, which we didn't call a defence review [*Options for Change*]. This was a mixture of high policy and the defence programme. I was put in charge of it. We ran a steering group, which I chaired. We had a group above us of all the top brass in the MoD which was run jointly by the chief of the defence staff and the permanent secretary. I worked to them and the secretary of state [Tom King]. This was the time of the fall of the Berlin Wall and the changes in Russia under Mr Gorbachev. There was considerable uncertainty over how East–West relations would develop. We were trying to devise a defence policy and programme to fit these circumstances. We developed several options, which we tried out on the secretary of state. If the secretary of state and the prime minister hadn't wanted it, then we would have done something different. That's what civil servants are for. We were giving them clear visions about things in an active dialogue, and we were pushing at the limits of what they wanted to do, but these were decisions that they took. They were their policies. They had ownership of them in the jargon and if they hadn't wanted them, I'd have gone and found some others, thank you very much.

Now they were looking for something new for me, you know, grooming me really to be the permanent secretary of defence and the chance fell to go and become permanent secretary of the Office of Public Service and Science in the Cabinet Office [1992–95]. It is interesting to take over a department when your predecessor [Peter Kemp] leaves in fairly spectacular fashion. Why has this man gone? Change manager loses out in battle with mandarins! You go to a department that is slightly shell-shocked. So I spent a fair amount of time cheering them up, explaining how much we loved them, explaining it had no significance for the change programme and pushing ahead with it. And we delivered it.

The post [permanent secretary, MoD, 1995–8] fell vacant and I was offered it. It was a big department, a massive job. If you are in charge of a big department, you are trying to give a sense of leadership to the whole department under ministers. You don't tend to get involved in those bits that are going well. So in a department like defence, the policy bit is a very well-run organisation. I used to leave them to get on with it. If it went wrong, or I thought it was going wrong, I would get involved. You spend a lot of time on broader civil service management, corporate issues across the whole service, and on people management, and financial management in the department. Your main role, in my view, is to say 'is what the department is doing coherent in a policy sense?' You think about the big picture and the coherence. You ask, 'do we have the planning and other systems to ensure that if we think we know where we are going, we're actually going to end up there?'

The job

Sir Robin Mountfield

In the DTI, I used to think there were three chunks to the job. There was a management job, there was the policy job and there was a representational job. Those three elements were still there in my permanent secretary job. They are probably not that different actually in proportions, roughly a third each with the reservation that the representational role in DTI was outwards to industry. In the Cabinet Office job it was mainly outwards to the rest of the civil service.

I certainly gave policy advice and to some extent played the policy origination role. For example, I claim authorship of the phrase 'joined-up government'. I think this is a hugely important agenda – trying to make government policy and public services work horizontally between departments and institutions as well as vertically within them. But now the job I think is much more about resource management and relatively less about policy management or policy advice. Policy management is part of resource management. It's a spectrum, not a black and white thing, but I think the emphasis has clearly shifted towards that management area.

It is wrong to look back, as some do, to a golden age in the 60s, but anyway that world has passed. It was a period when the civil service was the monolithic provider of advice and we are not in that world any more whether we like it or not. We have got, as a profession, to become accustomed to operating in a much more pluralist world of advice, where you have got the think tanks, the consultancies, you have got the political parties, you have got the individual pressure groups, you have much more serious public consultation, very much greater expectations built around that. The role of the civil service, if it has a unique role at all, becomes that of professional synthesiser of advice, rather than a professional originator of advice. I don't think we have necessarily done that as well as we should.

The succession of ministers was quite extraordinary through the DTI. I had twenty-nine secretaries of state in the course of my thirty-seven years in the civil service. In the major departments the personality of the secretary of state does matter. In some ways the transition between ministers of the same administration can be almost as great as the transition from one administration to the next. The differences between the Major administration and the current administration in some ways is probably less great than the difference between some of the three DTI secretaries of state of the Conservative government in the 1980s.

As a permanent secretary you become an orchestrator of advice, making sure that you have competent people doing particular jobs – you have got to have the right level of resources doing that particular subject.

That is one end of the management spectrum: it has always been part of the job. But now in terms of how the role has changed I have no doubt at all that systematic management has hugely increased in importance. There is a sense in which the agencies thing has withdrawn the permanent secretary from one level of management and taken him into a much more strategic level. I think on the whole that's been good.

Sir Richard Mottram

Ideally I think what you want is somebody who is very bright, by which I don't just mean high intellect, but a good thinking capacity because if you don't have that, you've had it really. The subject matter is just so difficult. You have got to have the capacity for logical thought, and for going from A to wherever you have to go in a structured way. My friends from industry who come in and work inside government say to me there is a striking difference between government and industry in terms of the average level of intellectual quality of the staff. Now, if you are going to lead a group of people like that, you've got to be clever because if not, you lack credibility with the best and it corrodes. The second quality that you need is integrity in relation to ministers, parliament, the public, the way arguments are presented, the use of public money.

I suppose I have this facility of being able to synthesise arguments to be put to ministers. For instance, in my time in the Cabinet Office, if there was a dispute between departments and issues to be addressed or a new issue had come up, you'd have a meeting, you would decide what the answer was, and a note by officials would be written which would address all the background and synthesise it all and come up with options and recommendations and so on. I was really good at this. I could do any subject even though I might not know too much about the subject matter. There is a vulnerability in that because I think you can get wrong decisions if people are over-confident about how far you can go on analytical skills alone. On the other hand, over the years I've discovered that lots of people can't analyse issues in this way, see the wood for the trees. It's actually a very small group of people who can do it.

What is absolutely right, and of fundamental importance, is that if ministers say to you 'I don't actually like the advice I'm getting, I think it's too narrow or whatever', then you say, 'well fine, I'll organise so you get the advice you want'. If they want to go outside the civil service, as they do for quite a lot of their advice, fine by me. All I ever say is it would be jolly helpful to know where the alternative advice is coming from.

As the permanent secretary, you mustn't fall into the trap of simply being caught up in the minister's entourage. You have got to sort of try and find a way of complementing. When you say how important is it to the minister and permanent secretary that they have a good relationship, I think it is very important because – this may sound pathetic but I will say it anyway – in some ways it is quite a lonely job for both of them. Actually, it is quite lonely being in charge of a department if it is a big department, and I think it is very lonely being a minister because being a minister in a big department is a fantastic-ally demanding thing. So, if you can develop a good relationship at the personal level, I think it is reinforcing for both of you.

What is good about ministers? Senior ministers are usually, in my experience, top-quality people. As a permanent secretary, I have worked with people of the calibre of, for example, William Waldegrave, Michael Portillo, George Robertson and John Prescott. Good ministers are quick on the uptake. You can spark off them. They are good company. They can do their job well. The most difficult thing is that they are very demanding and they get frustrated. They ask a lot of staff, but they are not always that hot at having an active dialogue with the staff, so you can get into quite difficult situations where they are dissatisfied with the service they are getting.

If you spend your whole life in the civil service, you actually have a very good idea about politics, not about being party political, I'm completely un-party political! But you develop a feel for the political. So the ministers that really give you a thrill, I suppose, are those who are very strategic because it's great, you know, to go off and do something new and really make a success of it. You are frustrated when ministers do stupid things and you are thinking, 'well, how could they do this? How could people who've had a lifetime in this profession, how could they make such a mess of the politics?'

When we did the strategic defence review, I really enjoyed that. That was a process where I actually didn't write any of the papers but where I said to myself what I want to do here is orchestrate a process where we will end up with a result where the secretary of state gets what he wants, not what I want, but what he wants. You are orchestrating a policy play.

You've got the network across the whole of your department, and you've got the network across Whitehall, and, to an extent, you've also got an international network. So you have to establish these relation-ships, keep them lubricated, keep the show on the road.

When I was in defence we had long since discovered joined-up government. It's presented as such a revolutionary idea but I had worked for my whole career in defence on the basis that we joined up everything we did with the Foreign Office and with the Cabinet Office and with 10 Downing Street. It was just deep in our culture: that this was the way you worked and we got it off to a fine art. I think it is more difficult on the civilian side of government. I suppose there's been a feeling too that the corporate management of the civil service has been given insufficient weight with the drive to greater delegation, which we are now putting right.

The changes

Sir Robin Mountfield

Reform is fine but you've got to do it with the grain. There's a great machine here. You can't just change it overnight. You've got to edge it into a new role. You've got to preserve the non-political role of the civil service when some of the changes are politically charged. I do not believe that we are significantly politicised. There are signs in one or two places, and we must be very careful about that. Generally, I think the civil service is in many ways much better now than we were fifteen years ago – more professional, more open, actually more competent.

Sir Richard Mottram

There is a certain sort of civil servant, who in the past did well, who over the last twenty years has been edged out from getting to the top. What stopped them getting to that level? It was that they were insufficiently able to move things along and they didn't see that the purpose was actually to change things. Nor could they lead and manage people. But we should guard against stereotypes. There is criticism of the 'mandarins' from outside and within the civil service, but I have worked with some remarkably gifted people with more traditional characteristics. Michael Quinlan, for example, is clever, fabulously clever, in the best sense, and an inspirational leader in an unusual way because we all have the idea that leadership is strutting your stuff and all that. He doesn't do that. He inspires people to be loyal to him.

Has there been any loss of institutional scepticism? There is a difficult balance to be drawn. You've got to give ministers advice that relates in some meaningful way to what they're after and what they are trying to do, and that must always be the case. You have an issue of 'is this person on message?' So I suppose people are very nervous about not being on message. I can't say it bothers me. I operate on the basis that I can say almost anything. All I ever think about is what is the best way of doing this in order to produce the right result. The right result isn't that I get my way, just that the points are registered and they're addressed. Heseltine was a wonderful example. The people that drove him up the wall were the people who came into the room and had nothing to say. He used to say to me, 'what is the point of these people?', 'what value have they added?' On the other hand, people that argue their corner and do it well, accept gracefully that they haven't won it and get on with what was decided; these people were gold dust.

I have been proud of what I have been involved in within the civil service over the years – trying to improve performance while sustaining all the key values that I joined it for. I've been proud, I suppose, that pre-eminently amongst civil servants still around, I helped to reshape the country's defence effort two or three times in ways which people say were responsive; they were strategic, we seized the chance of a change, we made something of it and we took ministers with us. We didn't sit around all day exchanging pieces of paper.

The meanings of change

How have the permanent secretaries received and enacted the reforms we have labelled governance? They would quickly point to some all too obvious changes. For a start, they stress that their job lays much greater emphasis on management. The term 'management' is variously under-stood. It does not cover hands-on management of services but rather putting in place organisation-wide systems and striking an oscillating balance in their own work between strategic or corporate management, financial management and human resource management. In addition, the permanent secretaries are all too conscious that they no longer have a monopoly of policy advice. Their role is now to manage the system for getting advice and to produce for the minister a synthesis of advice drawn from multiple sources. Also, they no longer initiate policy, in so far as they ever did. Instead, they operate the machine. Finally, they are often painfully aware that they are no longer 'statesmen in disguise' but public figures subject to the slings and arrows of outrageous newspapers, television commentators and parliamentary select committees. Running through their reaction to all these changes is a notion of constitutional propriety – civil servants are subordinate to ministers and do what ministers want.

The permanent secretaries express concern about the future of a permanent, neutral, anonymous civil service. They would admit to conserving their departments but also insist that they are managing change. Yet managing change, they might add in Whig fashion, is what the civil service always has been about. As Part argues:

> Then, as now, the administrative class spent most of their time initiating or implementing changes. It was – and is – their characteristic function, a point that has been overlooked by a number of prominent people who ought to know better.
>
> (1990: 20; see also 134)

They know their job has changed and they are all to greater or lesser degrees managers and public spokespersons for their department, and, on occasion, for the government.

We would argue, in particular, that they have managed change by relating the reforms to the traditional themes of the generalist and of efficiency. So with Sir Richard Mottram's managerial and leadership track-record go some of the classical qualities of the mandarin. He made his career as a policy specialist with all the essential skills for working with ministers. He has finely tuned political antenna that make him despair of the less gifted minister. He now works across the civil service, recognising he has a corporate responsibility as well as a departmental one. He highlights the ability of top civil servants to synthesise advice, a classical trait of the generalist. Both men insist that their job has many sides to it and the skill is to balance the conflicting demands and multiple roles, not to specialise in any one. They would agree with Sir Richard Wilson (1998) that 'we have a tradition that is rooted in pragmatism and flexibility'.

The persistence of the theme of the generalist also appears in the connotations of the phrase 'a good chap'. It implies a clubbable, closed elite, although they are members of a work-based network rather than of London clubs. But it also implies some important, even meritorious, traits. Good chaps are decent and reasonable. They can be trusted and are loyal. Mottram's loyalty was put on uncomfortable public display during the Ponting trial, where he appeared as a witness for the prosecution and was pilloried by the *Guardian* for his pains. Similarly, when the secretary of state at the Department of the Environment, Transport and the Regions, Stephen Byers, was embroiled in controversy for allegedly dismissing his press secretary, Martin Sixsmith, Mottram's public statement about the dismissal can be seen as an act of loyalty above and beyond the call of duty. And loyalty is extended not only to ministers but to other colleagues. Mountfield's affection and loyalty to Dennis Proctor shone through every word. The corollary of trusting ministers and civil servant colleagues is that they trust you. And trust is not just a matter of personal loyalty. It is also about being trusted to get on with the job, of being kept in the loop and of respect for one's judgement.

The concern with efficiency in the civil service also provides a context within which the permanent secretaries receive and construct reforms such as Next Steps agencies. These reforms are based on separating operational management in the agency from policy in the core department. Such separation can appear as an extension of the idea of 'hiving-off', which was rediscovered in 1968 though it was not new even then. The permanent secretaries understood the reforms in part as freeing them from operational management so they could concentrate on their classical tasks. Similarly, Sir Richard Mottram clearly domesticates 'joined-up' governance by assimilating it to established practices within the Ministry of Defence, practices he understands as part of his concern with efficiency.

In sum, the civil servants domesticate the successive waves of reform by filtering them through their traditional beliefs about the generalist and efficiency. The beliefs and practices of civil servants have changed but the changes have been refracted through familiar prisms. These prisms are sustained in part through the socialisation of young entrants to the civil service. This induction to the traditions of the civil service is informal. Robin Mountfield is an arts graduate from Oxford. Richard Mottram did social sciences at Keele. Such differences did not matter, as Mottram observed. Each had a mentor when they joined the service. Each had patrons as they progressed through its ranks. Both worked in a private office. Both had a stint in the Cabinet Office. Robin Mountfield was explicitly told that a stint in the Treasury would enhance his chances of promotion to permanent secretary. They share the norms and values of the higher civil service. The point is easily illustrated. Both men comment that you learn the rules and you are 'socialised into the idea of a profession'. Richard Mottram identifies three codes he had to learn – about personal behaviour, the job and its values and 'the framework of the acceptable'.

Of course, the permanent secretaries recognise that the reforms do not simply constitute an extension of the traditional themes of the generalist and of efficiency. Rather they see the reforms as posing widely recognised dilemmas to these themes. Fragmentation of the civil service threatens efficiency. Politicisation threatens the public sector ethos, and is threatened by it. Thus, Sir Robin Butler stressed: 'the need to maintain a degree of cohesion across the service as a whole; and to preserve a non-political civil service with a shared sense of the essential values and ethics that make our system work' (Butler 1993: 404). The core values to be preserved are: 'an impartial, apolitical public service, and its traditions of propriety, non-politicisation and selection and promotion on merit' (Butler 1992: 8).

Fragmentation poses a dilemma for traditional notions of efficiency in the civil service. Although agencies freed the core of operational responsibilities, in so doing they fragmented departments, creating worries about both the vertical links in departments and the horizontal links between departments. So, Sir Robin Mountfield suggests the call for joined-up government can be understood as a call to strengthen the corporate identity of the service. The dilemma is to reconcile decentralisation and the freedom to manage with co-ordination from the centre to achieve government policy objectives where, in the jargon, 'wicked issues' span departments and agencies.

Politicisation might pose a dilemma for the generalist and the public sector ethos. Now that civil service appointments are increasingly made by open competition, there are fears that the newcomers will not be socialised in the service's traditions. They will not have sat across the desk from a mentor learning the rules of the Whitehall village game. They will not have had a patron to advise them on career development. They will not have worked the rites of passage through a private office, the Treasury and the Cabinet Office. Thus, the public service ethos could be eroded. Loyalty might become conditional and contingent and formal mechanisms of co-ordination may replace the glue of trust and shared codes. The search for the can-do manager will increase the opportunity for, and the temptation to make, political appointments. The uneasy mix of private adviser with public spokesperson reinforces these fears. As the top civil servants become the ever-more prominent spokespersons for departments, and therefore government policy, there will be ever-greater temptation to appoint people of known political sympathies. One member of the senior civil service commented as follows.

> I am very pessimistic about the future of the non-political civil service. I think it is in its last five or seven years. I think it will survive until after the election. I would not be confident it would last another parliament. I mean there is a perfectly respectable argument that ministers are entitled to look for a degree of commitment to their policies from their principal advisers that is incompatible with a non-political service. On the other hand I think there are great strengths in our system. Somebody has to ask the sceptical questions. I don't think it has happened yet though I think there is a bit of a shadow there. Some of the younger officials see their future lying in demonstrating their passion for policies. That is very natural. A thrusting young guy of 40 or something, to show yourself enthusiastic about a government that looks as though it is going to be there for another seven, eight, nine years, it is a very natural thing to do. So that is why I am gloomy about it.

In a similar vein, Sir Robert Armstrong restated the constitutional position that the duty of the individual civil servant was to serve the Minister of the Crown in charge of the department. And Sir Richard Wilson (2002) defines the character of the civil service as integrity, political impartiality, merit, ability to work for successive governments and public service. On public service he comments:

> What attracts people to the Civil Service is the wish to make a contribution to the community. We have some of the best, most challenging jobs in the economy at every level. This gives us a deeply committed workforce.

Echoes of these sentiments can be found in the interviews. Sir Robin Mountfield joined the civil service out of a vague sense of public service and cares with a passion, some might say with a dangerous enthusiasm, for a service he served for all his life and sees as being on the cusp of major change. For him, the ideals of neutrality, permanence and expertise – yes, there is a strong sense of professionalism – confront the pressures favouring politicisation and a loss of institutional scepticism. Similarly, Sir Richard Mottram refers often to his 'profession' and insists on the importance of integrity in one's dealings with ministers, parliament and the public. Previously, recruits were socialised into these traditions in a taken-for-granted way. Now they will have to be sent on training courses.

Conclusion

Our ethnographic study of the permanent secretaries goes some way toward unpacking recent changes in the beliefs, traditions and, thus, practices of the higher civil service. The interviews showed how the beliefs of permanent secretaries have changed even if their objective characteristics have not. The successive waves of public sector reform associated with Thatcherism and New Labour posed dilemmas for the tradition of the civil service. But that tradition also provided resources with which the civil service could respond to the reforms. On the one hand, the reforms made permanent secretaries more convinced of the importance of management, more concerned to synthesise than initiate advice on policy, and more aware of the public context. On the other hand, however, the permanent secretaries defined the reforms in terms drawn from their tradition so, for example, management was constructed as strategic management, a notion congenial to the generalist.

Of course, interviewees can be self-serving and misleading: the validity and reliability of 'facts' can always be disputed. And of course we have presented a specific reading of the changing beliefs of permanent secretaries that fits our earlier analysis of civil service traditions. However, we are prepared to defend the proposition that an adequate study of political life must be grounded in accounts of the beliefs, preferences and practices of actors; and explanations of these beliefs, actions and practices by looking at the relevant traditions and dilemmas. Then whether our account is better than (say) the managerialist interpretation is a function of its relationship to the criteria of comparison discussed in Chapter 2. Does it account for more of the 'facts'? Does it open new lines of inquiry?

Political scientists, we believe, would be well advised to explore the continuing process of reform using the historical and ethnographic practices we have tried to illustrate. We believe these practices can be used to analyse any aspect of British government, ministers as much as civil servants, the lowest of the low as well as the great and the good. It remains next to recap the route travelled and to explain what gains are to be had from adopting an interpretive approach.

Notes

1 For general introductions to ethnography, elite interviews and related qualitative approaches, which are relevant to political science, see Dexter 1970; Eckstein 1975; Fenno 1990; Geertz 1973; Glaser and Strauss 1967; Hammersley and Atkinson 1983; Sanjek 1990; Silverman 1997; and Yin 1994. For applications to

British government see Heclo and Wildavsky 1974; McPherson and Raab 1988; and Rhodes 1997a: Chapter 9.

2 The interviews followed the order used in the text; that is, social background, recruitment, socialisation, career pattern, the interwoven tasks of policy advice, management and diplomacy, and interpreting change. We use only the departmental secretaries' words – any comments we have appear in brackets – and all attributed quotes were agreed with the departmental secretary before publication. However, we chose which extracts to use and we turned these extracts into continuous text. So, when we claim 'this section lets the departmental secretaries speak for themselves', we need to add 'through us as authors'.

3 We know of only one other study which relies on and reproduces in-depth interviews, and that was with middle-level management not the administrative elite (Silverman and Jones 1976).

4 On the Ponting affair see Ponting 1985 and Norton-Taylor 1985. On the sinking of the *Belgrano* see Foreign Affairs Committee 1985.

10 Conclusions

On governance again

Our interpretive approach to British governance does not read off actions from allegedly objective social facts about institutions or people. Rather it leads us to explore the historical and contingent patterns of belief that inform current governmental practices in Britain. So, instead of describing reified institutions with an alleged path-dependency, we decentred the relevant traditions and explored how they were modified in response to dilemmas. Our decentred theory prompted us to distinguish several competing strands in the British governmental tradition. It also led us to suggest that civil servants, with service providers and citizens, construct governance as much as politicians. So, we examined the broad patterns of belief that inform the changing practices of the higher civil service as well as the changing reform programmes of political movements. We now return to the broader themes of the book and summarise our arguments on the relative merits of positivist and interpretive approaches.

To recap briefly, we took as our starting point the claim there has been a shift from government by a unitary state to governance by and through networks. In this period the boundary between state and civil society changed. It can be understood as a shift from hierarchies, or the bureaucracies of the welfare state, through the marketisation reforms of the Conservative governments of Thatcher and Major to networks and the joined-up government of New Labour. This emphasis on networks contrasts markedly with accounts of British government rooted in the Westminster model.

Second, we used our anti-foundational approach, with its notions of tradition and dilemma, to decentre this governance story; that is, to identify the several ways in which individuals construct governance. Ethnography and history are the best tools respectively for recovering and explaining other people's constructions of what they are doing: that is, thick descriptions of individual beliefs and preferences.

Finally, we have also argued that governance is contingent and contested and so variously constructed. Table 10.1 summarises four narratives of governance: intermediate institutions, networks of communities, return to the organic constitution and joined-up government.

Table 10.1 Narratives of governance

Traditions	Tory	Liberal	Whig	Socialist
Narrative of reform	Preserving traditional authority	Restoring markets and combating state overload	Evolutionary change	Redefining the bureaucratic state
Narrative of governance	Wrecked intermediate institutions	Building networks of communities	Return to the organic constitution	Joining-up government
Examples				
(a) Practitioner	Gilmour 1992	Willetts 1992	Bancroft 1983	Mandelson and Liddle 1996
(b) Official report	Not applicable in 1980s and 1990s	Efficiency Unit 1988	Cm. 2627 1994	Cm. 4310 1999

We can unpack this table quickly because we described each narrative and tradition earlier. So we give brief examples of how each tradition interprets public sector reform.

Inspired by the Tory tradition, Gilmour (1992: 198–224) portrays Thatcher's public sector reforms as a 'series of tactical battles' that wrecked Britain's intermediate institutions, such as the monarchy, the church, the civil service, the judiciary, the BBC and local government. These 'barriers between state and citizen', he argues, were torn down in the drive to create an enterprise culture and a free market state. Gilmour values the pluralism of intermediate institutions and wants to return to moderation in the exercise of power. The Conservative Party encompasses the paternal statism of the High Tories and economic liberalism but during the 1980s and 1990s, the former has been a submerged tradition. Official reports did not articulate the High Tory reverence for the old values.

For Liberals such as Norman Tebbitt, former Secretary of State for Trade and Industry and former chair of the Conservative Party, Gilmour's belief that intermediate institutions such as local government were a check and balance on Westminster is 'an entirely new and quite false constitutional theory'. The Thatcher reforms drew on economic liberalism to address bureaucratic inefficiency. In her own words, Margaret Thatcher (1993: 48) 'preferred disorderly resistance to decline rather than comfortable accommodation to it' and the public sector was not insulated from her reforming zeal. The recurrent liberal concerns with business-like efficiency, setting clear policy objectives and recruiting better managers, pervade various official reports of the last two decades (see, for example, the Efficiency Unit 1988: 3–5).

Not all Liberals focus on reforming public management. Willetts (1992: 71) wants to claim community as a core principle in the Liberal tradition. He rejects the idea of community embodied in the nation state for the notion of an 'overlapping network of communities'. He denies that free markets destroy community. On the contrary, liberalism reconciles markets and community with the idea of 'micro-conservatism' or 'the particular network of communities which gives each individual life meaning'. The role of the state is to sustain 'a political order in which this multiplicity of communities can survive' (ibid.: 105). Micro-communities populate the boundary between state and civil society, an image with a close affinity to nineteenth-century notions of governance as private collectivism.

The Whig tradition lauds the capacity of British political institutions to incorporate and moderate changes. Its response to public sector reform, to return to the example provided by Hennessy, is 'wherever possible' to use 'traditional and familiar institutions for new purposes' and so to 'go with the grain of Westminster and Whitehall and their traditions'. Empathy with the British constitution leads to calls for a return to the organic constitution. In a similar vein Lord Bancroft (1983: 8), a former Head of the Home Civil Service, argues 'for organic institutional change, planned at a digestible rate' so that reforms work with, and so perpetuate, all that is salutary in Britain's constitution and political practice. The White Paper, *The Civil Service: Continuity and Change* (Cm. 2627 1994) is a testament to Whig consolidation, reaffirming the civil service's commitment to integrity, impartiality and loyal service to the government of the day.

New Labour rejects the command bureaucracy model of Old Labour with its emphasis on hierarchy, authority and rules. Peter Mandelson, former Secretary of State for Northern Ireland, and Roger Liddle explicitly reject the 'municipal socialism' and 'centralised nationalisation' of the past (Mandelson and Liddle 1996: 27). New Labour 'does not seek to provide centralised "statist" solutions to every social and economic problem'. Instead New Labour promotes the idea of networks of institutions and individuals acting in partnerships held together by relations of trust. It favours joined-up government or delivering public services by steering networks of organisations where the currency is not authority (bureaucracy) or price competition (markets) but trust. It exemplifies the shift from the providing state of Old Labour and the minimal state of Thatcherism to the enabling state and the continuing socialist commitment to making the state work. Such White Papers as *Modernising Government* (Cm. 4310 1999) with its emphasis on joining-up clearly expresses this commitment.

In some ways, our interpretation of British governance resembles a metanarrative that describes or embraces the Tory, Liberal, Whig and Socialist stories. Yet, as we said earlier, the resemblance of our interpretation to a metanarrative is superficial. Our interpretive approach provides a distinctive, alternative analysis, rather than an account of the field as a whole. It is just that the interpretive nature of our alternative analysis requires us to unpack and explain other theories and stories, hence the superficial resemblance to a metanarrative. As a distinct alternative, we offer a decentred and interpretive approach rooted in the concepts of belief, tradition and dilemma. Our approach inspires a narrative of reform as a series of contingent responses to dilemmas constructed in many ways. And it inspires a narrative of governance as the changing practices produced through the diverse, contingent ways in which politicians, civil servants, service providers and citizens construct and respond to reform. In an important sense, therefore, there is no such thing as governance, but only the differing constructions of the several traditions. That is to say, there is no necessary logical or structural process determining the form governance takes, neither a process based on the intrinsic rationality of markets nor one based on the path dependency of institutions. In an equally important sense, however, governance consists of the diverse actions and practices inspired by the varied beliefs and traditions we have discussed. Patterns of governance arise as the contingent products of diverse actions and political struggles informed by the beliefs of the agents as they in turn arise against a backcloth of traditions and dilemmas. These conclusions apply whether we are talking about the civil service, public sector reform, governing structures or state–civil society relations. There may be some agreement that the boundary between state and civil society is being redrawn, and the form and extent of state intervention is changing, but there is little agreement on how, why or whether it is desirable.

In Chapter 1 we noted the emphasis of historians on a broad concept of governance as the relation of the state to civil society. Although the historians we referred to differ in detail, they share the theme of governance as private collectivism being eroded by successive periods of centralisation fuelled by the two world wars. The New Right's reinventing of the minimal state and New Labour's discovery of networks are attempts to find a substitute for the voluntaristic bonds diminished by state intervention and the erosion of intermediate institutions such as local government. We are witnessing the search for an extended role for civil society in an era of large organisations. Appeals to networks can be seen as a counterweight to the centralising trends of the 1960s and 1970s.

We claim four main advantages for our interpretive approach and its governance narrative. First, our narrative identifies important empirical gaps in the Westminster model by identifying key changes in British government. In effect we challenge the central notions of the Westminster model. In place of the classical model of a unitary state characterised by a strong executive and parliamentary sovereignty, we posit a shift to a differentiated polity with a power-dependent core executive hollowed out by internal differentiation and international interdependence.

Second, our interpretive approach resolves theoretical difficulties that beset more positivist versions of the governance narrative. It decentres institutions, avoiding the unacceptable suggestion that they fix the behaviour of individuals within them rather than being products of that behaviour. It replaces unhelpful phrases such as path-dependency with an analysis of change rooted in the beliefs and preferences of individual actors. And yet it allows political scientists to offer aggregate studies by using the concepts of tradition and dilemma.

Third, our approach opens up new research agendas. It poses distinctive questions about British government: for example, about reshaping the state through the beliefs and preferences of key actors. It also introduces distinctive techniques for addressing these questions. It points to ethnography as a means of capturing beliefs and actions, and history as a means of explaining such beliefs and actions.

Finally, our interpretive approach identifies key theoretical issues that confront policy making and policy implementation in the 1980s and 1990s; for example, the issues of pluralising policy-making and the mix of governing structures. It also lends some support to bottom-up forms of decision-making as appropriate means for addressing many of these issues.

The governance narrative is a valuable corrective to the traditional Westminster model. We compare the two as an exercise in 'edification'. The governance narrative offers the hope of finding 'new, better, more interesting, more fruitful ways of speaking about' British government (Rorty 1980: 360). It does so by decentring networks and exploring how their informal authority supplements and supplants the more formal authority of government. We use the notion of governance to develop a more diverse view of state authority in its relationship to civil society.

Our interpretation of British governance offers a distinctive narrative. It also raises important issues for further research. Although there are equivalent trends in other advanced industrial democracies, we know little or nothing about how national governmental traditions shape responses to these trends (but see Bevir *et al.* 2003, forthcoming). We can identify the different approaches to network management but all these tools of central steering meet problems. Although there is a large democratic shortfall in governance, we know little about the prospects for democratising particular domains. Also we know little about the ethnography of government. Although reducing the size of the civil service and improving efficiency are long-standing policies, we do not how such change has affected the beliefs and practices of middle-level managers, supervisors and employees. All policies have multiple stakeholders. A decentred approach provides thick descriptions focusing on the beliefs and preferences of these stakeholders. No such accounts exist, whether the subject is management reform or minister–permanent secretary relationships.

Earlier, we asked, following Coleridge, 'what is the meaning of it?' Now we have both described and decentred a general account of governance (see Chapters 3 and 4). We have challenged attempts to use an abstract, monolithic concept of governance to account for a broad range of developments in various states (see Chapter 5); we have explored the waves of governance associated with the New Right and New Labour (see Chapters 6 and 7); and presented our historical and ethnographic reconstructions of the civil service's constructions of the relevant reforms and changes (see Chapters 8 and 9). We had no expectation that we could provide a true account of an objective process unaffected by the mentalities of particular individuals. Rather, we have related governance to the actions of many individuals; described the conflicting but overlapping stories that inform the actions of these individuals; and used the concepts of tradition and dilemma to explain why these actors construct their worlds as they do. Individuals are bearers of traditions and they enact and remake practices in their everyday lives. We argue governing practices can only be understood through the beliefs and actions of individuals located in traditions and in response to dilemmas. Political ethnography enables us to tell the stories of different individuals. Historical analysis is the way to uncover the traditions and dilemmas that shape these stories.

We prefer an interpretive approach with its governance narrative to the positivism lurking within most accounts of the Westminster model. Our reasons for doing so have appeared throughout, but we can restate them briefly using the criteria of comparison enjoined by our anti-foundational epistemology. First, the governance narrative is comparatively accurate and comprehensive in its coverage of shared 'facts'. We believe the story of a shift from hierarchies to markets to networks commands a large measure of agreement between academics and practitioners, even if the language varies, encompassing terms such as joining-up, holistic governance and partnerships. Second, we believe our approach and narrative are consistent with other norms of reasoning. We have shown how anti-foundationalism prompts an interpretive approach that takes mentalities seriously and so decentres mainstream accounts of institutions and governance. We have then unpacked governance as several narratives each located in specific traditions and dilemmas. Finally, we believe our approach will prove to be fruitful, progressive and open. It will open a wide range of new areas and styles of research about the beliefs, preferences and actions of many political actors – from prime minister to individual citizens – as they preserve and modify traditions and practices – from Toryism and parliament to, say, New Age travellers and forms of protest.

To end, let us turn to the implications of our governance narrative for practitioners. New patterns of governance bring new problems. Marketisation undermines trust, co-operation and reciprocity in networks. Organisational complexity obscures accountability. The search for co-operation impedes efficient service delivery. Perhaps, as Stoker (2000b) suggests, all we can tell the practitioner is to 'keep on "muddling through" . . . in an appropriately thoughtful and reflexive manner'. Perri (1997: 70) accuses this analysis of fatalism. Yet he is insufficiently cautious about the provisional nature of knowledge in the social sciences and his optimism for the latest managerial fashion is misplaced. But his tool view of governance, with its stress on choosing between and managing resource allocation, is widespread. Its prominence is clear from the large and growing literature on how to manage networks. We would argue, in contrast, that the research frontier for the study of governance should not be drawn this tightly. Steering networks is not the only or even the most important question. While a preference for relevance has always been strong in the study of British government, governance is not just about corporate management and marketisation but also the changing nature of government and how to understand such changes. The interpretive approach, as we have shown, suggests several ways of broadening the research agenda to encompass these topics.

Besides, one important lesson of an interpretive approach for those advising government is that there is no tool kit they can use to steer networks. Practitioners might learn from political scientists by listening to and telling stories. Although we can offer only provisional knowledge, this awareness of our limits does not render such knowledge useless. If we cannot offer universal solutions, we can define and redefine problems in novel ways. We can tell policy-makers and administrators distinctive stories about their world and how it is governed (see, for example, Rein 1976). The language of networks challenges the language of managerialism, markets and contracts. The language of interpretation and narratives challenges the language of positivist social science.

In short, therefore, we provide a language for redescribing the world. We open the door to an understanding of how several actors have constructed the meaning, and so nature, of recent government changes. In particular, we challenge the dominant, managerial discourse about networks. Too often, political scientists reduce the analysis of governance to managerial skills. In no way do we wish to suggest that learning how to steer networks is unimportant. We do want to suggest, however, that steering networks is about understanding participants' stories as much as more technical means. To work with governance as networks adequately, we need a decentred exploration of traditions and dilemmas.

Simple solutions such as joining-up or holistic governance may have an appealing elegance. Governments will always seek simplicity – but they should distrust it. Our narrative of governance makes no apology for describing a complex world in at least some of its complexity because there are no simple solutions, whether based on hierarchies, markets or networks. We hope that our governance narrative is edifying. We are convinced it is provisional.

Bibliography

'The Administrators' (1964) *The Reform of the Civil Service*. London: Fabian Society, Tract 355.

Alford, R. and Friedland, R. (1985) *Powers of Theory: Capitalism, the State and Democracy*. Cambridge: Cambridge University Press.

Anderson, Sir John (1946) 'The Machinery of Government', *Public Administration*, 24: 147–56.

Anderson, P. (1992) *English Questions*. London: Verso. See especially 'Origins of the Present Crisis', pp. 15–47, originally published in 1964.

Anderson, P. (1974) *Lineages of the Absolutist State*. London: New Left Books.

Armstrong, Sir Robert (1985) *The Duties and Responsibilities of Civil Servants in Relation to Ministers. Note by the Head of the Civil Service*. London: Cabinet Office, 25 February.

Aucoin, P. (1995) *The New Public Management: Canada in Comparative Perspective*. Quebec: Institute for Research on Public Policy.

Balogh, T. (1959) 'Apotheosis of the Dilettante', in H. Thomas (ed.) *The Establishment*. London: Anthony Blond.

Bancroft, Lord (1983) 'Whitehall: Some Personal Reflections', Suntory-Toyota lecture, London School of Economics and Political Science, 1 December.

Bancroft, Lord (1984) 'Whitehall and Management: A Retrospect', *Royal Society of Arts Journal*, 132, 5: 367–79.

Bang, H.P. and Sørensen, E. (1999) 'The Everyday Maker: a New Challenge to Democratic Governance', *Administrative Theory and Praxis*, 21, 3: 325–41.

Barberis, P. (1996) *The Elite of the Elite*. Aldershot: Dartmouth.

Barker, A. (1997) 'Political Responsibility for UK Prisons – Ministers Escape Again', *Public Administration*, 76, 1: 1–23.

Barker, Sir Ernest (1944) *The Development of Public Services in Western Europe, 1660–1930*. London: Oxford University Press.

Barker, R. (1994) *Politics, Peoples and Governments. Themes in British Political Thought since the Nineteenth Century*. London: Macmillan.

Barnett, C. (1986) *The Audit of War*. London: Macmillan.

Barry, A., Osborne, T. and Rose, N. (eds) (1996) *Foucault and Political Reason*. London: UCL Press.

Barthes, R. (1981) 'The Discourse of History', *Comparative Criticism*, 3: 7–20.

Bauman, Z. (1978) *Hermeneutics and Social Science: Approaches to Understanding*. London: Hutchinson.

Beer, S. (1965) *Modern British Politics*. London: Faber. All page references are to the 1982 edition.

Beer, S. (1982) *Britain Against Itself*. London: Faber.

Beloff, M. (1975) 'The Whitehall Factor: The Role of the Higher Civil Service 1919–39', in G. Peele and C. Cook (eds) *The Politics of Reappraisal 1918–1939*. London: Macmillan.

Berger, P. and Luckman, T. (1971) *The Social Construction of Reality: A Treatise in the Sociology of Knowledge*. Harmondsworth: Penguin Books.

Berman, M. (1982) *All That Is Solid Melts Into Air*. London: Verso.

Bevir, M. (1999a) *The Logic of the History of Ideas*. Cambridge: Cambridge University Press.

Bevir, M. (1999b) 'Foucault, Power and Institutions', *Political Studies*, 47: 345–59.

Bevir, M. (1999c) 'Humanism in and against The Order of Things', *Configurations*, 7: 191–209.

Bevir, M. (2000a) 'Derrida and the Heidegger Controversy: Global Friendship Against Racism', *Critical Review of International Social and Political Philosophy*, 3: 121–38.

Bevir, M. (2000b) 'Socialism, Civil Society, and the State in Modern Britain', in F. Trentmann (ed.) *Paradoxes of Civil Society: New Perspectives on Modern German and British History*. Providence, RI: Berghahn Books.

Bevir, M. (2000c) '"New Labour: A Study in Ideology', *British Journal of Politics and International Relations*, 2, 3: 277–301.

Bevir, M. (2001) 'Prisoners of Professionalism: On the Construction and Responsibility of Political Studies', *Public Administration*, 79, 2: 469–89.

Bevir, M. (2002) 'Sidney Webb: Utilitarianism, Positivism, and Social Democracy', *Journal of Modern History*, 74, 2: 217–52.

Bevir, M. and O'Brien, D. (2001) 'New Labour and the Public Sector in Britain', *Public Administration Review*, 61: 535–47.

Bevir, M., Rhodes, R.A.W. and Weller, P. (eds) (2003) *Traditions Of Governance*. Special issue of *Public Administration*, 83, 1: forthcoming.

Birch, A.H. (1964) *Representative and Responsible Government*. London: Allen & Unwin.

Birch, A.H. (1989) 'The Theory and Practice of Modern British Democracy', in J. Jowell and D. Oliver (eds) *The Changing Constitution*. 2nd edition. Oxford: Clarendon Press.

Blaas, P.B.M. (1978) *Continuity and Anachronism: Parliamentary and Constitutional Development in Whig Historiography and in the Anti-Whig Reaction Between 1890 and 1930*. The Hague: Martinus Nijhoff.

Blair, T. (1994) 'Reforming Welfare – Building on Beveridge'. Speech, Southampton Institute, UK, 13 July.

Blair, T. (1995a) *Let Us Face The Future*. London: Fabian Society, Fabian Pamphlet 571.

Blair, T. (1995b) 'Socialist Values in the Modern World'. Speech, Sedgefield, UK, 28 January.

Blair, T. (1996) *New Britain: My Vision of a Young Country*. London: Fourth Estate.

Blair, T. (1998a) *The Third Way: New Politics for a New Century*. London: Fabian Society, Fabian Pamphlet No. 588.

Blair, T. (1998b) *The Observer*, 31 May.

Blair, T. (1999) 'Modernising Public Services'. Speech to the Charter Mark Awards, Central Hall, Westminster, 26 January.

Blake, R. (1985) *The Conservative Party from Peel to Thatcher*. London: Fontana.

Blom-Hansen, J. (1997) 'A "New Institutional" Perspective on Policy Networks', *Public Administration*, 77: 669–93.

Bloom, A. (1987) *The Closing of the American Mind*. New York: Simon and Schuster.

Bogason, P. and Toonen, T.A.J. (eds) (1998) *Comparing Networks*. Special issue of *Public Administration*, 76, 2.

Bogdanor, V. and Skidelsky, R. (eds) (1970) *The Age of Affluence 1951–64*. London: Macmillan.

Börzel, T.J. (1998) 'Organising Babylon: On the Different Conceptions of Policy Networks', *Public Administration*, 76: 253–73.

Boyle, E., Crosland, A. and Kogan, M. (1971) *The Politics of Education*. Harmondsworth: Penguin Books.

Braun, R. (1975) 'Taxation, Sociopolitical Structure and State Building: Great Britain and Brandenburg-Prussia', in Tilly, C. (ed.) *The Formation of National States in Western Europe*. Princeton, NJ: Princeton University Press.

Bridges, Sir Edward (1950) *Portrait of a Profession*. Cambridge: Cambridge University Press. Reprinted in R.A. Chapman and A. Dunsire (eds) *Style in Administration*. London: Allen & Unwin.

Bridges, Sir Edward (1956) 'Administration: What Is It and How Can It Be Learnt?', in A. Dunsire (ed.) *The Making of an Administrator*. Manchester: Manchester University Press.

Brittan, S. (1975) 'The Economic Contradictions of Democracy', *British Journal of Political Science*, 5, 2: 129–59.

Brown, G. and Wright, T. (1995) 'Introduction', in G. Brown and T. Wright (eds) *Values, Visions and Voices: an Anthology of Socialism*. Edinburgh: Mainstream Publishing.

Bulmer, S. and Burch, M. (1996) *The British Core Executive and European Integration: A New Institutionalist Perspective*. Manchester: Department of Government, University of Manchester, EPRU Paper No. 4.

Bulpitt, J.G. (1983) *Territory and Power in the United Kingdom*. Manchester: Manchester University Press.

Bulpitt, J.G. (1986) 'The Discipline of the New Democracy: Mrs Thatcher's Domestic Statecraft', *Political Studies*, 34: 19–39.

Bunbury, Sir Henry (1971) [1928] 'Efficiency as an Alternative to Control', in R.A. Chapman and A. Dunsire (eds) *Style in Administration*. London: Allen & Unwin.

Burch, M. and Holliday, I. (1996) *The British Cabinet System*. Hemel Hempstead: Prentice Hall, Harvester Wheatsheaf.

Burrow, J. (1981) *A Liberal Descent: Victorian Historians and the English Past*. Cambridge: Cambridge University Press.

Burrow, J. (1988) *Whigs and Liberals: Continuity and Change in English Political Thought*. Oxford: Clarendon Press.

Butler, Sir Robin (1992) 'Managing the New Public Services: Towards a New Framework?', *Public Policy and Administration*, 7, 3: 1–14.

Butler, Sir Robin (1993) 'The Evolution of the Civil Service', *Public Administration*, 71: 395–406.

Butler, Sir Robin (1997) 'The Changing Civil Service', paper to the ESRC Whitehall Conference on 'Future Whitehall', Church House, Westminster.

Cabinet Office (1994a) *Next Steps: Moving On* (The Trosa Report). London: Cabinet Office.

Cabinet Office (1994b) *Civil Service Management Code*. London: HMSO.

Cabinet Office (1997) *Ministerial Code. A Code of Conduct and Guidance on Procedures for Ministers*. London: Cabinet Office.

Cabinet Office (1998) *Service First: The New Charter Programme*. London: Cabinet Office.

Cabinet Office (1999a) *Modernising Government Action Plan*. London: Cabinet Office.

Cabinet Office (1999b) *Professional Policy-making for the Twentieth Century*. Report by the Strategic Policy-making Team. London: Cabinet Office.

Cabinet Office (1999c) *Civil Service Reform*. Report to the Prime Minister from Sir Richard Wilson, Head of the Home Civil Service. London: Cabinet Office, 15 December.

Cabinet Office (2000) *Wiring It Up*. London: Cabinet Office.

Cadbury Report (1992) *The Report of the Committee on the Financial Aspects of Corporate Governance*. London: Gee & Co.

Chapman, B. (1963) *British Government Observed*. London: Allen & Unwin.

Chapman, L. (1978) *Your Disobedient Servant*. London: Chatto & Windus.

Chapman, R.A. (1970) *The Higher Civil Service in Britain*. London: Constable.

Chapman, R.A. and Greenaway, J.R. (1980) *The Dynamics of Administrative Reform*. London: Croom Helm.

Chapman, R.A. (1988) *Ethics in the British Civil Service*. London: Routledge.

Chapman, R.A. and O'Toole, B.J. (1995) 'The Role of the Civil Service: A Traditional View in a Period of Change', *Public Policy and Administration*, 10, 2: 3–20.

Chester, D.N. (1975) 'Political Studies in Britain: Recollections and Comments', *Political Studies*, 23, 151–64.

Chester, Sir Norman (1981) *The English Administrative System 1780–1870*. Oxford: Clarendon Press.

Christensen, Jørgen Grønnegaard (1998) 'Bureaucratic Autonomy, Formal Institutions and Politics'. Paper to the annual meeting of the American Political Science Association, Boston, 3–6 September.

Christensen, T. (1995) 'The Scandinavian State Tradition and Public Administration'. Paper to the Annual Meeting of the American Political Science Association, Chicago, 31 August–3 September.

Christensen, T. and Lægreid, P. (1998) 'Administrative Reform Policy: The Case of Norway', *International Review of Administrative Sciences*, 64, 3: 457–75.

CIPFA (Chartered Institute of Public Finance and Accountancy) (1994) *Corporate Governance in the Public Services*. London: CIPFA.

Clark, D. (1997) 'Delivering Better Government from the Bottom Up'. Speech by the Chancellor of the Duchy of Lancaster, 17 June, Queen Elizabeth Conference Centre, London.

Clarke, P. (1996) *Hope and Glory. Britain 1900–1990*. Harmondsworth: Penguin Books.

Cd. 9230 (1918) *Report of the Machinery of Government Committee* (Haldane). London: HMSO.

Cmnd 3638 (1968) *The Civil Service. Vol. 1 Report of the Committee 1966–68* (Fulton). London: HMSO.

Cmnd 4506 (1970) *The Reorganisation of Central Government*. London: HMSO.

Cmnd 8616 (1982) *Efficiency and Effectiveness in the Civil Service*. London: HMSO.

Cm. 1599 (1991) *The Citizen's Charter. Raising the Standard*. London: HMSO.

Cm. 2627 (1994) *The Civil Service. Continuity and Change*. London: HMSO.

Cm. 2748 (1995) *The Civil Service. Taking Forward Continuity and Change*. London: HMSO.

Cm. 2811 (1995) *Department of National Heritage Annual Report 1995*. London: HMSO.

Cm. 2850 (1995) *Standards in Public Life: The First Report of the Committee on Standards in Public Life* (Nolan). London: HMSO.

Cm. 3658 (1997) *Scotland's Parliament*. London: Stationery Office.

Cm. 3818 (1997) *Your Right To Know*. London: Stationery Office.

Cm. 3889 (1998) *Next Steps Report 1997*. London: Stationery Office.

Cm. 4011 (1998) *Modern Public Services for Britain: Investing in Reform. Comprehensive Spending Review: New Public Spending Plans 1999–2002*. London: Stationery Office.

Cm. 4014 (1998) *Modern Local Government: In Touch with the People*. London: Stationery Office.

Cm. 4181 (1998) *Public Services for the Future: Modernisation, Reform, Accountability*. London: Stationery Office.

Cm. 4273 (1999) *Next Steps Report 1998*. London: Stationery Office.

Cm. 4310 (1999) *Modernising Government*. London: Stationery Office.

Cm. 4444 (1999) *Memorandum of Understanding and Supplementary Agreements between the United Kingdom Government, Scottish Ministers and the Cabinet of the National Assembly for Wales*. London: Stationery Office.

Cm. 5511 (2002) *Your Region, Your Choice: Revitalising the English Regions*. London: Stationery Office.

Cohen, E.W. (1965) *The Growth of the British Civil Service*. London: Cass.

Collingwood, R. (1978) [1939] *An Autobiography*. With a new introduction by Stephen Toulmin. Oxford: Oxford University Press.

Collingwood, R. (1993) [1946] *The Idea of History*. Revised edition. Oxford: Oxford University Press.

Collingwood, R.G. (1965) *Essays in the Philosophy of History*. Austin: Texas University Press.

Collini, S., Winch, D. and Burrow, J. (1983) *That Noble Science of Politics*. Cambridge: Cambridge University Press.

Committee of Public Accounts (1994) *The Proper Conduct of Public Business*. London: HMSO.

Committee of Public Accounts (1997) *The Former Yorkshire Regional Health Authority: The Inquiry Commissioned by the NHS Chief Executive*. London: Stationery Office.

Cowling, M. (1963) *The Nature and Limits of Political Science*. Cambridge: Cambridge University Press.

Crewe, I. (1989) 'Has the Electorate Become Thatcherite?', in R. Skidelsky (ed.) *Thatcherism*. Oxford: Blackwell.

Crick, B. (1964) *The Reform of Parliament*. London: Weidenfeld & Nicolson.

Cromwell, V. (1966) 'Interpretations of Nineteenth Century Administration', *Victorian Studies*, 9: 245–55.

Cromwell, V. (ed.) (1977) *Revolution or Evolution*. London: Longman.

Cronin, J. (2001) 'Labour's "National Plan": Inheritances, Practices, Legacies', *European Legacy*, 6: 215–32.

Dale, H.E. (1941) *The Higher Civil Service of Great Britain*. Oxford: Oxford University Press.

Davis, G. (1998) 'Australian Administrative Tradition', in J.M. Shafritz (ed.) *International Encyclopaedia of Public Policy and Administration*. Boulder, CO: Westview Press.

Day, P. and Klein, R. (1997) *Steering But Not Rowing? The Transformation of the Department of Health: A Case Study*. Bristol: Policy Press.

Dearlove, J. (1982) 'The Political Science of British Politics', *Parliamentary Affairs*, 35: 436–54.

Dearlove, J. and Saunders, P. (1984) *Introduction to British Politics*. Cambridge: Polity Press.

Defence Committee (1986) *Westland plc: The Government's Decision Making. Fourth Report. Session 1985–86*. London: HMSO.

Demetriadi, Sir Stephen (1921) *Inside a Government Office*. London: Cassell.

Denham, J. (1999) Speech to the CIPFA, Public Management and Policy Association Conference on an 'An Epidemic of Zones: Illness or Cure?', International Conference Centre, Birmingham.

Department for Education and Employment (1998) 'New Year, New Deal, New Hope', Press Release, 5 January.

Derrida, J. (1976) *Of Grammatology*. Baltimore: Johns Hopkins University Press.

Dexter, L. (1970) *Elite and Specialized Interviewing*. Evanston, IL: Northwestern University Press.

Dicey, A.V. (1914) *Lectures on the Relations Between Law and Public Opinion During the Nineteenth Century*. 2nd edition. London: Macmillan.

Douglas, J. (1976) 'The Overloaded Crown', *British Journal of Political Science*, 6, 4: 483–505.

Dowding, K. (1995) 'Model or Metaphor? A Critical Review of the Policy Network Approach', *Political Studies*, 43: 136–58.

Dowding, K. (2001) 'There Must Be an End to Confusion', *Political Studies*, 49: 89–105.

Dowse, R.E. and Hughes, J.A. (1986) *Political Sociology*. 2nd edition. London: Wiley.

Drewry, G. and Butcher, T. (1991) *The Civil Service Today*. 2nd edition. Oxford: Blackwell.

Dreyfus, H. and Rabinow, P. (1982) *Michel Foucault: Beyond Structuralism and Hermeneutics*. Chicago: Chicago University Press.

Dunkley, P. (1980) 'The Emigration and the State, 1803–1842: The Nineteenth Century Revolution in Government Reconsidered', *Historical Journal*, 23: 353–80.

Dunleavy, P. and Hood, C. (1994), 'From Old Public Administration to New Public Management', *Public Money and Management*, 14, 3: 9–16.

Dunsire, A. (1993) 'Modes of Governance', in J. Kooiman (ed.) *Modern Governance*. London: Sage.

Dyson, K.H.F. (1980) *The State Tradition in Western Europe*. Oxford: Martin Robertson.

Eckstein, H. (1975) 'Case Study and Theory in Political Science', in F.I. Greenstein and N. Polsby (eds) *Handbook of Political Science. Volume 4. Strategies of Inquiry*. Reading, MA: Addison-Wesley: 79–137.

The Economist (1999) 'Thoroughly Modern Government', 3 April: 28–9.

Efficiency Unit (1988) *Improving Management in Government: The Next Steps*. London: HMSO.

Efficiency Unit (1993) *Career Management and Succession Planning Study* (Oughton). London: HMSO.

Elder, N., Thomas, A.H. and Arter, D. (1982) *The Consensual Democracies? The Government and Politics of the Scandinavian States*. Oxford: Martin Robertson.

English, R. and Kenny, M. (eds) (2000) *Rethinking British Decline*. London: Macmillan.

Epstein, L. (1987) 'Review Article: Books for Teaching British Politics', *British Journal of Political Science*, 17: 93–107.

Evans, P.B., Rueschemeyer, D. and Skocpol, T. (1985) 'On the Road Towards a More Adequate Understanding of the State', in P.B. Evans, D. Rueschemeyer and T. Skocpol (eds) *Bringing The State Back In*. Cambridge: Cambridge University Press.

Fenno, R.F. (1990) *Watching Politicians: Essays on Participant Observation*. Berkeley: Institute of Governmental Studies, University of California.

Ferlie, E. and Pettigrew, A. (1996) 'Managing Through Networks: Some Issues and Implications for the NHS', *British Journal of Management*, 7: 81–99.

Finer, H. (1946) *The Theory and Practice of Modern Government*. Two volumes. 2nd edition. London: Methuen.

Finer, S.E. (1952a) 'Patronage and the Public Service', *Public Administration*, 30: 329–60.

Finer, S.E. (1952b) *The Life and Times of Sir Edwin Chadwick*. London: Methuen.

Finer, S.E. (1956) 'The Individual Responsibility of Ministers', *Public Administration*, 34: 377–96.

Finer, S.E. (1970) *Comparative Government*. London: Allen Lane, The Penguin Press.

Finer, S.E. (1972) 'The Transmission of Benthamite Ideas 1820–50', in G. Sutherland (ed.) *Studies in the Growth of Nineteenth Century Government*. London: Routledge & Kegan Paul.

Finer, S.E. (ed.) (1975a) *Adversary Politics and Electoral Reform*. London: Anthony Wigram.

Finer, S.E. (1975b) 'State and Nation Building in Europe: The Role of the Military', in C. Tilly (ed.) *The Formation of National States in Western Europe*. Princeton, NJ: Princeton University Press.

Finer, S.E. (1980) 'Princes, Parliaments and the Public Service', *Parliamentary Affairs*, 33: 353–72.

Finer, S.E. (1987) 'Thatcherism and British Political History', in K. Minogue and M. Biddiss (eds) *Thatcherism: Personality and Politics*. London: Macmillan.

Finlayson, A. (1999) 'Third Way Theory', *Political Quarterly*, 70, 3: 271–9.

Fischer, W. and Lundgreen, P. (1975) 'The Recruitment and Training of Administrative and Technical Personnel', in C. Tilly (ed.) *The Formation of National States in Western Europe*. Princeton, NJ: Princeton University Press.

Flynn, R., Williams, G. and Pickard, S. (1996) *Markets and Networks: Contracting in Community Health Services*. Buckingham: Open University Press.

Foreign Affairs Committee (1985) *Events of the Weekend of 1st and 2nd of May 1982*. Third Report. Session 1984–5. London: HMSO.

Foster, C. and Plowden, F. (1996) *The State Under Stress*. Buckingham: Open University Press.

Foucault, M. (1972) *The Archaeology of Knowledge*. London: Tavistock.

Foucault, M. (1973) *The Birth of the Clinic: An Archaeology of Medical Perception*. London: Tavistock.

Foucault, M. (1977) *Discipline and Punish: The Birth of the Prison*. London: Tavistock.

Foucault, M. (1978–85) *The History of Sexuality*. Three volumes. New York: Pantheon.

Foucault, M. (1982) 'The Subject and Power', in H. Dreyfus and P. Rabinow (eds) *Michel Foucault: Beyond Structuralism and Hermeneutics*. Chicago: Chicago University Press.

Foucault, M. (1986) *The Order of Things: An Archaeology of the Human Sciences*. London: Routledge.

Foucault, M. (1991) 'Governmentality', in G. Burchell, C. Gordon and P. Miller (eds) *The Foucault Effect: Studies in Governmentality*. London: Harvester Wheatsheaf.

Frances, J. *et al.* (1991) 'Introduction', in G. Thompson, J. Frances, R. Levacic, and J. Mitchell (eds) *Markets Hierarchies and Networks: The Co-ordination of Social Life*. London: Sage.

Freeden, M. (1999) 'The Ideology of New Labour', *Political Quarterly*, 70: 42–51.

Fry, G.K. (1969) *Statesmen in Disguise*. London: Macmillan.

Fry, G.K. (1979) *The Growth of Government*. London: Cass.

Fry, G.K. (1981) *The Administrative 'Revolution' in Whitehall*. London: Croom Helm.

Fry, G.K. (1985) *The Changing Civil Service*. London: Allen & Unwin.

Fry, G.K. (1993) *Reforming the Civil Service: the Fulton Committee on the British Civil Service 1966–68*. Edinburgh: Edinburgh University Press.

Fry, G.K. (1995) *Policy and Management in the British Civil Service*. London: Prentice Hall, Harvester Wheatsheaf.

Gadamer H.-G. (1979) *Truth and Method*. Translated by W. Glen-Doepel. London: Sheed & Ward.

Gaffney, D., Pollock, A.M., Price, D. and Shaoul, J. (1999) 'NHS Capital Expenditure and the Private Finance Initiative – Expansion or Contraction?', *British Medical Journal*, 319, 3 July: 48–51.

Gamble, A. (1988) *The Free Economy and the Strong State*. London: Macmillan.

Gamble, A. (1990) 'Theories of British Politics', *Political Studies*, 38: 404–20.

Gamble, A. (1994) [1985] *Britain in Decline*. 4th edition. London: Macmillan.

Garrett, J. (1972) *The Management of Government*. Harmondsworth: Penguin Books.

Geertz, C. (1973) *The Interpretation of Cultures*. New York: Basic Books.

Giddens, A. (1990) *The Consequences of Modernity*. Cambridge: Polity Press.

Giddens, A. (1993) *New Rules of Sociological Method*. 2nd revised edition. Cambridge: Polity Press.

Giddens, A. (1998) *The Third Way*. Cambridge: Polity Press.

Gilmour, I. (1978) *Inside Right*. London: Quartet.

Gilmour, I. (1992) *Dancing with Dogma: Britain under Thatcherism*. London: Simon & Schuster.

Glaser, B. and Strauss, A. (1967) *The Discovery of Grounded Theory*. Chicago: Aldine.

Goodin, R. and Klingemann, H. (1996) (eds) *A New Handbook of Political Science*. Oxford: Oxford University Press.

Gould, J. and Anderson, D. (1987) 'Thatcherism and British Society', in K. Minogue and M. Biddiss (eds) *Thatcherism: Personality and Politics*. London: Macmillan.

Gowan, P. (1987) 'The Other Face of Reform'. London: Unpublished MA Thesis, London School of Economics and Political Science. All page references are to the thesis. A shortened version was published as: 'The Origins of the Administrative Elite', *New Left Review*, 162: 4–34.

Grant, W.P., Paterson, W. and Whitson, C. (1988) *Government and the Chemical Industry: A Comparative Study of Britain and West Germany*. Oxford: Clarendon Press.

Gray, A. and Jenkins, B. (1998) 'New Labour, New Government? Change and Continuity in Public Administration and Government 1997', *Parliamentary Affairs*, 51, 2: 111–30.

Greaves, H.R.G. (1947) *The Civil Service in the Changing State*. London: Harrap.

Greenleaf, W.H. (1983a) *The British Political Tradition. Volume 1. The Rise of Collectivism*. London: Methuen.

Greenleaf, W.H. (1983b) *The British Political Tradition. Volume 2. The Ideological Heritage*. London: Methuen.

Greenleaf, W.H. (1987) *The British Political Tradition. Volume 3. A Much Governed Nation, Parts 1 and 2*. London: Methuen.

Greve, C. (1997) 'Governance by Contract. Creating Public–Private partnerships in Denmark'. Paper to the European Group of Public Administration Annual Conference, 10–13 September, Leuven, Belgium.

Greve, C. (1998) 'Exploring Contracts and Boards as Reinvented Institutions for Bridging the Gap Between Politics and Non-state Governance'. Paper to the ECPR Joint Sessions, Workshop on 'Political Institutions: Beyond the State', 23–27 March, University of Warwick, Coventry, UK.

Greve, C. and Jensen, L. (2000) 'Central Government Reforms and Best Practice: the Case of Denmark', in W. Jann and C. Reichard (eds) *Central State Government Reform – An International Survey*. Washington, DC: Brookings Institute.

Greve, C. and Jespersen, P.K. (1998) 'New Public Management and its Critics. Alternative Roads to Flexible Service Delivery to Citizens'. Paper to the European Group of Public Administration Annual Conference, 14–17 September, Paris.

Habermas, J. (1987) *The Philosophical Discourse of Modernity*. Cambridge: Polity Press.

Hailsham, Lord (1978) *The Dilemma of Democracy*. London: Collins.

Hall, P.A. (1986) *Governing the Economy: The Politics of State Intervention in Britain and France*. Cambridge: Polity Press.

Hall, P.A. (1993) 'Policy Paradigms, Social Learning and the State: The Case of Economic Policy Making in Britain', *Comparative Politics*, 25, 3: 185–96.

Hall, P. and Taylor, R. (1996) 'Political Science and the Three Institutionalisms', *Political Studies*, 44: 936–57.

Hall, S. (1980) 'Popular-democratic versus Authoritarian Populism', in A. Hunt (ed.) *Marxism and Democracy*. London: Lawrence & Wishart.

Hall, S. (1983) 'The Great Moving Right Show', in S. Hall and M. Jacques (eds) *The Politics of Thatcherism*. London: Lawrence & Wishart.

Hall, S. and Jacques, M. (eds) (1983) *The Politics of Thatcherism*. London: Lawrence & Wishart.

Hall, S. and Schwarz, B. (1985) 'State and Society, 1880–1930', in M. Langan and B. Schwarz (eds) *Crises in the British State 1880–1930*. London: Hutchinson.

Hammersley, M. (1991) *Reading Ethnographic Research. A Critical Guide*. Harlow, Essex: Longman.

Hammersley, M. and Atkinson, P. (1983) *Ethnography: Principles in Practice*. London: Routledge.

Hansen, K. (1997) 'The Municipality Between Central State and Local Self-Government: Towards a New Municipality', *Local Government Studies*, 23, 4: 44–69.

Harris, J. (1990) 'Society and State in Twentieth-century Britain,' in F.M.L. Thompson (ed.) *The Cambridge Social History of Britain 1750–1950. Volume 3. Social Agencies and Institutions*. Cambridge: Cambridge University Press.

Harris, J.S. and Garcia, T.V. (1966) 'The Permanent Secretaries: Britain's Top Administrators', *Public Administration Review*, 26, 1: 31–44.

Harrison, B. (1996) *The Transformation of British Politics*. Oxford: Oxford University Press.

Hart, J. (1965) 'Nineteenth Century Social Reform: a Tory Interpretation of History', *Past and Present*, 31: 39–61.

Hart, J. (1972) 'The Genesis of the Northcote–Trevelyan Report', in G. Sutherland (ed.) *Studies in the Growth of Nineteenth-Century Government*. London: Routledge & Kegan Paul.

Hay, C. (1996) *Re-Stating Social and Political Change*. Buckinhgam: Open University Press.

Hay, C. (2003, forthcoming) *Political Analysis*. Basingstoke: Palgrave.

Hay, C. and Marsh, D. (2000) *Demystifying Globalisation*. London: Macmillan.

Hay, C. and Richards, D. (2000) 'The Tangled Webs of Westminster and Whitehall: The Discourse, Strategy and Practice of Networking within the British Core Executive', *Public Administration*, 78, 1: 1–28.

Hay, C. and Rosamund, B. (2002) 'Globalisation, European Integration and the Discursive Construction of Economic Imperatives', *Journal of European Public Policy*, 9, 2: 147–67.

Hay, C. and Wincott, D. (1998) 'Structure, Agency and Historic Institutionalism', *Political Studies*, 46: 951–7.

Hayek, F.A. (1991) [1944] *The Road to Serfdom*. London: Routledge & Kegan Paul.

Hayward, J. (1986) 'The Political Science of Muddling Through: The De Facto Paradigm?', in J. Hayward and P. Norton (eds) *The Political Science of British Politics*. Brighton: Wheatsheaf Books.

Hayward, J. (1991) 'Cultural and Contextual Constraints upon the Development of Political Science in Great Britain', in D. Easton, J.G. Gunnell and L. Graziano (eds) *The Development of Political Science: A Comparative Survey*. London: Routledge.

Hayward, J., Barry, B. and Brown, A. (2000) *The British Study of Politics in the Twentieth Century*. Oxford: Oxford University Press, for the British Academy.

Hazell, R. and Morris, B. (1999) 'Machinery of Government: Whitehall', in R. Hazell (ed.) *Constitutional Futures*. Oxford: Oxford University Press.

Heady, F. (1984) *Public Administration: A Comparative Perspective*. 3rd edition. New York and Basel: Marcel Dekker.

Heath, A. et al. (1991) *Understanding Political Change*. Oxford: Pergamon Press.

Heath, E. (1998) *The Course of My Life*. London: Hodder & Stoughton.

Hechter, M. (1975) *Internal Colonialism*. London: Routledge.

Heclo, H. and Wildavsky, A. (1974) *The Private Government of Public Money*. London: Macmillan.

Held, D. (1991) 'Democracy, the Nation State and the Global System', *Economy and Society*, 20: 138–72.

Hennessy, P. (1986a) *Cabinet*. Oxford: Blackwell.

Hennessy, P. (1986b) 'Michael Heseltine, Mottram's Law and the Efficiency of Cabinet Government', *Political Quarterly*, 57, 2: 137–43.

Hennessy, P. (1989) *Whitehall*. London: Secker & Warburg.

Hennessy, P. (1992) *Never Again*. London: Jonathan Cape.

Hennessy, P. (1995) *The Hidden Wiring: Unearthing the British Constitution*. London: Victor Gollancz.

Hennessy, P. (1996) '"Shadow and Substance": Premiership for the Twenty-first Century', Gresham College, Rhetoric Lectures, 1995–6. Lecture 6, 5 March 1996.

Hennessy, P. (1998) 'The Blair Style of Government', *Government and Opposition*, 33, 1: 3–20.

Henney, A. (1984) *Inside Local Government. The Case for Radical Reform*. London: Sinclair Browne.

Hennock, E.P. (1973) *Fit and Proper Persons: Ideal and Reality in Nineteenth Century Urban Government*. London: Edward Arnold.

Hindmoor, A. 1998. 'The Importance of Being Trusted: Transaction Costs and Policy Network Theory', *Public Administration*, 76: 25–44.

Hirst, P. (1990) *Representative Democracy and Its Limits*. Cambridge: Polity Press.

Hirst, P. and Thompson, G. (1995) 'Globalization and the Future of the Nation State', *Economy and Society*, 24: 408–42.

Hirst, P. and Thompson, P. (1999) *Globalisation in Question*. 2nd edition. Cambridge: Polity Press.

Hogwood, B.W., Judge, D. and McVicar, M. (2000) 'Agencies and Accountability', in R.A.W. Rhodes (ed.) *Transforming British Government. Volume 1. Changing Institutions*. London: Macmillan.

Honderich, T. (1991) *Conservatism*. Harmondsworth: Penguin Books.

Hood, C. (1991) 'A Public Management for All Seasons?', *Public Administration*, 69: 3–19.

Hood, C. (1995) 'Contemporary Public Management: A New Global Paradigm?', *Public Policy and Administration*, 10, 2: 104–17.

Hood, C. (1996) 'Exploring Variations in Public Management Reforms of the 1980s', in H.A.G.M. Bekke, J.L. Perry and T.A.J. Toonen (eds) *Civil Service Systems in Comparative Perspective*. Bloomington: Indiana University Press.

Hood, C., James, O. and Scott, C. (2000) 'Regulation in Government: Has it Increased, is it Increasing, Should it be Diminished?', *Public Administration*, 78, 2: 283–304.

Hood, C., James, O., Jones, G., Scott, C. and Travers, T. (1998) 'Regulation Inside Government: Where the New Public Management Meets the Audit Explosion', *Public Money and Management*, 18, 2: 61–8.

Hooghe, E. (1996) (ed.) *Cohesion and European Integration: Building Multi-Level Governance*. Oxford: Clarendon Press.

Hoskyns, Sir John (1983) 'Whitehall and Westminster: An Outsider's View', *Parliamentary Affairs*, 36: 137–47.

Hughes, E. (1949) 'Sir Charles Trevelyan and Civil Service Reform 1853–55', *English Historical Review*, 64: 52–8 and 206–34.

Hume, L.J. (1981) *Bentham and Bureaucracy*. Cambridge: Cambridge University Press.

Husserl, E. (1931) *Ideas: General Introduction to Pure Phenomenology*. London: George Allen and Unwin.

Hutton, W. (1996) *The State We're In*. London: Vintage.

Jacoby, H. (1973) *The Bureaucratisation of the World*. London: University of California Press.

Jenkins, W.I. (1993) 'Reshaping the Management of Government: The Next Steps Initiative in the United Kingdom', in F.L. Seidle (ed.) *Rethinking Government: Reform or Revolution?* Quebec: Institute for Research on Public Policy.

Jensen, H.N., Jensen, L. and Knudsen, T. (1999) 'The Changing Role of the Danish Senior Civil Service'. Paper to the Workshop on 'The Changing Role of the Civil Service, Nuffield College, Oxford: 15–16 January.

Jensen, L. (1998a) 'Cultural Theory and Democratizing Functional Domains: The Case of Danish Housing', *Public Administration*, 76: 117–39.

Jensen, L. (1998b) 'Interpreting New Public Management: The Case of Denmark', *Australian Journal of Public Administration*, 57, 4: 55–66.

Jessop, B. (1990) *State Theory*. Pennsylvania: Pennsylvania State University Press.

Jessop, B. (1995) 'The Regulation Approach, Governance and Post-Fordism: An Alternative Perspective on Economic and Political Change?', *Economy and Society*, 24, 3: 307–33.

Jessop, B. (1997) 'The Governance of Complexity and the Complexity of Governance: Preliminary Remarks on Some Problems and Limits of Economic Guidance', in A. Amin and J. Hausner (eds) *Beyond Market and Hierarchy: Interactive Governance and Social Complexity*. Cheltenham: Edward Elgar.

Jessop, B. (1999) 'Governance Failure', in G. Stoker (ed.) *The New Management of Local Governance: Audit of an Era of Change in Britain*. London: Macmillan.

Jessop, B., Bonnett, K., Bromley, S. and Ling, T. (1988) *Thatcherism*. Cambridge: Polity Press.

Johnson, N. (1975) 'The Place of Institutions in the Study of Politics', *Political Studies*, 23: 271–83.

Johnson, N. (1977) *In Search of the Constitution*. Oxford: Pergamon Press.

Johnson, N. (1989) *The Limits of Political Science*. Oxford: Clarendon Press.

Jordan, G. (1990) 'Sub-governments, Policy Communities and Networks. Refilling the Old Bottles?', *Journal of Theoretical Politics*, 2: 319–38.

Jordan, G. and Schubert, K. (eds) (1992) *Policy Networks*. Special issue of the *European Journal of Political Science*, 21, 1 and 2.

Jordan, M., Maloney, W. and McLaughlin, A. 1994. 'Characterising Agricultural Policy Making', *Public Administration*, 72: 505–26.

Jørgensen, Torben Beck (1993) 'Modes of Governance and Administrative Change', in J. Kooiman (ed.) *Modern Governance*. London: Sage.

Jørgensen, Torben Beck (1999) 'The Public Sector in an In-between Time', *Public Administration*, 77, 3: 565–84.

Jørgensen, Torben Beck and Hansen, Claus-Arne (1995) 'Agencification and De-agencification in Danish Central Government: Contradictory Developments – Or Is There an Underlying Logic?', *International Review of Administrative Sciences*, 61: 549–63.

Kamenka, E. (1989) *Bureaucracy*. Oxford: Blackwell.

Kavanagh, D. (1990a) *Thatcherism and British Politics. The End of Consensus?* 2nd edition. Oxford: Oxford University Press.

Kavanagh, D. (1990b) *British Politics: Continuity and Change*. 2nd edition. Oxford: Oxford University Press.

Kavanagh, D. (1991) 'Why Political Science Needs History', *Political Studies*, 39: 479–95.

Kavanagh, D. and Seldon, A. (2000) 'The Power Behind the Prime Minister: The Hidden Influence of No. 10', in R.A.W. Rhodes (ed.) *Transforming British Government. Volume 2. Changing Roles and Relationships*. London: Macmillan.

Keir, Sir David Lindsay (1961) *The Constitutional History of Modern Britain Since 1485*. 6th edition. London: A. & C. Black.

Kellner, P. and Lord Crowther-Hunt (1980) *The Ruling Servants*. London: Macdonald Futura.

Kenis, P. and Schneider, V. (1991) 'Policy Networks and Policy Analysis: Scrutinizing a New Analytical Toolbox', in B. Marin and R. Mayntz (eds) *Policy Networks: Empirical Evidence and Theoretical Considerations*. Frankfurt am Main: Campus Verlag.

Kerr, P. (2001) *Post-war British Politics: From Conflict to Consensus*. London: Routledge.

Kickert, W.J.M (1993) 'Autopoiesis and the Science of (Public) Administration: Essence, Sense and Nonsense', *Organization Studies*, 14: 261–78.

Kickert, W.J.M (1997b) 'Public Governance in the Netherlands: An Alternative to Anglo-American "Managerialism"', *Public Administration*, 75: 731–52.

Kickert, W.J.M. (1997a) 'Public Management in the United States and Europe', in W.J.M. Kickert (ed.) *Public Management and Administrative Reform in Europe*. Aldershot: Edward Elgar.

Kickert, W.J.M., Klijn, E.-H. and Koppenjan, J.F.M. (1997a) 'Managing Networks in the Public Sector: Findings and Reflections', in W.J.M. Kickert, E.-H. Klijn and J.F.M. Koppenjan (eds) *Managing Complex Networks: Strategies for the Public Sector*. London: Sage.

Kickert, W.J.M., Klijn, E.-H., and Koppenjan, J.F.M. (eds) (1997b) *Managing Complex Networks: Strategies for the Public Sector*. London: Sage.

King, A. (1975) 'Overload: Problems of Governing in the 1980s', *Political Studies*, 23: 284–96.

King, A. (1985) 'Margaret Thatcher: The Style of a Prime Minister', in A. King (ed.) *The British Prime Minister*. 2nd edition. London: Macmillan.

Kingdom, J. (1991) *Government and Politics in Britain*. Cambridge: Polity Press.

Kingsley, J.D. (1944) *Representative Bureaucracy*. Yellow Springs, OH: Antioch Press.

Kirchhoff, H. (1995) 'A Light in the Darkness of the Holocaust? A Reply to Gunnar S. Paulsson', *Journal of Contemporary History*, 30: 465–79.

Kitson-Clark, G. (1973) ' "Statesmen in Disguise": Reflections on the History of the Neutrality of the Civil Service', in P. Stansky (ed.) *The Victorian Revolution*. New York: Watts.

Kjellberg, F. (1988) 'Local Government and the Welfare State: Reorganisation in Scandinavia', in B. Dente and F. Kjellberg (eds) *The Dynamics of Institutional Change. Local Government Reorganisation in Western Democracies*. London: Sage.

Klijn, E.-H., Koopenjan, J. and Termeer, K. (1995) 'Managing Networks in the Public Sector: A Theoretical Study of Management Strategies in Policy Networks', *Public Administration*, 73: 437–54.

Knudsen, T. (1991) 'State Building in Scandinavia: Denmark in a Nordic Context', in T. Knudsen (ed.) *Welfare Administration in Denmark*. Copenhagen: Ministry of Finance.

Knudsen, T. (1999) 'How Informal Can You Be? The Case of Denmark?', in V. Wright, B.G. Peters and R.A.W. Rhodes (eds) *Administering the Summit: Administration of the Core Executive in Developed Countries*. London: Macmillan.

Knudsen, T. and Rothstein, B. (1994) 'State Building in Scandinavia', *Comparative Politics*, 27: 203–20.

Kooiman, J. (ed.) (1993a) *Modern Governance*. London: Sage.

Kooiman, J. (1993b) 'Findings, Speculations and Recommendations', in J. Kooiman (ed.) *Modern Governance*. London: Sage.

Koselleck, R. (1998) 'Social History and Begriffsgeschichte', in I. Hampsher-Monk, K. Tilmans and F. van Vree (eds) *History of Concepts: Comparative Perspectives*. Amsterdam: University of Amsterdam Press.

Kramer, R.M. and Tyler, T. (eds) (1996) *Trust in Organizations: Frontiers of Theory and Research*. London: Sage.

Labour Party (1991) *Made in Britain: A New Economic Policy for the 1990s*. London: Labour Party.

Labour Party (1994) *Rebuilding the Economy*. London: Labour Party.

Labour Party (1996) *Getting Welfare to Work*. London: Labour Party.

Lacan, J. (1977) 'The Function and Field of Speech and Language in Psychoanalysis', in *Ecrits: A Selection*. London: Tavistock.

Landers, B. (1999) 'Encounters with the Public Accounts Committee: A Personal Memoir', *Public Administration*, 77, 1: 197–213.

Larson, A. (1992) 'Network Dyads in Entrepreneurial Settings: A Study of Governance Exchange Relationships', *Administrative Science Quarterly*, 37: 76–104.

Laski, H.J. (1938) *Parliamentary Government in England*. London: Allen & Unwin.

Laumann, E.O. and Knoke, D. (1987) *The Organizational State: Social Choice in National Policy Domains*. Madison, WI: University of Wisconsin Press.

Lee, J.M. (1977) *Reviewing the Machinery of Government 1942–1952. An Essay on the Anderson Committee and its Successors*. London: Birkbeck College, mimeo.

Leftwich, A. (1984) 'On the Politics of Politics', in A. Leftwich (ed.) *What is Politics?* Oxford: Blackwell.

Leftwich, A. (1993) 'Governance, Democracy and Development in the Third World', *Third World Quarterly*, 14: 605–24.

Le Galès, P. (1998) 'Regulations and Governance in European Cities', *International Journal of Urban and Regional Research*, 22: 482–506.

Le Galès, P. and Thatcher, M. (eds) (1995) *Les réseaux de politique publique. Débat autour des policy networks*. Paris: Editions L'Harmatton.

Leys, C. (1983) *Politics in Britain*. London: Heinemann.

Lijphart, A. (1984) *Democracies*. New Haven, CT: Yale University Press.

Lindberg, L., Campbell, J.L. and Hollingsworth, J.R. (1991) 'Economic Governance and the Analysis of Structural Change in the American Economy', in J. Campbell, J.R. Hollingsworth and L. Linberg (eds) *Governance of the American Economy*. Cambridge: Cambridge University Press.

Linklater, M. and Leigh, D. (1986) *Not With Honour: The Inside Story of the Westland Scandal*. London: Sphere.

Loughlin, J. and Peters, B.G. (1997) 'State Traditions, Administrative Reform and Regionalization', in M. Keating and J. Loughlin (eds) *The Political Economy of Regionalism*. London: Frank Cass.

Loughlin, M. (1992) *Public Law and Political Theory*. Oxford: Clarendon Press.

Low, S. (1904) *The Governance of England*. London: Fisher Unwin.

Lowe, R. (1999) *The Welfare State in Britain*. 2nd edition. London: Macmillan.

Lowe, R. and Rollings, N. (2000) 'Modernising Britain, 1957–64: A Classic Case of Centralisation and Fragmentation?', in R.A.W. Rhodes (ed.) *Transforming British Government. Volume 1. Changing Institutions*. London: Macmillan.

Lowndes, V. and Skelcher, C. (1998) 'The Dynamics of Multi-organisational Partnerships: An Analysis of Changing Modes of Governance', *Public Administration*, 76: 313–33.

Luhmann, N. (1982) *The Differentiation of Society*. New York: Columbia University Press.

Lyon, M. (1994) *Postmodernity*. Buckingham: Open University Press.

Lyotard, J.-F. (1984) *The Postmodern Condition: A Report on Knowledge*. Minneapolis: University of Minnesota Press.

MacDonagh, O. (1961) *A Pattern of Government Growth: The Passenger Acts and the Enforcement, 1800–1860*. London: MacGibbon and Kee.

MacDonagh, O. (1973) [1958] 'The Nineteenth Century Revolution in Government: A Reappraisal', pp. 5–25 and 355–8. The page references are to the reprinted version in P. Stansky (ed.) *The Victorian Revolution*. New York: Watts. The paper appeared originally in *Historical Journal*, 1: 52–67.

MacDonagh, O. (1977) *Early Victorian Government*. London: Weidenfeld and Nicolson.

MacIntyre A. (1983) 'The Indispensability of Political Theory', in D. Miller and L. Siedentop (eds) *The Nature of Political Theory*. Oxford: Clarendon Press.

Mackenzie, W.J.M. (1961) *Theories of Local Government*. London: London School of Economics and Political Science, Greater London Papers No. 2.

Mackenzie, W.J.M. and Grove, J.W. (1957) *Central Administration in Britain*. London: Longmans, Green.

Mackintosh, M. (1999) 'Two Economic Discourses in the New Management of Local Governance: "Public Trading" and "Public Business"', in G. Stoker (ed.) *The New Management of British Local Governance*. London: Macmillan.

McLennan, G. (1995) *Pluralism*. Buckingham: Open University Press.

MacLeod, R. (1988) 'Introduction', in R. MacLeod (ed.) *Government and Expertise*. Cambridge: Cambridge University Press.

McPherson, A. and Raab, C. (1988) *Governing Education*. Edinburgh: Edinburgh University Press.

Madgwick, P. (1986) 'Prime Ministerial Power Revisited', *Social Studies Review*, 1, 5: 28–35.

Mandelson, P. and Liddle, R. (1996) *The Blair Revolution: Can New Labour Deliver?* London: Faber & Faber.

March, J.G. and Olsen, J.P. (1984) 'The New Institutionalism: Organisational Factors in Political Life', *American Political Science Review*, 78.

March, J.G. and Olsen, J.P. (1989) *Rediscovering Institutions: The Organizational Basis of Politics*. New York: The Free Press.

Marin, B. and Mayntz, R. (eds) (1991) *Policy Networks: Empirical Evidence and Theoretical Considerations*. Frankfurt am Main: Campus Verlag.

Marquand, D. (1988) *The Unprincipled Society*. London: Cape.

Marquand, D. (1989) 'The Paradoxes of Thatcherism', in R. Skidelsky (ed.) *Thatcherism*. Oxford: Blackwell.

Marsh, D. (ed.) (1999) *Comparing Networks*. Buckingham: Open University Press.

Marsh, D. and Rhodes, R.A.W. (eds) (1992a) *Policy Networks in British Government*. Oxford: Clarendon Press.

Marsh, D. and Rhodes, R.A.W. (eds) (1992b) *Implementing Thatcherite Policies*. Buckingham: Open University Press.

Marsh, D. and Smith, M. (2000) 'The Role of Networks in an Understanding of Whitehall: Towards a Dialectical Approach', *Political Studies*, 48, 1: 4–21.

Marsh, D., Buller, J., Hay, C., Johnston, J., Kerr, P., McAnulla, S. and Watson, M. (1999) *Post-war British Politics in Perspective*. Cambridge: Polity Press.

Marsland, D. (1996) *Welfare State or Welfare?* Basingstoke: Macmillan.

Marwick, A. (1995) 'Two Approaches to Historical Study: The Metaphysical (Including "Postmodernism") and the Historical', *Journal of Contemporary History*, 30: 5–35.

Menon, A. and Wright, V. (1998) 'The Paradoxes of "Failure": British EU Policy Making in Comparative Perspective', *Public Policy and Administration*, 13, 4: 46–66.

Metcalfe, L. and Richards, S. (1991) *Improving Public Management*. 2nd edition. London: Sage.

Middlemas, K. (1979) *Politics in Industrial Society: The Experience of the British System Since 1911*. London: André Deutsch.

Miliband, R. (1969) *The State in Capitalist Society*. London: Weidenfeld & Nicolson.

Miliband, R. (1972) *Parliamentary Socialism*. London: Merlin Press.

Miliband, R. (1982) *Capitalist Democracy in Britain*. Oxford: Oxford University Press.

Mill, J.S. (1910) [1861] *Considerations on Representative Government*. London: Dent.

Mill, J.S. (1969) [1840] 'Coleridge', in *Essays on Ethics, Religion and Society*. The Collected Works of John Stuart Mill. Volume 10. Edited by J.M. Robson. Toronto: University of Toronto Press.

Ministry of Finance (1993) *Nyt syn på den offentlige sektor*. København: Ministry of Finance.

Ministry of Finance (1998) *Forholdet mellem minister og embedsmænd.* København: Betænkning 1354.

Minogue, K. (1989) 'The Emergence of the New Right', in R. Skidelsky (ed.) *Thatcherism.* Oxford: Blackwell.

Moore, B. (1969) *Social Origins of Democracy and Dictatorship.* Harmondsworth: Penguin Books.

Mount, F. (1992) *The British Constitution Now: Recovery or Decline?* London: Mandarin.

Mueller, H.E. (1984) *Bureaucracy, Education and Monopoly: Civil Service Reforms in Prussia and England.* London: University of California Press.

Muir, R. (1910) *Peers and Bureaucrats.* London: Constable.

Mulgan, G. (2001) Speech to the 'Conference on Joined-Up Government', British Academy, London, 30 October.

Murray, C. (1990) *The Emerging British Underclass.* London: Institute for Economic Affairs.

Murray, C. (1994) *Underclass: The Crisis Deepens.* London: Institute for Economic Affairs.

Nairn, T. (1981) [1977] *The Break Up of Britain.* Revised edition. London: Verso.

Namier, Sir Lewis (1961) *England in the Age of the American Revolution.* 2nd edition. London: Macmillan.

Namier, Sir Lewis (1974) [1955] *Personalities and Power.* Westport, CT: Greenwood Press [London: Hamish Hamilton].

Naschold, F. (1995) *The Modernisation of the Public Sector in Europe: A Comparative Perspective on the Scandinavian Experience.* Helsinki: Ministry of Labour.

Nash, G.D. (1969) *Perspectives on Administration: The Vistas of History.* Berkeley, CA: Institute of Governmental Studies, University of California.

Nielsen, K. and Pedersen, O.K. (1988) 'The Negotiated Economy: Ideal and History', *Scandinavian Political Studies*, 11, 2: 79–101.

Niskanen, W. *et al.* (1973) *Bureaucracy: Servant or Master?* London: Institute for Economic Affairs.

Norton, A. (1994) *The International Handbook of Local and Regional Government. A Comparative Analysis of Advanced Democracies.* Aldershot: Edward Elgar.

Norton, P. (1983) 'The Norton Model', in D. Judge (ed.) *The Politics of Parliamentary Reform.* London: Heinemann.

Norton, P. (1984) *The British Polity.* New York: Longman.

Norton, P. (1991) 'In Defence of the Constitution: A Riposte to the Radicals', in P. Norton (ed.) *New Directions in British Politics? Essays on the Evolving Constitution.* Aldershot: Edward Elgar.

Norton, P. (1996) 'Constitutional Change', *Talking Politics*, 9, 1: 17–22.

Norton, P. (2000) 'Barons in a Shrinking Kingdom: Senior Ministers in British Government', in R.A.W. Rhodes (ed.) *Transforming British Government. Volume 2. Changing Roles and Relationships.* London: Macmillan.

Norton, P. and Hayward, J. (1986) 'Retrospective Reflections', in J. Hayward and P. Norton (eds) *The Political Science of British Politics.* Brighton: Wheatsheaf Books.

Norton-Taylor, R. (1985) *The Ponting Affair.* London: Cecil Wolf.

Oakeshott, M. (1962) 'Political Education', in *Rationalism in Politics and Other Essays.* Oxford: Oxford University Press.

Oakeshott, M. (1975) *On Human Conduct*. Oxford: Clarendon Press.

Oakeshott, M. (1983) *On History and Other Essays*. Oxford: Oxford University Press.

OECD (1993) *Public Management: OECD Country Profiles*. Paris: OECD.

OECD (1995) *Governance in Transition: Public Management Reform in OECD Countries*. Paris: OECD, PUMA.

OECD (1996) *Ministerial Symposium on the Future of the Public Services*. Paris, OECD.

O'Halpin, E. (1989) *Head of the Civil Service. A Study of Sir Warren Fisher*. London: Routledge.

Olsen, J.P. (1983) *Organized Democracy. Political Institutions in a Welfare State – The Case of Norway*. Oslo: Universitetsforlaget.

Olsen, J.P. and Peters, B.G. (1996) *Lessons from Experience*. Oslo: Scandinavian University Press.

One Nation Group (1954) *Change is our Ally*. London: Conservative Political Centre.

Osborne, D. and Gaebler, T. (1992) *Reinventing Government*. Reading, MA: Addison-Wesley.

O'Toole, L. (1997) 'Treating Networks Seriously: Practical and Research-based Agendas in Public Administration', *Public Administration Review*, 57, 1: 45–52.

Page, E. (1990) 'The Political Origins of Self-government and Bureaucracy: Otto Hintze's Conceptual Map of Europe', *Political Studies*, 38: 39–55.

Painter, C., Isaac-Henry, K. and Rouse, J. (1997) 'Local Authorities and Non-elected Agencies: Strategic Responses and Organizational Networks', *Public Administration*, 75: 225–45.

Parker, M. (1992) 'Post-modern Organisations or Postmodern Organization Theory', *Organization Studies*, 13: 1–17.

Parker, R.S. (1979) 'The Public Service Inquiries and Responsible Government', in R.F.I. Smith and P. Weller (eds) *Public Service Inquiries in Australia*. Brisbane: University of Queensland Press.

Parris, H. (1969) *Constitutional Bureaucracy*. London: Allen & Unwin.

Parris, H. (1973) [1960] 'The Nineteenth-Century Revolution in Government: A Reappraisal Re-appraised', in P. Stansky (ed.) *The Victorian Revolution*. New York: Watts.

Part, A. (1990) *The Making of a Mandarin*. London: Deutsch.

Paulsson, Gunnar S. (1995) 'The "Bridge over the Øresund": The Historiography on the Expulsion of the Jews from Nazi-Occupied Denmark', *Journal of Contemporary History*, 30: 431–64.

Pearson, R. and Williams, G. (1984) *Political Thought and Public Policy in the Nineteenth Century*. London: Longman.

Pedersen, P.K., Sørensen, H.D. and Vestergaard, J.B. (1997) 'The Contract Management Project in Denmark', in OECD, *Benchmarking, Evaluation and Strategic Management*. Paris: OECD.

Perez-Diaz, V.M. (1993) *The Return of Civil Society*. Cambridge, MA: Harvard University Press.

Perkin, H.J. (1969) *Origins of Modern English Society, 1780–1880*. London: Routledge & Kegan Paul.

Perri 6 (1997) *Holistic Government*. London: Demos.

Peters, B.G. (1993) 'Managing the Hollow State', in K.J. Eliassen and J. Kooiman (eds) *Managing Public Organizations*. London: Sage.

Peters, B.G. (1995) 'Introducing the Topic', in B.G. Peters and D.J. Savoie (eds) *Governance in a Changing Environment*. Montreal and Kingston: Canadian Centre for Management Development and McGill-Queen's University Press.

Peters, B.G. (1996) *The Future of Governing: Four Emerging Models*. Lawrence, KS: University of Kansas Press.

Peters, B.G. (1997) 'A North American Perspective on Administrative Modernisation in Europe', in W.J.M. Kickert (ed.) *Public Management and Administrative Reform in Western Europe*. Aldershot, Edward Elgar.

Plowden, W. (1994) *Ministers and Mandarins*. London: Institute for Policy Research.

Pollitt, C. (1993) *Managerialism and the Public Services*. 2nd edition. Oxford: Blackwell.

Pollitt, C. (1995) 'Justification by Works or by Faith? Evaluating the New Public Management', *Evaluation*, 1, 2: 133–54.

Pollitt, C. and Bouckaert, G. (2000) *Public Management Reform: A Comparative Analysis*. Oxford: Oxford University Press.

Pollitt, C. and Summa, H. (1997) 'Trajectories of Reform: Public Management in Four Countries', *Public Money and Management*, 17, 1: 7–18.

Ponting, C. (1985) *The Right to Know*. London: Sphere.

Porter, B. (1994) *Britannia's Burden: The Political Evolution of Modern Britain, 1851–1990*. London: Edward Arnold.

Powell, J. Enoch and Maude, A. (eds) (1954) *Change is our Ally*. London: Conservative Political Centre.

Powell, W. (1991) 'Neither Market Nor Hierarchy: Network Forms of Organisation', in G. Thompson, J. Frances, R. Levacic, and J. Mitchell (eds) *Markets, Hierarchies and Networks: The Co-ordination of Social Life*. London: Sage.

Power, M. (1994) *The Audit Explosion*. London: Demos.

Public Accounts Committee (1994) *The Proper Conduct of Public Business*. London: HMSO.

Public Service Committee (1996) *Ministerial Accountability and Responsibility*. HC 313. Session 1995–96. London: Stationery Office.

Pugh, M. (1994) *State and Society: British Political and Social History 1870–1992*. London: Edward Arnold.

Putnam, H. (1981) *Reason, Truth, and History*. Cambridge: Cambridge University Press.

Qualter, T.N. (1980) *Graham Wallas and the Great Society*. London: Macmillan.

Quine, W. (1960) *Word and Object*. Cambridge, MA: MIT Press.

Reed, M. (1992) *The Sociology of Organisations: Themes, Perspectives and Prospects*. London: Harvester Wheatsheaf.

Reed, M. (1993) 'Organisations and Modernity: Continuity and Discontinuity in Organization Theory', in J. Hassid and M. Parker (eds) *Post-modernism and Organisations*. London: Sage.

Rein, M. (1976) *Social Science and Public Policy*. Harmondsworth: Penguin Books.

Rhodes, R.A.W. (1973) '"Wilting in Limbo": Anthony Trollope and the Nineteenth Century Civil Service', *Public Administration*, 51: 207–19.

Rhodes, R.A.W. (1988) *Beyond Westminster and Whitehall*. London: Unwin-Hyman. Reprinted Routledge, 1992.

Rhodes, R.A.W. (1992) 'Beyond Whitehall: Researching Local Governance', *Social Sciences*, 13, November: 2.

Rhodes, R.A.W. (1996) 'The New Governance: Governing without Government', *Political Studies*, 44: 652–67.

Rhodes, R.A.W. (1997a) *Understanding Governance*. Buckingham: Open University Press.

Rhodes, R.A.W. (1997b) 'It's the Mix that Matters: From Marketisation to Diplomacy', *Australian Journal of Public Administration*, 56: 40–53.

Rhodes, R.A.W. (1997c) 'Shackling the Leader? Coherence, Capacity and the Hollow Crown', in P. Weller, H. Bakvis and R.A.W. Rhodes (eds) *The Hollow Crown: Countervailing Trends in Core Executives*. London: Macmillan.

Rhodes, R.A.W. (1998) 'Different Roads to Unfamiliar Places: UK Experience in Comparative Perspective', *Australian Journal of Public Administration*, 57: 19–31.

Rhodes, R.A.W. (1999) [1981] *Control and Power in Central–Local Government Relationships*. Farnborough: Gower. Reprinted (Aldershot: Ashgate) with a new Preface and three extra chapters.

Rhodes, R.A.W. (ed.) (2000a) *Transforming British Government*. Two volumes. London: Macmillan.

Rhodes, R.A.W. (ed.) (2000b) 'New Labour's Civil Service: Summing-up Joining-up', *Political Quarterly*, 71, 2, 2000: 151–66.

Rhodes, R.A.W. (2001) 'Unitary States', in Neil J. Smelser and Paul B. Baltes (eds) *International Encyclopaedia of the Social and Behavioural Sciences*. Oxford: Pergamon Press.

Rhodes, R.A.W. (2002) 'Putting People Back Into Networks', *Australian Journal of Political Science*, 37, 3: 399–415.

Rhodes, R.A.W. and Weller, P. (2001) (eds) *The Changing World of Top Officials: Mandarins or Valets?* Buckingham: Open University Press.

Richards, D. (1997) *The Civil Service under the Conservatives 1979–97*. Brighton: Sussex Academic Press.

Richards, S. (1993) 'Memorandum', submitted by Professor Sue Richards, Director of the Public Management Foundation, to Treasury and Civil Service Committee, *Role of the Civil Service, Volume II, Minutes of Evidence and Appendices*. London: HMSO. 6th Report. HC 390–II. Session 1992–3: 277–80.

Richter, M. (1995) *The History of Political and Social Concepts: A Critical Introduction*. New York: Oxford University Press.

Riddell, P. (1989) *The Thatcher Decade*. Oxford: Blackwell.

Riddell, P. (1997) 'Advising the Prime Minister'. Paper to the ESRC Conference on 'Future Whitehall', Church House, London.

Riddell, P. (2000) 'A Portrait of the Whitehall Programme'. Report to the Economic and Social Research Council, Swindon, unpublished.

Ridley, F.F. (1988) *Specialists and Generalists*. London: Allen & Unwin.

RIPA (Royal Institute of Public Administration) (1987) *Top Jobs in Whitehall: Appointments and Promotions in the Senior Civil Service*. London: RIPA.

Robson, W.A. (ed.) (1937) *The British Civil Servant*. London: Allen & Unwin.

Rorty, R. (1980) *Philosophy and the Mirror of Nature*. Oxford: Blackwell.

Rose, R. (1982) *Understanding the United Kingdom*. London: Longman.

Rose, R. (1985) *Politics in England: Change and Persistence*. 4th edition. London: Faber.

Rosen, F. (1983) *Jeremy Bentham and Representative Government*. Oxford: Clarendon Press.

Rosenau, J.N. (1992) 'Governance, Order and Change in World Politics', in J.N. Rosenau and E.-O. Czempiel (eds) *Governance without Government: Order and Change in World Politics*. Cambridge: Cambridge University Press.

Rosenau, P.M. (1992) *Post-modernism and the Social Sciences, Insights, Inroads and Intrusions*. Princeton: Princeton University Press.

Rowe, M. (1999) 'Joined Up Accountability: Bringing the Citizen Back In', *Public Policy and Administration Review*, 14, 2: 91–102.

Rueschemeyer, D. and Evans, P.B. (1985) 'The State and Economic Transformation: Toward an Analysis of the Conditions Underlying Effective Intervention', in P.B. Evans, D. Rueschemeyer and T. Skocpol (eds) *Bringing The State Back In*. Cambridge: Cambridge University Press.

Ryan, A. (1972) 'Utilitarianism and Bureaucracy: The Views of J.S. Mill', in G. Sutherland (ed.) *Studies in the Growth of Nineteenth-Century Government*. London: Routledge & Kegan Paul.

Sanjek, R. (ed.) (1990) *Fieldnotes: The Making of Anthropology*. Ithaca, NY: Cornell University Press.

Scharpf, F.W. (1997) *Games Real Actors Play: Actor Centred Institutionalism in Policy Research*. Boulder, CO: Westview Press.

Scruton, R. (1984) *The Meaning of Conservatism*. 2nd edition. London: Macmillan.

Sharpe, L.J. (1981) 'Theories and Values of Local Government', in L.D. Feldman (ed.) *Politics and Government of Urban Canada*. 4th edition. London: Methuen.

Shepherd, R. (1996) *Enoch Powell: A Biography*. London: Hutchinson.

Shils, E. (1981) *Tradition*. Chicago: University of Chicago Press.

Siim, B. (1998) *Vocabularies of Citizenship and Gender: The Danish Case*. Aarlborg University, GEP Working Paper No. 6.

Silverman, D. (1997) (ed.) *Qualitative Research: Theory, Method, Practice*. London: Sage.

Silverman, D. and Jones, J. (1976) *Organizational Work*. London: Collier-Macmillan.

Sisson, C.H. (1959) *The Spirit of British Administration*. London: Faber & Faber.

Skidelsky, R. (1989) 'Introduction', in R. Skidelsky (ed.) *Thatcherism*. Oxford: Blackwell.

Skinner, Q. (1970) 'Conventions and the Understanding of Speech-acts', *Philosophical Quarterly*, 20: 118–38.

Skinner, Q. (1988) 'Social Meaning and the Explanation of Social Action', in J. Tully (ed.) *Meaning and Context: Quentin Skinner and His Critics*. Cambridge: Polity Press.

Skocpol, T. (1979) *State and Social Revolutions*. London: Cambridge University Press.

Skocpol, T. (1985) 'Bringing the State Back In: Strategies of Analysis in Current Research', in P.B. Evans, D. Rueschemeyer and T. Skocpol (eds) *Bringing The State Back In*. Cambridge: Cambridge University Press.

Smellie, K.B. (1950) *A Hundred Years of English Government 1832–1939*. 2nd edition. London: Duckworth.

Smith, B.C. (1969) 'The Justification of Local Government', in L.D. Feldman and M.D. Goldrick (eds) *Politics and Government of Urban Canada*. Ontario: Methuen.

Smith, Joshua Toulmin (1849) *Government by Commissions Illegal and Pernicious.* London: S. Sweet.

Smith, M.J. (1998) 'Theoretical and Empirical Challenges to British Central Government', *Public Administration*, 76, 3: 45–72.

Smith, M.J. (1999a) *Prime Ministers, Ministers and Civil Servants: Complexity in the Core Executive.* London: Macmillan.

Smith, M.J. (1999b) 'Institutionalising the "Eternal Return": Textbooks and the Study of British Politics', *British Journal of Politics and International Relations*, 1, 1: 106–18.

Smith, S. (2000) 'The Discipline of International Relations: Still an American Social Science?', *British Journal of Politics and International Relations*, 3: 374–402.

Stansky, P. (ed.) (1973) *The Victorian Revolution.* New York: Watts.

Stapleton, J. (1991) 'Localism and Centralism in the Webbs' Political Thought', *History of Political Thought*, 12: 147–65.

Stewart, J. (1993) 'Defending Public Accountability', *Demos Newsletter*, 35, November: 5–10.

Stoker, G. (1991) *The Politics of Local Government.* 2nd edition. London: Macmillan.

Stoker, G. (1998a) 'Governance as Theory: Five Propositions', *International Social Science Journal*, 155: 17–28.

Stoker, G. (1998b) 'Theory and Urban Politics', *International Political Science Review*, 19: 119–29.

Stoker, G. (1999a) 'Introduction: The Unintended Costs and Benefits of New Management Reform for British Local Government', in G. Stoker (ed.) *The New Management of British Local Governance.* London: Macmillan.

Stoker, G. (ed.) (1999b) *The New Management of British Local Governance.* London: Macmillan.

Stoker, G. (ed.) (2000a) *The New Politics of British Local Governance.* London: Macmillan.

Stoker, G. (2000b) 'Urban Political Science and the Challenge of Urban Governance', in J. Pierre (ed.) *Debating Governance.* Oxford: Oxford University Press.

Sutherland, G. (1970) 'Recent Trends in Administrative History', *Victorian Studies*, 13: 408–11.

Sutherland, G. (ed.) (1972) *Studies in the Growth of Nineteenth-Century Government.* London: Routledge & Kegan Paul.

Taylor, C. (1971) 'Interpretation and the Sciences of Man', *Review of Metaphysics*, 25, 1: 3–51.

Taylor, Sir Henry (1927) [1836] *The Statesman.* Cambridge: Heffer.

Thain, C. and Wright, M. (1995) *The Treasury and Whitehall: The Planning and Control of Public Expenditure 1976–1993.* Oxford: Oxford University Press.

Thane, P. (1990) 'Government and Society in England and Wales, 1750–1914', in F.M.L. Thompson (ed.) *The Cambridge Social History of Britain 1750–1950. Volume 3. Social Agencies and Institutions.* Cambridge: Cambridge University Press.

Thatcher, M. (1993) *The Downing Street Years.* London: HarperCollins.

Theakston, K. (1998a) 'New Labour, New Whitehall?', *Public Policy and Administration*, 13, 1: 13–33.

Theakston, K. (1998b) 'Labour and the Civil Service', in G. Taylor (ed.) *The Impact of New Labour.* London: Macmillan.

Theakston, K. (1999) *Leadership in Whitehall*. London: Macmillan.

Theakston, K. (2000) 'Permanent Secretaries: Comparative Biography and Leadership in Whitehall', in R.A.W. Rhodes (ed.) *Transforming British Government. Volume 2. Changing Roles and Relationships*. London: Macmillan.

Theakston, K. and Fry, G.K. (1989) 'Britain's Administrative Elite: Permanent Secretaries 1900–1986', *Public Administration*, 67: 129–47.

Thelen, K. and Steinmo, S. (1992) 'Historical Institutionalism in Comparative Perspective', in S. Steinmo, K. Thelen and F. Longstreth (eds) *Structuring Politics*. Cambridge: Cambridge University Press.

Thomas, K. (1978) 'The United Kingdom', in R. Grew (ed.) *Crises of Political Development in Europe and the United States*. Princeton: Princeton University Press.

Thomas, R. (1978) *The British Philosophy of Administration*. London: Longman.

Thompson, E.P. (1978) *The Poverty of Theory*. New York: Monthly Press Review. See especially, 'The Peculiarities of the English', pp. 245–301, originally published in 1965.

Thompson, F.M.L. (ed.) (1990) *The Cambridge Social History of Britain 1750–1950. Volume 3. Social Agencies and Institutions*. Cambridge: Cambridge University Press.

Thompson, G. (1993) 'Network Co-ordination', in R. Maidment and G. Thompson (eds) *Managing the United Kingdom*. London: Sage.

Thompson, G., Frances, J., Levacic, R. and Mitchell, J. (eds) (1991) *Markets Hierarchies and Networks: the Co-ordination of Social Life*. London: Sage.

Thomson, D. (1950) *England in the Nineteenth Century*. Harmondsworth: Penguin Books.

Tilly, C. (1975a) 'Western State-making and Theories of Political Transformation', in C. Tilly, (ed.) *The Formation of National States in Western Europe*. Princeton: NJ: Princeton University Press.

Tilly, C. (ed.) (1975b) *The Formation of National States in Western Europe*. Princeton: NJ: Princeton University Press.

Tivey, L. (1988) *Interpretations of British Politics*. London: Harvester Wheatsheaf.

Treasury and Civil Service Committee (1994) *Role of the Civil Service*. London: HMSO.

Tricker, R.I. (1984) *International Corporate Governance*. Englewood Cliffs, NJ: Prentice Hall.

Tully, J. (ed.) (1988) *Meaning and Context: Quentin Skinner and his Critics*. Cambridge: Polity Press.

Verney, D. (1991) 'Westminster Model', in V. Bogdanor (ed.) *The Blackwell Encyclopaedia of Political Science*. Corrected paperback edition. Oxford: Blackwell.

Vickers, Sir Geoffrey (1968) [1965] *The Art of Judgement*. London: Methuen.

Vincent, A. (1998) 'New Ideologies for Old?', *Political Quarterly*, 69: 48–58.

Vincent-Jones, P. (1999) 'Competition and Contracting in the Transition from CCT to Best Value: Towards a more Reflexive Regulation?', *Public Administration*, 77, 2: 273–91.

Waarden, F. van (1992) 'Dimensions and Types of Policy Networks', *European Journal of Political Research*, 21: 29–52.

Waldegrave, W. (1993) *Public Service and the Future: Reforming Britain's Bureaucracies*. London: Conservative Political Centre.

Walker, D. (1999) 'Methods in the Zones Mosaic?', *Public Finance*, 11–17 June: 24–6.

Waller, M. (1992) 'Evaluating Policy Advice', *Australian Journal of Public Administration*, 51, 4: 440–6.

Watson, S. (1992) *Is Sir Humphrey Dead? The Changing Culture of the Civil Service*. Bristol: School for Advanced Urban Studies, Working Paper No. 103.

Webb, S. and Webb, B. (1963) [1906] *The Parish and the County*. London: Frank Cass.

Weber, M. (1978) *Economy and Society: An Outline of Interpretative Sociology*. Two volumes. Berkeley: University of California Press.

Weller, P. (1985) *First Among Equals*. Sydney: Allen & Unwin.

Weller, P. (1989) *Malcolm Fraser, the Westminster System and the Separation of Powers*. Brisbane: Griffith University, Research Lecture Series.

Weller, P., Bakvis, H. and Rhodes, R.A.W. (eds) (1997) *The Hollow Crown: Countervailing Trends in Core Executives*. London: Macmillan.

Whalen, H. (1969) 'Ideology, Democracy and the Foundations of Local Self-government', in L.D. Feldman and M.D. Goldrick (eds) *Politics and Government of Urban Canada*. Ontario: Methuen.

White, H. (1973) *Metahistory: The Historical Imagination in Nineteenth-Century Europe*. Baltimore: Johns Hopkins University Press.

White, H. (1978) *Tropics of Discourse*. Baltimore: Johns Hopkins University Press.

White, H. (1987) *The Content of the Form: Narrative Discourse and Historical Representation*. Baltimore: Johns Hopkins University Press.

White, H. (1995) 'Response to Arthur Marwick', *Journal of Contemporary History*, 30: 233–46.

Wilks, S. and Wright, M. (1987) 'Conclusion: Comparing Government–Industry Relations: States, Sectors, and Networks', in S. Wilks and M. Wright (eds) *Comparative Government Industry Relations*. Oxford: Clarendon Press.

Willetts, D. (1992) *Modern Conservatism*. Harmondsworth: Penguin Books.

Williams, D. and Young, T. (1994) 'Governance, the World Bank and Liberal Theory', *Political Studies*, 42: 84–100.

Willson, F.M.G. (1955) 'Ministries and Boards: Some Aspects of Administrative Development Since 1832', *Public Administration*, 33: 43–58.

Wilson, C.D. (ed.) (1948) *Essays in Local Government*. Oxford: Blackwell.

Wilson, G. (1994) 'The Westminster Model in Comparative Perspective', in I. Budge and D. McKay (eds) *Developing Democracy*. London: Sage.

Wilson, Sir Richard (1998) 'Modernising Government: The Role of the Senior Civil Service'. Speech to the Senior Civil Service Conference, October.

Wilson, Sir Richard (1999) 'The Civil Service in the New Millennium'. Speech, May.

Wilson, Sir Richard (2001) 'Modernisation and Change in Public Services'. Speech to the Chartered Institute for Personnel and Development, Harrogate, 25 October.

Wilson, Sir Richard (2002) 'Portrait of a Profession Revisited'. Speech. 26 March.

Winch, P. (1958) *The Idea of a Social Science*. London: Routledge & Kegan Paul.

Wistow, G., Knapp, M., Hardy, B. and Allen, C. (1994) *Social Care in a Mixed Economy*. Buckingham: Open University Press.

Wittgenstein, L. (1972) *Philosophical Investigations*. Translated by G. Anscombe. Oxford: Blackwell.

World Bank (1992) *Governance and Development.* Washington, DC: World Bank.

Wright, P. (1987) *Spycatcher.* Victoria, Australia: Heinemann.

Wright, V. (1994) 'Reshaping the State: Implications for Public Administration', *West European Politics*, 17: 102–34.

Wright, V. (1997) 'The Paradoxes of Administrative Reform', in W. Kickert (ed.) *Public Management and Administrative Reform in Western Europe.* Aldershot: Edward Elgar.

Wright, V. and Hayward, J.E.S. (2000) 'Governing from the Centre: Policy Co-ordination in Six European Core Executives', in R.A.W. Rhodes (ed.) *Transforming British Government. Volume 2. Changing Roles and Relationships.* London: Macmillan.

Yin, R.K. (1994) *Case Study Research: Design and Methods.* 2nd edition. London: Sage.

Young, H. (1989) *One of Us.* London: Macmillan.

Index

LIBRARY, UNIVERSITY OF CHESTER